Copyright © 2023 by Trient Press

All rights reserved. No part of this publication may be reproduced, distributed, or transmitted in any form or by any means, including photocopying, recording, or other electronic or mechanical methods, without the prior written permission of the publisher, except in the case of brief quotations embodied in critical reviews and certain other noncommercial uses permitted by copyright law. For permission requests, write to the publisher, addressed "Attention: Permissions Coordinator," at the address below.

Criminal copyright infringement, including infringement without monetary gain, is investigated by the FBI and is punishable by up to five years in federal prison and a fine of $250,000.

Except for the original story material written by the author, all songs, song titles, and lyrics mentioned in the novel The Entrepreneurial Mindset are the exclusive property of the respective artists, songwriters, and copyright holder.

Trient Press
3375 S Rainbow Blvd
#81710, SMB 13135
Las Vegas, NV 89180

Ordering Information:
Quantity sales. Special discounts are available on quantity purchases by corporations, associations, and others. For details, contact the publisher at the address above.
Orders by U.S. trade bookstores and wholesalers. Please contact Trient Press:
Tel: (775) 996-3844; or visit www.trientpress.com.

Printed in the United States of America

Publisher's Cataloging-in-Publication data
Ruscsak, M.L.
A title of a book :The Entrepreneurial Mindset
ISBN
Hardcover   979-8-88990-169-3
Paperback   979-8-88990-170-9
E-book   979-8-88990-171-6

Introduction

Chapter 1: The Foundations of Entrepreneurship

Chapter 2: Cultivating an Entrepreneurial Mindset

Chapter 3: Vision and Goal Setting

Chapter 4: Innovation and Creativity

Chapter 5: Decision-Making and Problem-Solving

Chapter 6: Financial Acumen

Chapter 7: Building and Leading Teams

Chapter 8: Marketing and Branding

Chapter 9: Navigating Challenges and Setbacks

Chapter 10: Scaling and Growth

Chapter 11: The Entrepreneur's Journey

Chapter 12: Social Responsibility and Ethical Entrepreneurship

Conclusion

Appendices

Dear Aspiring Entrepreneurs,

As you stand on the precipice of one of life's most exhilarating paths – entrepreneurship – I write to you with a blend of excitement, admiration, and solidarity. This journey upon which you are embarking is not just a career choice; it is a voyage into the very depths of innovation, creativity, and self-discovery.

Embrace the Adventure with Open Arms

Your journey will be a tapestry woven with threads of uncertainty, challenge, and triumph. Embrace uncertainty as your companion; it is in the unknown that the greatest discoveries are made. Celebrate each small victory – these are the milestones that will pave your path to success. Remember, entrepreneurship is not just about building a business; it's about sculpting your character and discovering your true potential.

Cultivate Unyielding Resilience

Do not fear failure, for in the entrepreneurial odyssey, it is an invaluable teacher. Each setback is a lesson that shapes your strategy and strengthens your resolve. Build resilience as your fortress – it will be your shelter during storms. And in times of doubt, seek support. The entrepreneurial community is a tapestry of camaraderie and wisdom – tap into it.

Let Passion Fuel Your Journey

Let your passion be the beacon that guides you through turbulent and calm waters alike. Hold fast to your vision; it is the anchor that will keep you grounded. In the ever-evolving landscape of business, adaptability and innovation are your sails; let them catch the winds of change and propel you forward.

Commit to Lifelong Learning

In the world of entrepreneurship, learning never ceases. Every experience, every interaction is an opportunity to grow. The stories of fellow entrepreneurs are like stars in the night sky – let their light guide you. And never lose your curiosity; it is the compass that leads to innovation.

Foster Meaningful Connections

Build bridges, not just to carry your dreams but to forge lasting relationships. The connections you make are more than professional networks; they are the pillars of your entrepreneurial journey. Attend events, engage in communities, and never underestimate the power of a conversation.

Find Harmony in the Chaos

While entrepreneurship is demanding, balance it with the melody of personal well-being. Your health, your relationships, your passions – they are the symphony that adds richness to your life. Make time for yourself, for it is in these moments of pause that you will find clarity and inspiration.

In Conclusion: A Clarion Call to Brave Hearts

To each of you about to embark on this remarkable journey – you are stepping into a world brimming with potential and promise. It is a path that will challenge you, but also one that will offer rewards beyond measure. You have the power to create, to innovate, and to transform not just your life, but the world around you.

So, step forward with courage, with passion, and with an unwavering belief in your dreams. The world of entrepreneurship is not just waiting for you; it needs you. Your ideas, your vision, and your energy are the catalysts for change and progress.

Welcome to the adventure of a lifetime. Here's to your journey, your growth, and the indelible mark you will leave on the tapestry of entrepreneurship.

With heartfelt encouragement and best wishes,

Introduction

Welcome to a journey like no other, a voyage into the heart of business adventure and innovation. This isn't just a book; it's a gateway to a realm where ideas ignite realities, and dreams take flight on the wings of action. You're about to embark on an exploration into the essence of what it means to be an entrepreneur, a dive into the mindset that has powered some of the greatest business triumphs in history.

Imagine standing at the edge of a vast ocean of possibilities. In front of you lies uncharted territory, waiting to be discovered and shaped by your vision and effort. This is the entrepreneurial landscape – dynamic, exhilarating, and brimming with potential. Here, success is not just about having a groundbreaking idea or substantial capital; it's about cultivating a mindset that turns barriers into stepping stones and challenges into opportunities.

So, what exactly is this entrepreneurial mindset? Picture it as a unique blend of qualities – resilience, creativity, vision, and an unwavering belief in one's ability to make a difference. It's about seeing the world not just for what it is, but for what it could be, and then having the courage and determination to make that vision a reality.

In these pages, you'll find more than just theories and anecdotes. You'll encounter a vibrant tapestry of stories, insights, and experiences that illuminate the path of the entrepreneur. From the audacious spirit of startup founders to the calculated strategies of seasoned business moguls, we'll explore the diverse ways in which the entrepreneurial mindset manifests and flourishes.

As we navigate through this exciting landscape, you'll learn how to foster and harness this mindset in your own entrepreneurial endeavors. Whether you're taking your first steps into the business world or looking to elevate your existing venture, this book is designed to be your guide, mentor, and inspiration.

Get ready to be engaged, encouraged, and informed. Get ready to be enthused about the endless possibilities that await you. The entrepreneurial journey is as much about personal growth as it is about business success. It's a journey of discovery, learning, and above all, a journey of transformation. Let's begin this adventure together and unlock the power of the entrepreneurial mindset. The path to business success and personal fulfillment awaits!

Defining the Entrepreneurial Mindset

Now, let's delve deeper into the essence of the entrepreneurial mindset. Imagine it as a canvas, each stroke representing a unique trait that together forms the masterpiece of an entrepreneur's spirit. This mindset isn't a one-size-fits-all; rather, it's a dynamic and evolving set of attitudes and qualities that empower individuals to navigate the complex and often tumultuous world of business.

1. Visionary Thinking: At the heart of the entrepreneurial mindset is visionary thinking. Entrepreneurs are dreamers who dare to imagine a different world. They see opportunities where others see obstacles, envisioning new solutions to old problems. Think of it as the ability to not just foresee the future but to actively shape it with innovative ideas and bold actions.

2. Resilience and Grit: The path of entrepreneurship is strewn with challenges and setbacks. Resilience is the entrepreneur's armor, a steadfast determination that keeps them standing firm in the face of adversity. Grit is their driving force, the inner strength that fuels persistence even when the odds seem insurmountable.

3. Adaptability and Flexibility: In the ever-changing landscape of business, adaptability is key. Successful entrepreneurs are agile, constantly learning and evolving to stay ahead of the curve. They're not just prepared for change; they embrace it, using it as a catalyst for growth and innovation.

4. A Passion for Learning: Entrepreneurs are perpetual students of life and business. Their passion for learning drives them to continuously acquire new knowledge, skills, and experiences. This insatiable curiosity keeps them on the cutting edge, always ready to explore new ventures and ideas.

5. Risk-Taking and Courage: Entrepreneurship is about taking calculated risks. It's about having the courage to step out of the comfort zone and venture into the unknown. Entrepreneurs understand that risk and reward are two sides of the same coin, and they're not afraid to bet on themselves and their visions.

6. A Focus on Execution: Ideas alone don't lead to success; execution does. Entrepreneurs are doers, not just thinkers. They turn their visions into reality through meticulous planning, unwavering dedication, and relentless execution. They understand that action is the bridge between dreams and achievements.

As you journey through this book, keep in mind that the entrepreneurial mindset is not just for those starting a business. It's a way of thinking and being that can enhance every aspect of your life. It's about being proactive, resourceful, and resilient in the face of life's many challenges.

So, whether you're an aspiring entrepreneur or simply looking to inject some entrepreneurial spirit into your personal or professional life, embrace these qualities. Nurture them, develop them, and watch as they transform not just the way you do business, but the way you view and engage with the world around you.

Welcome to the world of the entrepreneurial mindset – a world where dreams are the seeds of reality, where resilience paves the path to success, and where every challenge is an opportunity in disguise. Let's embark on this transformative journey together and unlock the limitless potential that lies within you.

The Importance of Mindset in Business Success

Understanding the entrepreneurial mindset is only the beginning. Its true power lies in its profound impact on business success. Mindset is the invisible architect of all entrepreneurial endeavors, shaping decisions, strategies, and ultimately, outcomes. Let's explore why this mindset is so crucial in the business world.

1. Driving Innovation: In the realm of business, innovation is the key to staying relevant and competitive. An entrepreneurial mindset fosters an environment where new ideas are not just encouraged but celebrated. It's this mindset that leads to groundbreaking products, disruptive business models, and revolutionary market strategies. Entrepreneurs don't just follow trends; they create them.

2. Overcoming Challenges: The journey of entrepreneurship is often fraught with hurdles. A robust mindset turns these challenges into valuable learning experiences. It's not about never failing; it's about rising every time you fall. This resilience is what separates successful entrepreneurs from the rest. They view challenges as opportunities to grow, adapt, and emerge stronger.

3. Building Strong Relationships: Business is not just about transactions; it's about relationships. An entrepreneurial mindset emphasizes the importance of networking, collaboration, and emotional intelligence. It's about building alliances, understanding customer needs, and fostering a team culture that values creativity and teamwork.

4. Continuous Improvement: The world of business is dynamic, and resting on one's laurels is not an option for the successful entrepreneur. This mindset is characterized by a relentless pursuit of excellence and continuous improvement. It involves critically analyzing every success and failure, always looking for ways to do better, be more efficient, and provide greater value.

5. Inspiring Leadership: At its core, entrepreneurship is about leadership – leading a vision, a team, a market trend. An entrepreneurial mindset is instrumental in inspiring and motivating others. It's about setting a vision that others believe in, guiding with empathy and integrity, and creating a culture where each team member feels valued and driven to contribute to the collective goal.

6. Adapting to Change: In business, change is the only constant. Entrepreneurs thrive on change; they anticipate it, adapt to it, and often, are the catalysts for it. This mindset equips entrepreneurs with the agility to pivot when necessary, embrace technological advancements, and stay ahead in a rapidly evolving global market.

In essence, the entrepreneurial mindset is much more than a set of traits – it's a way of life. It influences every decision, shapes every strategy, and determines the trajectory of every entrepreneurial venture. It's the foundation upon which businesses are built, grown, and sustained.

As we progress through this book, remember that cultivating an entrepreneurial mindset is not a one-time effort; it's a continuous journey of growth, learning, and self-discovery. It's about being open to new experiences, ready to tackle new challenges, and willing to embrace change, all while staying true to your vision and values.

Embark on this journey with an open mind and a willing heart, and watch as the entrepreneurial mindset transforms not just your business, but every facet of your life. Let's continue to explore and embrace this powerful mindset, unlocking the door to limitless possibilities and unparalleled success in the world of business.

Overview of the Book

Now that we've introduced the entrepreneurial mindset and its significance in business success, let's outline what you can expect from the rest of this book. Each chapter is designed not only to inform and educate but also to inspire and engage. This book is a mosaic of knowledge, experiences, and insights, carefully crafted to guide you on your entrepreneurial journey.

Chapter 1: The Foundations of Entrepreneurship

We begin by exploring the roots of entrepreneurship. This chapter delves into the historical evolution of entrepreneurship, examining how it has shaped modern business practices. We'll also look at the psychological aspects that drive entrepreneurial behavior and the societal impact of entrepreneurial ventures.

Chapter 2: Cultivating an Entrepreneurial Mindset

Building upon our understanding of what constitutes an entrepreneurial mindset, this chapter focuses on how to develop and nurture these traits in yourself. From embracing risk and failure to fostering creativity and innovation, we'll provide practical strategies to cultivate a mindset geared for entrepreneurial success.

Chapter 3: Vision and Goal Setting

Vision is the compass that guides the entrepreneurial journey. In this chapter, we discuss how to create a compelling vision for your business and set achievable goals. We'll cover techniques for effective goal setting and how to align your personal and business aspirations for maximum impact.

Chapter 4: Innovation and Creativity

Here, we dive into the heart of what makes businesses stand out – innovation and creativity. This chapter offers insights into fostering a culture of innovation within your organization and practical tips for nurturing creative thinking.

Chapter 5: Decision-Making and Problem-Solving

Effective decision-making and problem-solving are crucial skills for any entrepreneur. This chapter provides frameworks and strategies to enhance these skills, helping you navigate complex business landscapes with confidence and clarity.

Chapter 6: Financial Acumen

Understanding finance is key to entrepreneurial success. This chapter breaks down fundamental financial concepts and explores various funding sources and strategies. We'll also look at financial planning and management essentials for startups and growing businesses.

Chapter 7: Building and Leading Teams

No entrepreneur succeeds alone. This chapter focuses on the art of team building and leadership. Learn about different leadership styles, how to build high-performance teams, and strategies for fostering a positive and productive work environment.

Chapter 8: Marketing and Branding

Discover the power of branding and marketing in this chapter. We'll explore how to understand your market, build a strong brand identity, and develop effective marketing strategies that resonate with your audience.

Chapter 9: Navigating Challenges and Setbacks

Challenges are an inevitable part of the entrepreneurial journey. This chapter discusses common obstacles entrepreneurs face and offers strategies for building resilience and turning setbacks into growth opportunities.

Chapter 10: Scaling and Growth

Growth is the goal of every entrepreneurial venture. Here, we'll explore strategies for scaling your business, managing growth challenges, and planning for long-term success.

Chapter 11: Social Responsibility and Ethical Entrepreneurship

In this chapter, we delve into the role of ethics and social responsibility in entrepreneurship. Explore how to build a business that not only generates profits but also contributes positively to society.

Chapter 12: The Entrepreneur's Personal Journey

Finally, we take a personal look at the life of an entrepreneur. Balancing work and personal life, dealing with stress, and staying motivated – this chapter covers the personal aspects of entrepreneurship.

Each chapter is filled with real-life examples, case studies, interactive exercises, and practical advice to not only inform you but also inspire and challenge you. This book is more than a guide; it's a companion on your journey to entrepreneurial success. Whether you're just starting out or looking to take your business to the next level, 'The Entrepreneurial Mindset' is your roadmap to success. Let's turn the page and begin this exciting journey together!

Chapter 1: The Foundations of Entrepreneurship

Welcome to the first chapter of our exhilarating journey - 'The Foundations of Entrepreneurship'. This chapter serves as the bedrock upon which your understanding of the entrepreneurial world will be built. Here, we'll delve into the historical, psychological, and societal facets of entrepreneurship, piecing together the puzzle of what makes this endeavor so unique and impactful.

The Historical Tapestry of Entrepreneurship

Our journey begins with a voyage through time, tracing the evolution of entrepreneurship across ages and cultures. Imagine walking through the bustling marketplaces of ancient civilizations, where the seeds of trade and commerce were first sown. Fast forward to the industrial revolutions, witnessing the birth of modern corporations and the rise of influential entrepreneurs who shaped the course of history. This historical perspective is not just about dates and events; it's a narrative of human ingenuity and the relentless pursuit of progress.

Psychology Behind the Entrepreneurial Spirit

Next, we dive into the human mind. What drives an individual to take risks, to innovate, to forge their own path? We'll explore the psychological traits common among successful entrepreneurs - their motivations, their fears, their mindset. This is a journey into the heart of ambition and resilience, understanding how the entrepreneur's mind works, how they view challenges, and what fuels their relentless drive.

Societal Impact and the Role of the Entrepreneur

The entrepreneurial journey is not an isolated one; it significantly impacts society. Here, we'll examine how entrepreneurs have shaped economies, changed societal norms, and influenced cultural trends. We'll explore the symbiotic relationship between entrepreneurship and society, understanding how one feeds into and shapes the other. This section isn't just about business impact; it's about the entrepreneur's role as a change agent, an innovator, and often, a visionary leader.

Entrepreneurial Traits and Their Relevance Today

As we conclude this chapter, we'll reflect on how the foundational traits of entrepreneurship are more relevant today than ever. In an ever-evolving business landscape marked by technology and globalization, these traits remain the guiding stars for aspiring entrepreneurs. We'll connect the historical and psychological insights to present-day scenarios, illustrating how these timeless qualities continue to drive success in the modern entrepreneurial world.

This chapter is not just an introduction to entrepreneurship; it's an invitation to view the world through the lens of an entrepreneur. It's an opportunity to understand the deep roots of this dynamic field and appreciate its profound impact on our world. As we turn these pages, let's embark on this journey with curiosity, eagerness to learn, and an openness to be inspired by the countless stories of determination, innovation, and success that define the essence of entrepreneurship.

Prepare to be enlightened, inspired, and equipped with the foundational knowledge that will pave the way for the rest of your entrepreneurial journey. Let's dive into the fascinating world of entrepreneurship and uncover the secrets that lie at its very core!

Historical Perspectives on Entrepreneurship

Embark with me now on a captivating journey through time, as we unravel the rich tapestry of entrepreneurship's history. This journey isn't just a chronological account of events; it's a story of human aspiration, ingenuity, and the relentless pursuit of progress. Here, in the annals of history, lie the roots of modern entrepreneurship.

The Birth of Trade and Commerce

Let us delve deeper into the origins of trade and commerce, where the first seeds of entrepreneurship were sown. This narrative isn't merely about the exchange of goods; it's a saga of human ingenuity and the dawn of economic civilization.

✧ Mesopotamia: The Cradle of Early Trade

Mesopotamia, a land nestled between the Tigris and Euphrates rivers, is often celebrated as the cradle of civilization. But it was also here, in the bustling city-states of Sumer and Babylon, where the seeds of organized trade and entrepreneurship were first sown.

Vibrant Marketplaces of Sumer and Babylon

Step back in time and envision the ancient city-states of Mesopotamia, specifically Sumer and Babylon, where the dawn of commerce brought forth a vibrancy and energy that would lay the foundations of modern trade. In Sumer, often hailed as one of civilization's earliest cradles, the marketplaces buzzed with activity, serving as the nucleus of economic life. Narrow, winding streets were lined with stalls and shops, where merchants, known for their business acumen, displayed a range of goods from daily essentials to exotic luxuries. These were the grounds where some of the first commercial transactions were pioneered, setting the stage for more complex trade systems.

In contrast, Babylon, famed for its architectural marvels, hosted grander marketplaces, acting as significant nodes in an expansive network of ancient trade routes. Here, a diverse array of traders and customers from across the known world gathered, trading everything from local grains and textiles to spices and jewels from distant lands. Babylon's markets were not just trading posts but crucibles of international trade, with Babylonian merchants emerging as key intermediaries in what was becoming a global marketplace.

Beyond mere trade, these marketplaces were vibrant centers of innovation and cultural exchange. Artisans and craftsmen shared techniques and ideas, advancing their crafts, while the influx of diverse cultures enriched the Mesopotamian civilization, turning these markets into cultural melting pots. Socially, these markets were the heartbeats of Sumer and Babylon, where people from all societal strata converged for business, news, and social interaction, playing a crucial role in shaping societal norms and structures.

Reflecting on these bustling marketplaces, one can discern the early blueprints of our modern economic systems. From introducing standardized weights and measures to pioneering credit and lending systems, these markets laid the groundwork for the evolution of trade and commerce. Their legacy, transcending their historical context, continues to influence contemporary market dynamics, reminding us of the timeless principles of effective commerce: diversity in trade, innovation, and a robust social fabric.

Thus, the vibrant markets of Sumer and Babylon stand as a testament to the enduring human spirit of entrepreneurship, innovation, and community, marking the beginning of an economic saga that continues to this day.

> The Bustling Economic Life in Sumer

In the rich tapestry of ancient Mesopotamia, the city-states of Sumer and Babylon emerged as beacons of commerce and culture, each boasting marketplaces that transcended mere trade hubs. In Sumer, the world's oldest known city, the marketplace was a bustling nucleus where commerce, art, and innovation fused seamlessly. Artisans and craftsmen, adept in their trades, transformed raw materials into wares of both utility and aesthetic appeal – be it intricately woven textiles, exquisitely crafted jewelry, or aesthetically pleasing pottery. These vibrant markets were more than exchange centers; they were the crucibles of modern trade practices. Here, the Sumerians not only honed the arts of negotiation and valuation but also pioneered the use of cuneiform script for recording transactions, laying down the early principles of business documentation.

Simultaneously, in Babylon, the grandeur of its markets mirrored the city's stature as a commercial colossus. These sprawling bazaars attracted a diverse array of traders and merchants from far and wide, creating a dynamic tapestry of cultural and economic exchange. Overflowing with exotic spices, precious metals, and luxurious fabrics, Babylon's markets were a display of the city's opulence and sophistication. Moreover, Babylon's strategic position in the vast network of trade routes accentuated its role as a pivotal hub for the international exchange of goods and ideas, with its merchants serving dual roles as traders and cultural ambassadors.

Both in Sumer and Babylon, these marketplaces transcended their commercial roles, evolving into vital centers for social and cultural dynamics. They were melting pots of diverse ideas and cultures, fostering an environment ripe for innovation and creativity, thus significantly contributing to the economic and cultural development of Mesopotamia. In these ancient markets, where art and commerce interwove seamlessly, foundational principles of modern commerce were laid, illustrating the deep-rootedness of trade and entrepreneurship in human civilization.

As one meandered through these markets, they transformed into the social media platforms of their era – alive with the hustle of negotiations, the latest news, and the shared experiences of daily life. These markets were where diverse social classes and cultures mingled, breaking down barriers and weaving a rich tapestry of community and mutual understanding. The economic dynamics within these marketplaces were not static; they were reflective of evolving societal structures, where concepts like supply and demand, branding, and customer relations were not merely theoretical but part of the lived experience.

In essence, the marketplaces of Sumer and Babylon were much more than centers of commerce; they were the pulsating hearts of their cities, brimming with innovation, learning, and community spirit. They were spaces where business was an adventure, learning was interactive, and every visit was a journey into the rich landscape of human interaction and innovation, laying down the timeless principles of commerce and trade that continue to resonate in our modern economic systems.

> ➤ Foundation for Modern Economic Systems

In the bustling marketplaces of ancient Mesopotamia, particularly in the renowned city-states of Sumer and Babylon, we find the genesis of modern economic systems. These historic trading hubs were more than mere aggregations of merchants and goods; they were the forerunners of the contemporary central trading hub concept. Their significance lies not only in their historical context but also in their foundational role in shaping today's global economy. These markets demonstrated the importance of a centralized location for trade, where a diverse range of goods and services could be exchanged. This centralization not only facilitated economic transactions but also fostered a vibrant commercial environment, encouraging the growth and development of businesses.

Moreover, the diversity in goods and services offered in these ancient marketplaces highlights another fundamental aspect of modern economies. From exotic spices and luxurious textiles in Babylon to intricate jewelry and functional pottery in Sumer, the variety of products available was astonishing. This diversity was not just a testament to the extensive trade networks but also an early indication of market segmentation and specialization – concepts that are pivotal in today's business world. The wide range of goods catered to different needs and preferences, a principle that modern businesses continue to adhere to, emphasizing the value of catering to a diverse customer base.

Furthermore, innovation was a cornerstone of these ancient marketplaces. Artisans and traders in Sumer and Babylon were not just passive sellers; they were innovators and creators, constantly seeking new methods, materials, and ideas to improve their wares and attract customers. This culture of innovation, deeply ingrained in the marketplaces, mirrors the modern business emphasis on innovation as a key driver of growth and success. The spirit of innovation that permeated these ancient markets laid the groundwork for continuous improvement and advancement in business practices.

In addition to the economic aspects, the social interaction that characterized these markets was crucial in shaping the dynamics of trade and commerce. The marketplaces were social hubs, where people from various backgrounds and cultures converged, exchanged ideas, and built relationships. This aspect of social connectivity, essential in the ancient markets, remains relevant in today's business world, where networking, relationship building, and cultural exchange are integral to commercial success. The marketplaces of Sumer and Babylon fostered a sense of community and mutual dependence, underscoring the importance of social interaction in business.

Lastly, the enduring spirit of entrepreneurship and commerce that thrived in these ancient marketplaces is a testament to their lasting impact. The bustling streets of Sumer and Babylon, with their vibrant mix of traders, artisans, and customers, showcased the fundamental principles of business: innovation, exchange, and social connectivity. These principles have been pivotal to human progress since the dawn of civilization and continue to underpin the modern business world. The legacy of these ancient marketplaces is a reminder that the foundations of today's global economy were laid millennia ago in the vibrant trading hubs of Mesopotamia.

> The Role of Merchants and Artisans

In the thriving marketplaces of ancient Mesopotamia, merchants and artisans stood as the vanguard of early entrepreneurship, playing roles far more complex than mere traders. These individuals were the lifeblood of the markets, possessing an acute understanding of the value of goods not just in their immediate vicinity but across distant lands. They were the bearers of commodities that spoke of their regions' richness – grains harvested from the fertile crescent, textiles woven with mesmerizing designs, and pottery that epitomized the blend of functionality and artistry. Their trade extended beyond local boundaries, connecting diverse cultures and economies through the exchange of these valuable goods.

These early entrepreneurs were masters of multiple trades, embodying skills that spanned crafting, production, negotiation, and salesmanship. The artisan in Sumer or Babylon was not just a creator but also a savvy businessperson, understanding the market's demands and tailoring their crafts accordingly. Their ability to adapt their products to suit various needs and preferences was a testament to their versatility and business acumen. They were not just selling products; they were offering pieces of their culture and artistry, each item carrying a story of its origin and craftsmanship.

Negotiation and salesmanship were as crucial to their trade as the crafting of their goods. These merchants and artisans were adept in the art of persuasion, understanding the psychology of their customers, and tailoring their sales techniques to different individuals. This skill was vital in a world without fixed prices, where haggling was the norm, and a sale's success often hinged on the seller's ability to negotiate effectively. They were the pioneers of customer relationship management, building trust and rapport with their clientele, which was crucial for sustaining their businesses in the competitive marketplaces.

Moreover, these merchants and artisans were not just participants in the marketplace; they were its creators and sustainers. They were responsible for driving innovation within their trades, constantly experimenting with new materials, techniques, and designs to stay ahead in the market. Their pursuit of excellence and innovation was not just for personal gain but also contributed to the advancement of their respective crafts. This continuous improvement and adaptation to market trends are reminiscent of modern entrepreneurial practices.

In essence, the role of merchants and artisans in the ancient marketplaces of Mesopotamia was multifaceted and integral to the economic and cultural vitality of their societies. They were the earliest embodiments of entrepreneurship, combining creativity, craftsmanship, strategic business thinking, and customer engagement. Their contributions went beyond mere trading; they were pivotal in shaping the economic landscapes of their times, laying the foundations for future generations of entrepreneurs and artisans. Their legacy is a testament to the enduring spirit of entrepreneurship and the multifaceted role of merchants and artisans in the tapestry of commerce.

> Innovation in Trade Practices

In the bustling markets of ancient Mesopotamia, entrepreneurs were not just traders but innovators who laid the groundwork for modern trade and commerce. One of their most significant contributions was the establishment of systems of weights and measures. In an era where trade was predominantly based on bartering, the introduction of standardized weights and measures was revolutionary. It brought a sense of fairness and transparency to transactions, allowing both parties to agree on the value of goods with confidence. This standardization was crucial in building trust among traders, which is the bedrock of any successful economic system. By ensuring that a set amount of grain, textiles, or pottery had a universally recognized value, these entrepreneurs facilitated smoother and more efficient trade.

The development of cuneiform was another monumental achievement by Mesopotamian entrepreneurs. This early form of writing, initially created for recording economic transactions, stands as one of the first known instances of written expression. The implications of this development were far-reaching. By documenting transactions, these ancient entrepreneurs were laying the foundations of modern accounting and record-keeping practices. Cuneiform allowed for the tracking of sales, debts, and credits, bringing a new level of complexity and sophistication to business operations. It marked the transition from memory-based transactions to recorded history, changing the course of business administration.

Moreover, cuneiform's use in economic transactions highlights the Mesopotamians' understanding of the need for transparency and accountability in business. This early form of record-keeping ensured that transactions were not only remembered but could also be verified and referenced in the future. It was a pioneering step towards the development of contracts and legal documentation in business, aspects that are indispensable in today's economic world. The ability to refer back to written records of transactions reduced disputes and fostered a more reliable trading environment.

Furthermore, the advent of cuneiform and standardized weights and measures allowed Mesopotamian entrepreneurs to engage in more complex business transactions. With reliable records and standardized valuation of goods, they could undertake larger and more intricate trade deals, extending beyond local markets to distant regions. This development was crucial in facilitating the growth of businesses and the expansion of the economy. It enabled the tracking of inventory, management of large-scale trade operations, and even the planning of future business ventures based on past records.

In conclusion, the Mesopotamian entrepreneurs were not just participants in their economy; they were architects of the economic systems that would influence trade and commerce for millennia to come. Their innovations in establishing standardized weights and measures and developing cuneiform for economic transactions were pivotal in shaping the foundations of modern business practices. These advancements brought about a new era in trade, characterized by increased efficiency, reliability, and expansion, underscoring the ingenuity and forward-thinking of these early entrepreneurs.

> Strategic Trading and Economic Strategy

The trade networks of ancient Mesopotamia were a testament to the far-reaching vision and entrepreneurial spirit of its traders. These intrepid merchants were not content with the confines of their city-state walls; they were explorers, visionaries who ventured beyond familiar territories to establish expansive trade routes. Their journeys connected them with distant civilizations, from the lush valleys of the Indus to the grandeur of Ancient Egypt. This was not mere trading; it was the development of a strategic network that allowed for the flow of goods, ideas, and culture. These Mesopotamian traders displayed an understanding of global commerce and economic strategy that was remarkably advanced for their time, foreseeing the benefits of connecting with distant markets to enhance their own economic prosperity.

Within the bustling marketplaces of Mesopotamia, a dynamic environment of early entrepreneurship thrived. The merchants and artisans who conducted their business there were far from being mere cogs in an economic machine; they were the very architects of their trade system. Their contributions went beyond the simple act of selling and buying goods. They were innovators in trade practices, creators of business tools, and strategic thinkers in commerce. These individuals laid the foundational stones of trade and entrepreneurship, setting in motion practices and principles that have continued to shape economic systems throughout history.

Reflecting on the entrepreneurial spirit that characterized Mesopotamia's marketplace, one can't help but be inspired by their ingenuity and foresight. These early entrepreneurs were not just conducting business; they were paving the way for future generations. They embodied principles that are still relevant in today's business world – innovation in their crafts and trade methods, strategic planning in establishing far-reaching trade networks, and a relentless spirit of exploration that pushed them to seek new markets and opportunities.

The legacy of these Mesopotamian traders and artisans is a powerful reminder of the timeless nature of successful business principles. Their spirit of exploration, willingness to innovate, and strategic approach to commerce were the building blocks of their economic success. These qualities transcended the constraints of their era, offering lessons that remain pertinent in the modern business landscape. The ability to foresee market trends, adapt to new environments, and continually innovate are as crucial today as they were in the bustling marketplaces of ancient Mesopotamia.

In conclusion, the marketplaces of Mesopotamia serve as more than historical footnotes; they are beacons of entrepreneurial wisdom. The legacy of these early merchants and artisans continues to inspire and guide modern entrepreneurs. Their approach to business – marked by innovation, strategic thinking, and an adventurous spirit – demonstrates that the core principles of successful entrepreneurship are as enduring as civilization itself. As we navigate the complexities of modern commerce, we would do well to remember and draw inspiration from the pioneering spirit of these ancient Mesopotamian entrepreneurs.

- Egypt: Trade in the Land of the Pharaohs

In the realm of ancient trade, Egypt, with its mighty Nile and majestic Pharaohs, offers a unique and fascinating story. Here, in the land of pyramids and sphinxes, commerce was intricately linked to the central authority of the Pharaohs, yet it was propelled forward by the ingenuity and entrepreneurial spirit of its people. The Egyptian economy, while under the auspices of the Pharaohs, thrived due to the contributions of skilled artisans and savvy traders who mastered the art of crafting and selling goods that were coveted across the known world.

Egyptian artisans were renowned for their exquisite craftsmanship, particularly in creating luxurious goods. The jewelry made in ancient Egypt was not merely ornamental; it was a symbol of wealth, power, and divine protection, crafted with precision and imbued with meaning. Similarly, their skill in producing fine linen, known for its quality and durability, set Egyptian textiles apart in the ancient world. Papyrus, another significant Egyptian innovation, was a sought-after commodity, serving as the canvas for written communication and a precursor to modern paper. These goods were not just products of trade; they represented the pinnacle of Egyptian art and culture, making them highly desirable to other civilizations.

The trading ventures of ancient Egypt were often state-sponsored, reflecting the Pharaohs' interest in expanding their wealth and influence. These ventures were far-reaching, extending beyond the nation's borders through extensive networks of sea and land routes. Egyptian traders sailed across the Mediterranean and Red Seas, while overland caravans traversed deserts to reach distant lands. This expansive trade network facilitated the exchange of Egyptian goods for precious metals, exotic woods, and other luxury items from afar, enriching the Egyptian economy and culture.

However, being an entrepreneur in ancient Egypt required more than just skill in a craft or trade. These individuals had to adeptly navigate not only the physical challenges of long and perilous trade routes but also the complex hierarchies of power within their own society. Engaging in trade under the watchful eyes of the Pharaohs and their officials meant that entrepreneurs had to be astute in their dealings, balancing the demands of the state with the realities of the marketplace. Their ability to maneuver within these constraints while still pursuing profitable ventures showcased their exceptional business acumen.

In essence, trade in ancient Egypt was a complex interplay of state control and individual entrepreneurship. The luxurious goods that flowed from the workshops of Egyptian artisans to markets both near and far were a testament to the country's rich cultural heritage and its people's entrepreneurial spirit. These ventures not only filled the coffers of the Pharaohs but also laid the groundwork for Egypt's lasting legacy in the annals of global trade and commerce. The story of trade in the land of the Pharaohs is thus a vibrant chapter in the history of ancient entrepreneurship, highlighting the enduring human drive to create, trade, and prosper.

⋄ The Indus Valley: Pioneers of Urban Trade

The Indus Valley Civilization, a marvel of ancient human ingenuity, presents a captivating narrative in the history of trade and commerce. Spanning across what is now modern-day Pakistan and India, this civilization was distinguished by its exceptional urban planning and sophisticated trade systems. Cities like Harappa and Mohenjo-Daro stood as testament to the advanced knowledge in arts, crafts, and urban organization that characterized this civilization. These cities were not just population centers; they were bustling hubs of trade and economic activity, showcasing a level of advancement that was remarkable for their time.

The Indus Valley people were adept traders, engaging not only in local commerce but also in long-distance trade that connected them with distant civilizations, including Mesopotamia. This indicates a network of trade routes that spanned vast geographical distances, facilitating the exchange of goods and ideas far beyond their immediate region. The entrepreneurial spirit of the Indus Valley people was evident in the diversity of their crafts. They produced a wide range of goods, from fine pottery to intricate jewelry and high-quality textiles, which were sought after both locally and in distant lands.

A key aspect of the Indus Valley's trade system was their uniformity in weights and measures. This standardization was a groundbreaking innovation, ensuring fairness and consistency in trade transactions. It reflects an early understanding of the need for a regulated economic system, which is a fundamental principle in modern commerce. Additionally, the Indus Valley Civilization had a sophisticated system of trade and taxation, indicating a structured approach to economic management. This level of organization in their economic system was pioneering, laying the groundwork for future economic models and systems.

Moreover, the trade practices of the Indus Valley Civilization were more than just a means of economic survival; they represented a complex interplay of innovation, negotiation, and exploration. The entrepreneurs of this era were visionaries who not only navigated the physical trade routes but also mastered the intricate dynamics of supply and demand. Their understanding of economic and cultural relationships transcended mere transactional interactions and delved into strategic alliances and partnerships.

The entrepreneurial legacy of the Indus Valley Civilization offers invaluable lessons in the fundamentals of entrepreneurship such as innovation, risk-taking, and strategic thinking. These principles have been intrinsic to human progress since the dawn of civilization. Reflecting on the advanced urban planning, standardized trade systems, and far-reaching commercial networks of the Indus Valley, we are reminded of the deep-rooted nature of entrepreneurship in human history. Their achievements in commerce and trade are not just historical footnotes but are integral chapters in the story of human advancement, inspiring future generations to continue the journey of innovation and economic exploration.

The Rise of Merchant Ventures

As history unfolded, the emergence of the Silk Road marked a pivotal chapter in the annals of trade and entrepreneurship. This extensive network of trade routes, stretching from the heart of Asia to the Mediterranean, represented far more than a conduit for commerce. It was a grand tapestry interweaving diverse cultures, ideas, and innovations, a testament to the entrepreneurial spirit that drove early traders to venture beyond known horizons.

The Silk Road was not just a physical path traversing vast and varied landscapes; it was a bridge connecting distant worlds. Along this network, goods such as silk, spices, tea, and precious metals flowed from one civilization to another. But more importantly, it facilitated an unprecedented exchange of cultural and intellectual riches. Ideas in science, art, and philosophy, as well as technological and agricultural innovations, traveled alongside caravans, igniting a cross-pollination of knowledge that shaped civilizations.

The merchants who embarked on journeys along the Silk Road were quintessential entrepreneurs. They were far more than mere businessmen conducting transactions; they were bold adventurers who embraced the unknown. Braving perilous terrains, navigating through deserts, mountains, and across seas, they embodied resilience and adaptability. The risks they took were not just financial but also physical, as they traversed territories fraught with dangers from natural elements and bandits alike.

Furthermore, these traders were cultural ambassadors, playing a crucial role in the exchange and preservation of cultural heritages. They introduced languages, religions, customs, and artistic expressions to distant lands, weaving a rich tapestry of cultural diversity along the Silk Road. Their interactions fostered mutual understanding and respect among different cultures, breaking down barriers and building bridges of cultural exchange.

In essence, the Silk Road was a cradle of entrepreneurial endeavor, where the spirit of exploration, innovation, and cultural exchange flourished. The traders and adventurers who traversed this ancient network were not just partaking in commerce; they were shaping the course of human history. Their journeys and interactions along the Silk Road laid the foundations for our modern globalized world, demonstrating that the essence of entrepreneurship transcends time and geography. It is this enduring spirit of exploration, risk-taking, and cultural connection that continues to inspire and drive the entrepreneurial journeys of today.

The Rise of Merchant Ventures, particularly in the context of the Silk Road, is an enthralling subject, encompassing the multifaceted roles of merchants as entrepreneurs, cultural ambassadors, and pioneers of globalization.

Entrepreneurs and Risk Takers

The merchants on the Silk Road were the epitome of early entrepreneurs. Their role transcended mere trading; they were innovators and risk-takers. They developed new trading methods and routes, often investing not only their capital but also their lives. The Silk Road was fraught with perils, from treacherous terrains to bandit attacks, yet these merchants braved these challenges. This audacity to confront risks for potential economic gain is a defining characteristic of entrepreneurship.

Entrepreneurship as a Synthesis of Innovation and Risk

The Silk Road: A Testament to Entrepreneurial Innovation and Risk Management

The merchants of the Silk Road serve as a prime example of the synthesis between innovation and risk in entrepreneurship. These traders were not merely passive participants in the trade network; they actively sought innovative methods to enhance their trading practices. This quest for innovation was evident in their continuous efforts to find shorter or safer trade routes, develop new logistical solutions for efficient transportation of goods, and even create novel financial instruments to fund their ventures. In an era devoid of modern transportation or communication technologies, such innovations were not only beneficial but essential.

Moreover, these entrepreneurs faced a myriad of risks in their endeavors. To navigate this treacherous landscape, they adopted sophisticated risk management strategies. Forming caravans for safety, establishing networks of contacts along their routes for intelligence and assistance, and diversifying investments across various goods and routes were some of the key strategies employed. These measures laid the groundwork for fundamental principles in modern entrepreneurship, particularly in terms of risk management.

Investment for these traders extended beyond mere capital. It encompassed their time, energy, and often their entire livelihoods. This total immersion and commitment to their enterprise are emblematic of the entrepreneurial spirit, requiring a level of passion and dedication that is still relevant in contemporary entrepreneurial endeavors.

Risk as a Driving Force in Entrepreneurial Success

For the Silk Road merchants, embracing risk was not merely a necessity but a catalyst for growth and expansion. Venturing into unknown territories and establishing new trade relations allowed them to significantly expand their businesses. This approach mirrors the modern entrepreneurial ethos, where risk-taking is often a prerequisite for innovation and breakthroughs.

The Silk Road was fraught with uncertainties, ranging from natural disasters to political upheavals. The merchants' ability to navigate such unpredictable challenges underscores their resilience and adaptability - qualities that remain quintessential for entrepreneurs in any era. Additionally, not all ventures led to success. Some faced catastrophic losses, yet the ability to learn from these setbacks and persist is a testament to the enduring entrepreneurial spirit. Modern entrepreneurs often regard failure as a critical stepping stone to eventual success.

Conclusion: The Timeless Model of Entrepreneurship

In conclusion, the merchants of the Silk Road epitomize the essence of entrepreneurship. Their innovative approach to trade, coupled with an unwavering willingness to embrace risk, forms their legacy. It lies not just in the wealth they accumulated or the goods they traded, but in the enduring model of entrepreneurship they represent. They demonstrate that at the heart of successful entrepreneurship lies a blend of innovation, a deep understanding of risk, and the courage to venture into the unknown. This model continues to inspire and shape the entrepreneurial landscape today, reminding us that the core principles of entrepreneurship, combining innovation and risk-taking, are indeed timeless.

Cultural Ambassadors and Diplomats

The traders of the Silk Road were more than mere merchants of goods; they were also unofficial cultural ambassadors. In their extensive travels, they not only transported commodities but also became carriers of their own customs, beliefs, and languages, introducing them across the diverse regions they traversed. This role in cultural transmission was significant and multifaceted.

As these traders journeyed, they facilitated a two-way cultural exchange. They not only introduced their own customs and traditions to new areas but also absorbed elements of the cultures they encountered. This exchange extended to various aspects of life, from culinary practices to clothing styles. The impact of this dissemination was profound, often leading to the adoption and adaptation of these customs, thereby enriching the cultural tapestry of the societies they interacted with.

Beyond mere customs and traditions, these merchants played a pivotal role in the spread of religious beliefs and philosophical ideas. Major religious and philosophical systems, including Buddhism, Islam, Christianity, and others, traveled along the Silk Road, aided significantly by the traders. This movement of ideas was not a byproduct of trade but often a deliberate act, influenced by the traders' own religious or philosophical convictions.

In essence, the Silk Road traders' contribution to history extends beyond their economic impact. They were instrumental in the intercultural exchange, spreading not just material goods but also immaterial cultural, religious, and philosophical ideas. This exchange played a crucial role in shaping the cultural and intellectual landscapes of the regions connected by the Silk Road, showcasing the traders' historical significance as agents of cultural transmission and transformation.

❖ Ambassadors of Language and Art

Linguistic Exchange: Fostering Communication and Cultural Understanding

The traders of the Silk Road played a pivotal role as ambassadors of language. Language, in this context, was not merely a tool for trade negotiations; it was a vehicle for cultural exchange and understanding. As these merchants engaged with people from diverse linguistic backgrounds, they facilitated a two-way linguistic exchange. They shared their own languages and dialects, and in turn, absorbed new languages and dialects encountered along their routes. This dynamic exchange of languages was instrumental in the development of new lingua francas, serving as common languages that eased communication across different linguistic groups. Additionally, this interaction contributed significantly to the evolution of existing languages, enriching them with new words, phrases, and expressions. This linguistic interplay was a critical element in fostering not only commercial ties but also cultural understanding and integration among the regions connected by the Silk Road.

Artistic and Literary Exchange: The Cross-Pollination of Cultures

Moreover, the Silk Road traders were key agents in the exchange of artistic and literary traditions. As they traversed vast distances, they carried with them not just tangible goods but also intangible cultural treasures. Art forms, motifs, and literary works traveled with these merchants, leading to a significant cross-pollination of artistic and literary cultures. This exchange was not limited to the mere transfer of artistic objects or texts; it involved the sharing of ideas, styles, techniques, and narratives. The impact of this artistic and literary exchange was profound, significantly influencing the development of art and literature in various regions. For example, artistic motifs from one culture found their way into the fabric of another, and literary themes and styles were adapted and reinterpreted in different cultural contexts.

This rich exchange of art and literature contributed to the creation of a more interconnected and culturally diverse world. It played a crucial role in shaping the artistic and literary landscapes of the societies along the Silk Road, leaving a lasting impact on the development of world art and literature. The legacy of these traders, therefore, extends far beyond their commercial achievements. They were instrumental in fostering a vibrant and dynamic exchange of culture, art, and ideas, which continues to resonate in the rich tapestry of global cultural heritage.

✧ Unofficial Diplomats in Foreign Lands
The traders of the Silk Road, in their extensive travels and interactions, transcended their commercial roles to act as unofficial diplomats in foreign lands. Their everyday activities in trade and communication often went beyond mere business transactions; they served as vital conduits for mutual understanding and respect between diverse cultures. These traders, through their personal interactions and exchanges, played a crucial role in bridging societies that were geographically distant and culturally distinct.

Their presence in foreign lands, often marked by their adaptability and respect for local customs and practices, paved the way for a deeper level of cross-cultural engagement. As these merchants engaged with local populations, shared their customs, and learned from the cultures they interacted with, they fostered a sense of familiarity and mutual respect. This was not a structured or formal diplomatic effort; rather, it was an organic process driven by the necessities and opportunities of trade. However, the impact of their actions often had far-reaching consequences. The relationships and understandings developed through these interactions frequently laid the groundwork for more formal diplomatic relations between distant lands.

Economic and Political Implications: The Ripple Effect of Cultural Exchange
The cultural exchange facilitated by these Silk Road traders had significant economic and political implications. By fostering a better understanding and appreciation of different cultures, they indirectly

contributed to the establishment of more stable and prosperous trade relations. This was because trade is not merely a transaction of goods; it's also an exchange of trust, respect, and understanding. As these traders built relationships and established a rapport with their foreign counterparts, they created a foundation of trust that was crucial for sustainable and long-term economic interactions.

Moreover, the understanding and respect fostered by these traders often had broader political implications. In an age where formal diplomatic channels were limited or non-existent between many regions, these traders inadvertently served as liaisons, conveying not only goods but also ideas, customs, and even political sentiments. Their interactions helped to build a network of informal diplomatic ties, which could sometimes ease tensions and facilitate smoother political relations between diverse regions.

In conclusion, the traders of the Silk Road were much more than economic agents; they were pioneers of cross-cultural interaction, playing the role of unofficial diplomats in foreign lands. Through their efforts in fostering cross-cultural relationships, they not only enhanced trade and commerce but also laid the groundwork for better economic and political relations between diverse cultures, making a lasting impact on the course of global history.

Conclusion
In summary, the traders of the Silk Road were much more than economic agents; they were the vanguards of cultural exchange. Their travels facilitated the spread of customs, beliefs, languages, and artistic expressions, significantly impacting the cultural development of the regions they connected. They served as a bridge between civilizations, playing a role that went far beyond commerce and ventured into the realms of cultural and diplomatic exchange. This aspect of their legacy offers invaluable insights into the power of cultural diplomacy and the role of trade in fostering cross-cultural understanding and cooperation.

Pioneers of Globalization

The Silk Road can be seen as an early form of globalization. It connected disparate regions, leading to an exchange of not only goods but also ideas and technologies. This interaction was a precursor to the modern interconnected global economy. The merchants were, therefore, pioneers of this early globalization, fostering economic and cultural ties across vast distances.

Agents of Technological and Agricultural Exchange

The merchants traversing the Silk Road played a pivotal role as agents of change, particularly in the realms of technological and agricultural exchange. Their journeys across continents did not just involve the transportation of commodities; they were instrumental in the dissemination of innovative technologies and agricultural practices, which had profound impacts on the societies along their routes.

The Spread of Technological Innovations
One of the most significant aspects of these exchanges was the transmission of technological advancements. Technologies such as papermaking and printing, which originated in certain regions, were transported by these merchants to distant lands. This exchange was not a mere transfer of physical objects; it was the transmission of knowledge and skills. For instance, when papermaking technology traveled from China to the Middle East and later to Europe, it brought about a revolution in the way knowledge was recorded and disseminated. Similarly, the spread of printing technology played a crucial role in the democratization of knowledge, enabling the mass production of books and other written materials. These technologies significantly impacted the societies they reached, contributing to educational, cultural, and scientific advancements.

Agricultural Exchanges and Their Impact
In addition to technological innovations, these merchants were also vital in the exchange of agricultural products and techniques. As they

moved from region to region, they carried with them seeds, plants, and knowledge of agricultural practices. This exchange led to significant changes in food production and consumption patterns across continents. Crops that were indigenous to one region became staples in another, altering diets and agricultural practices. For example, the introduction of new varieties of grains, fruits, and vegetables led to more diverse and nutritious diets, which had far-reaching effects on public health and lifestyle.

Moreover, the transfer of agricultural techniques, such as irrigation methods and crop rotation, helped to improve agricultural productivity in regions that adopted them. These techniques, adapted to suit local conditions, enabled societies to better manage their agricultural resources and increase food production, leading to enhanced food security and economic stability.

Conclusion: A Catalyst for Societal Transformation
In conclusion, the merchants of the Silk Road were much more than carriers of goods; they were catalysts for widespread societal transformation. Through their role in the exchange of technological and agricultural innovations, they not only influenced trade and commerce but also shaped cultural, technological, and agricultural developments. The legacy of their contributions is evident in the way these exchanges brought about significant advancements in various societies, impacting everything from daily life and food habits to scientific progress and cultural growth. Thus, their role as agents of technological and agricultural exchange is a testament to the profound impact of the Silk Road on global history.

Impact on Modern Entrepreneurship

The entrepreneurial spirit of the Silk Road merchants, characterized by their adaptability, innovative approaches, and risk-taking attitudes, holds significant relevance in today's increasingly interconnected global economy. Modern entrepreneurs stand to gain considerable insight from studying these historical traders, particularly in how they navigated the complex and often uncertain landscapes of long-distance trade.

Lessons in Adaptability and Innovation

One of the key takeaways from the Silk Road merchants is their remarkable adaptability. In an ever-changing environment marked by diverse cultures, fluctuating market demands, and unpredictable risks, these merchants excelled in adjusting their strategies and practices. This adaptability is crucial in the modern business world, where rapid technological advancements and shifting market trends require a similar flexibility and willingness to evolve.

Their innovative approaches to overcoming challenges are equally instructive. Faced with the absence of modern transportation and communication technologies, these merchants developed groundbreaking methods in trade, logistics, and cultural diplomacy. Today's entrepreneurs can draw inspiration from this innovative spirit, applying creativity and resourcefulness in solving contemporary business challenges.

Cultural Intelligence in a Globalized Business Environment

The cultural intelligence displayed by the Silk Road merchants is another aspect that resonates strongly with modern entrepreneurship. Their success was partly due to their ability to navigate and respect the myriad of cultures they encountered. In today's globalized business environment, cultural intelligence is increasingly important. Entrepreneurs must understand and appreciate diverse cultural contexts to build successful international relationships and ventures.

Conclusion: A Timeless Legacy in Global Entrepreneurship

In conclusion, the merchants of the Silk Road were far more than mere traders of their time; they were pioneers who significantly shaped the economic, cultural, and technological landscapes. Their legacy provides profound insights into the essence of entrepreneurship, emphasizing the importance of adaptability, innovation, and cultural intelligence. These elements played a crucial role in the early stages of globalization and remain critical for understanding the evolution of global trade and commerce.

Their story is not just a historical account but a source of inspiration and learning for modern entrepreneurs. The challenges and triumphs of these ancient merchants mirror the complexities faced in today's global business environment, offering valuable lessons in resilience, innovation, and cross-cultural engagement. Their enduring impact highlights that the core principles of successful entrepreneurship are indeed timeless and continue to hold relevance in shaping the future of global business and trade.

The Age of Exploration and Expansion

Embark with me on a thrilling journey back to the Age of Exploration, an epoch that redefined the boundaries of the known world and marked a pivotal chapter in our collective story. This was a time when intrepid entrepreneurs were also bold explorers, setting sail on uncharted seas, driven by the allure of undiscovered lands and the promise of immense wealth. Picture the creak of wooden ships, the billow of sails against the vast, open ocean, and the indomitable spirit of adventurers seeking horizons beyond the edge of the map. This era was not merely about discovering new lands; it was about weaving a tapestry of global trade networks, intertwining distant continents through the exchange of exotic goods, groundbreaking ideas, and diverse cultures. The Age of Exploration was the dawning of a new era in human interaction, laying the foundational stones for the interconnected global economy we experience today.

As our narrative progresses, we enter the era of the Industrial Revolutions, a period of profound transformation that reshaped the very fabric of society. It was during this time that the world transitioned from agrarian economies to industrial behemoths. In this crucible of change, modern entrepreneurship was born and nurtured. Visionaries and innovators, figures like James Watt with his steam engine and Henry Ford with his assembly line, emerged not merely as businessmen but as architects of new industries. They revolutionized production methods, transforming how goods were manufactured and altering the rhythm of daily life. Their legacy transcends the tangible products they created; they were pioneers who reimagined the possibilities of business and innovation.

Imagine the bustling factories, the hum of machinery, and the sparks of creativity that ignited in these workshops and industrial complexes. Entrepreneurs of the Industrial Revolution were not just building businesses; they were constructing the future, piece by piece. Their ingenuity laid the groundwork for the technological advancements and economic systems that shape our modern world. They taught us that entrepreneurship is about more than creating products; it's about envisioning and realizing new ways of living and working.

The Industrial Revolution was a testament to human resilience and adaptability. As society grappled with the rapid changes brought about by industrialization, entrepreneurs were at the forefront, navigating uncharted territories in business and technology. They showed us that in times of change, the most potent tool we have is our ability to innovate and adapt.

As we look back at these monumental chapters in history, let us draw inspiration from the daring spirit of the explorers of the Age of Exploration and the transformative vision of the entrepreneurs of the Industrial Revolution. Their stories are not just historical accounts; they are enduring lessons in courage, innovation, and the relentless pursuit of progress. They remind us that the journey of entrepreneurship is an ever-evolving adventure, filled with opportunities to redefine the world and leave a lasting impact on the tapestry of human history.

The 20th Century and the Rise of the Corporate Giant

As we turn the pages of history to the dawn of the 20th century, we find ourselves in an era of colossal transformation and innovation. This period marked the rise of corporate titans, a time when ambitious entrepreneurs did not just build businesses; they built vast empires that would redefine the landscape of economies and societies alike. Picture the bustling streets of early 20th-century America, the clatter of industry, and the whispers of a new economic era taking shape.

In this dynamic backdrop, figures like John D. Rockefeller and Andrew Carnegie emerged, not merely as businessmen but as architects of industries that would shape the modern world. John D. Rockefeller, with his Standard Oil Company, didn't just capitalize on the oil industry; he revolutionized it. He constructed an empire that extended its influence far beyond oil, impacting every facet of American industry and economy. Similarly, Andrew Carnegie, the steel magnate, transformed the production of steel, not just fueling the construction of cities but also forging the very backbone of industrial America. Their endeavors went beyond mere profit-making; they were reshaping society, setting new standards for business, and redefining the meaning of corporate success.

But the 20th century brought with it more than just the rise of industrial magnates; it witnessed the birth of venture capitalism. This new dimension in entrepreneurship was like a gust of wind under the wings of innovation, providing the necessary capital and support for groundbreaking ideas and ventures. Venture capitalism emerged as a driving force, enabling dreamers and innovators to bring their visions to life. It was an era where the boldness of an idea, coupled with the right financial backing, could change the world.

This period was a breeding ground for innovation, where the courage to dream big was met with the resources to make those dreams a reality. The emergence of venture capitalism meant that entrepreneurship was no longer limited by the constraints of personal capital. It opened doors to wider possibilities, fostering an environment where creativity and innovation could thrive. It was during this time that the foundations of modern technology companies, the startups and tech giants we know today, were laid.

As we reflect on this transformative era, let us be inspired by the audacity and vision of the entrepreneurs of the 20th century. Their stories are not just tales of business success; they are narratives of shaping and reshaping the world. They remind us that entrepreneurship is about more than just creating a product or a service; it's about envisioning and building new realities. Their legacy teaches us that with determination, innovation, and the right support, the potential for change is boundless. The 20th century stands as a vibrant chapter in the ongoing story of entrepreneurship, encouraging us to dream big, embrace innovation, and relentlessly pursue the creation of something truly monumental.

The Digital Revolution and the New Age Entrepreneur

As we journey closer to our present day, we find ourselves amidst the exhilarating whirlwind of the digital revolution, a pivotal chapter in our saga of human progress and innovation. This era is characterized by a seismic shift, where technology becomes the driving force, opening doors to realms previously unimagined. In this digital epoch, enter a new breed of entrepreneurs – visionaries like Steve Jobs, Bill Gates, and Jeff Bezos. These individuals did not simply build companies; they spawned entirely new industries, fundamentally altering the fabric of how we live, work, and connect with each other.

Imagine the world before the advent of personal computing. It was a landscape ripe for revolution, and visionaries like Bill Gates and Steve Jobs stepped into this void. They saw potential where others saw impossibility. With the creation of Microsoft and Apple, they brought computing to the masses, democratizing technology and opening a world of possibilities. Similarly, Jeff Bezos, with the founding of Amazon, transformed how we shop, bringing the marketplace to our fingertips. These trailblazers did more than create products; they crafted new ways of living, embedding technology into our daily lives.

The digital revolution, powered by these entrepreneurial minds, is a testament to the unyielding power of human creativity and ambition. It is a revolution that continues to evolve, constantly pushing the boundaries of what is possible. These leaders showed us that with technology as our tool, we can reimagine and reshape our world. They were not just adapting to change; they were the architects of change, leveraging technology to build new paradigms.

This historical journey through the epochs of entrepreneurship reveals a common thread – the indomitable entrepreneurial spirit. It is a force fueled by resilience, vision, adaptability, and the audacity to venture into the unknown. These historical narratives are not just accounts of the past; they are a mosaic of lessons and inspirations that illuminate the essence of entrepreneurship. They remind us that to be an entrepreneur is to be a relentless seeker, a dreamer who dares to challenge the status quo.

As we reflect on these stories, let them ignite our imagination and guide our endeavors in the present and the future. They encourage us to embrace the spirit of innovation, to see beyond the horizon, and to boldly venture where no one has before. The legacy of these entrepreneurs teaches us that our journey in business and life is not just about creating or managing ventures; it is about embarking on a transformative journey that has the power to reshape our world. Let us carry forward this legacy, inspired by the past, to forge new paths and leave our mark in the ongoing story of human endeavor and progress.

The Psychology of the Entrepreneur

In the captivating world of entrepreneurship, the psychology of the entrepreneur emerges as a fascinating and vital realm to explore. This isn't just about business strategies or market trends; it's about delving into the minds of those who dare to dream and do. Entrepreneurs are a unique breed, their minds a blend of creativity, resilience, passion, and relentless determination. Let's embark on an enlightening journey to understand the psychological makeup of these trailblazers who not only build businesses but often change the course of industries and impact societies.

◆ The Creative Visionary

Let's dive deeper into the world of the creative visionary, the heart and soul of the entrepreneurial spirit. Envision an entrepreneur, not just as a business person, but as a modern-day alchemist, turning the mundane into the extraordinary. Their mind is a labyrinth of creativity, where ideas swirl and coalesce into visions of what could be. These individuals look at the world through a lens of endless possibilities, seeing opportunities where others see obstacles, solutions where others see problems.

➤ The Birth of Ideas

Imagine the birth of an idea, akin to a solitary spark that illuminates the vast expanse of the creative mind. This spark, often emerging from the most mundane of experiences – a casual conversation, a solitary walk, or a moment of quiet reflection – ignites the imagination of the visionary entrepreneur. In these seemingly trivial moments, connections are formed, dots are joined, and an idea begins to take shape. The mind of the entrepreneur is a rich soil, teeming with the seeds of potential; it is here that a simple thought can germinate into a concept capable of altering the world.

Picture these visionaries, not merely as business creators, but as artists of the future. Their canvas is boundless, unrestricted by the norms and conventions of the present. They are not mere spectators of the status quo; they are active challengers, constantly seeking to innovate, build, and bring forth change. Their visions are vivid tapestries of possibility, painted with the bold strokes of imagination and the fine lines of strategic planning. These visions are not idle daydreams but blueprints of a future they are determined to realize. They see a world that differs from the present, one that is improved by their contributions, and it's this vision that propels them forward, guiding their journey through the tumultuous yet exhilarating path of bringing their ideas to fruition.

In this process of creation, the entrepreneurial mind functions like an alchemist, transforming the lead of everyday life into the gold of groundbreaking innovation. Each step of the way, these entrepreneurs are guided by their vision, using it as a compass to navigate the complexities and challenges of turning their ideas into reality. The journey is rarely smooth; it is fraught with obstacles and setbacks. Yet, it is their unwavering commitment to their vision that keeps them steadfast, turning each hurdle into a stepping stone towards their ultimate goal.

This journey of the entrepreneur, from the inception of an idea to the realization of a vision, is a testament to the power of human creativity and determination. It's a narrative that inspires and motivates, reminding us that within each of us lies the potential to conceive ideas that can change the course of our lives and the world. These entrepreneurs teach us that the birth of an idea is just the beginning; it's the relentless pursuit of that idea, the courage to dream big, and the resilience to bring those dreams to life that truly define the entrepreneurial spirit.

Let this narrative of the birth and realization of ideas serve as an encouragement and a beacon of inspiration. It reminds us that the journey of entrepreneurship is accessible to all who dare to dream and are willing to embark on the journey of turning their dreams into reality. In the story of each entrepreneurial visionary, we find a reflection of our own potential to imagine, create, and transform – to paint our own visions of the future and to boldly bring them to life.

> From Dreamers to Doers

Embark on a journey with the entrepreneurs, the remarkable breed of individuals who transform the ethereal fabric of dreams into the tangible structures of reality. These are the people who do more than just envision futures; they build them. Picture an entrepreneur with an idea, a vision shimmering like a mirage on the horizon. This idea is not just a fleeting thought; it's a beacon guiding them. They are not mere dreamers lost in the clouds of imagination; they are doers, grounded in the resolve to make their dreams a reality.

The path from being dreamers to becoming doers is not a straight line; it's a winding road filled with obstacles, challenges, and sometimes, seemingly insurmountable barriers. But it is their unwavering belief in their vision that keeps these entrepreneurs steadfast in their journey. They possess a unique blend of optimism and pragmatism – the ability to see the world not just as it is, but as it could be, and the determination to make that vision a reality.

As architects of their dreams, entrepreneurs lay the foundation of their visions with the bricks of hard work, determination, and an unrelenting commitment to their goals. They understand that an idea, no matter how groundbreaking, is only as powerful as the effort put into realizing it. So, they roll up their sleeves and delve into the laborious process of creation, turning the abstract blueprints of their imagination into concrete realities.

This transformative process is akin to alchemy, where the base metals of effort and perseverance are transmuted into the gold of success and innovation. The journey of an entrepreneur is a testament to the power of human will and creativity. It's a narrative that underscores the fact that with enough determination and hard work, even the loftiest dreams can be grounded in reality.

Let this story of transformation from dreamers to doers inspire and motivate. It's a reminder that each one of us has the potential to not only dream but also to act, to not just imagine but also to create. The entrepreneurs' journey from concept to creation teaches us that while dreaming is essential, it is the doing that changes the world. It's a call to action – to take those first steps towards realizing our visions, to embrace the challenges and to persevere through the obstacles, and to join the ranks of those who dare to turn their dreams into reality.

- Igniting the Spark of Entrepreneurship

In the dynamic odyssey of entrepreneurship, the initial spark often ignites from the creative vision of the entrepreneur, a vision that transcends the conventional boundaries of business and aspires to forge change. Envision these entrepreneurs as not merely founders of companies but as catalysts of transformation, driven by an insatiable urge to create, innovate, and redefine. This spark, this initial burst of inspiration, is what sets them on their path – a path not just of commercial success, but of making a tangible, meaningful impact on the world.

These visionaries are propelled by a desire to solve problems in unprecedented ways, to venture into uncharted territories of thought and action. Their aspirations go beyond the mechanics of running a business; they are about birthing ideas that can elevate societies, revolutionize industries, and alter the course of history. Picture them as architects of the future, using their vision as a blueprint to construct realities that once lived only in the realms of imagination.

This drive to create and impact is not just about ambition; it's about a deep-seated belief in the power of ideas to improve lives. Entrepreneurs like these see potential where others see challenges, opportunities where others see obstacles. Their motivation lies in the conviction that their innovations can bring about positive change, be it through groundbreaking technology, revolutionary business models, or novel products that meet unaddressed needs.

Their journey is more than a pursuit of personal or financial achievement; it's a quest to leave a lasting imprint on society. Each step forward is guided by the desire to make a difference, to challenge the status quo, and to contribute something of value to the world. This is what fuels their relentless drive, their tireless work, and their unwavering dedication.

In essence, igniting the spark of entrepreneurship is about lighting the fire of innovation and impact. It's a reminder that entrepreneurship at its core is a force for change, a means to bring about a better, more efficient, more connected world. These entrepreneurs teach us that with creativity, passion, and determination, it's possible to turn visionary ideas into realities that not only shape businesses but also redefine the landscapes in which we live. Let their journeys inspire us to find our sparks, to nurture them, and to embark on our paths of innovation and impact.

➢ Inspiring Change and Innovation

In the tapestry of human progress, the creative visionary emerges not merely as an entrepreneur, but as a luminary of change and innovation, illuminating paths for others to follow. These individuals stand as towering beacons of inspiration, challenging us to look beyond the ordinary, urging us to see beyond the veil of the present into the realm of what could be. Their approach to innovation transcends the conventional boundaries of technology and products; it is a mindset, a unique way of perceiving the world and its myriad possibilities.

Imagine the creative visionary as a catalyst, sparking a flame of inspiration in all who encounter their story. They teach us that to innovate is to dare to dream, to venture beyond the comfort zones of current thinking and existing solutions. Their journeys are not linear narratives of success but are rich, multifaceted odysseys marked by moments of revelation, resilience, and reinvention. They encourage us to think bigger, not just in terms of scale but in terms of vision. To dream bolder, stretching the limits of our imagination, and to embrace the pursuit of our visions with unyielding passion and determination.

More than just architects of businesses, these visionaries are builders of the future, molding and shaping the contours of our world with their ideas and actions. Their stories are not confined to the annals of business success; they are compelling narratives of transformation, of turning the impossible into the possible, of reshaping industries, and, in many cases, influencing the very fabric of society. They remind us that at the heart of significant change and innovation lies a powerful vision, coupled with the courage to pursue it against all odds.

As we immerse ourselves in the world of these creative visionaries, let their journey ignite the latent spark of ambition and creativity within us. Let their unwavering commitment to their vision inspire us to embrace our inner entrepreneur. Their stories are not just a testament to what they have achieved; they are invitations for us to embark on our journeys of innovation and impact. They urge us to dream with audacity, to challenge the status quo, and to see the pursuit of our dreams not just as a possibility but as a responsibility.

In the end, the legacy of the creative visionary is a call to action – a call to each one of us to awaken our potential, to harness our unique talents and insights, and to boldly step forward as agents of change. Their stories stand as powerful reminders that each of us has within us the capacity to be visionaries in our own right, to inspire change and innovation in our spheres, and to contribute to the ever-unfolding story of human progress and ingenuity.

✧ Resilience in the Face of Adversity

In the exhilarating yet demanding journey of entrepreneurship, resilience emerges as a defining characteristic, a beacon of strength that guides entrepreneurs through the tumultuous seas of business. This resilience is not just a trait; it's a dynamic force, a muscle that grows more robust and more formidable with each challenge faced and overcome. As we venture into the world of entrepreneurship, we discover that the path is indeed laden with obstacles and setbacks. However, what distinguishes successful entrepreneurs is their extraordinary capacity to confront these adversities head-on, to learn from their failures, and to emerge from them not weakened, but stronger and more determined.

Picture resilience in the entrepreneurial world as a phoenix rising from the ashes. Each time an entrepreneur faces a setback, whether it's a failed venture, a rejected proposal, or an unexpected market shift, they do not see it as the end. Instead, they view these moments as invaluable learning opportunities, stepping stones that are integral to their journey. They understand that the road to success is not a straight line but a winding path filled with lessons to be learned and growth to be experienced. This resilient mindset allows them to navigate the highs and lows of their journey with a remarkable blend of grit and grace.

Entrepreneurs with this kind of resilience do not shy away from failure; they embrace it. They recognize that to innovate and break new ground, one must be willing to take risks and sometimes fail. But more importantly, they know that each failure brings them closer to their goals, equipping them with insights and experiences that cannot be gained any other way. This perspective transforms the very nature of setbacks, turning them from roadblocks into stepping stones, from moments of doubt into opportunities for development.

This resilient spirit is what propels entrepreneurs forward, fueling their persistence and driving their passion. It's what enables them to keep their vision in sight, even when the path becomes obscured by challenges. They tackle each obstacle with a tenacity and perseverance that is both inspiring and instructive. Their resilience is their compass, guiding them through uncharted territories and helping them stay the course, even when the going gets tough.

In essence, resilience in the face of adversity is the hallmark of true entrepreneurship. It's a quality that not only defines the entrepreneurial spirit but also inspires and encourages others to pursue their dreams. It teaches us that the journey of entrepreneurship is not about avoiding failure but about learning to rise every time we fall. It's a reminder that in the world of business, as in life, our greatest growth often comes from our most challenging experiences. Let the resilience of entrepreneurs be a source of inspiration and motivation, urging us to face our challenges with courage, to learn from our setbacks, and to keep moving forward with unwavering determination and hope.

✧ A Passion That Fuels Persistence

In the enthralling narrative of entrepreneurship, passion stands as the indefatigable engine that propels entrepreneurs forward, fueling their journey through thick and thin. This passion transcends mere enthusiasm for a product or service; it's a deep-seated drive that burns within, propelling them towards their vision of making a meaningful impact. Whether it's about revolutionizing an industry, breathing life into a groundbreaking invention, or contributing to societal change, their passion is the force that keeps them anchored to their mission, even in the face of daunting challenges.

Picture this passion as a relentless current, driving entrepreneurs through the often turbulent waters of their ventures. It's this unwavering passion that gets them out of bed each morning, ready to tackle the day's challenges, and it's what keeps them up at night, planning and dreaming of what's next. It's a passion so potent that it becomes infectious, spreading to their teams, their customers, and beyond, igniting a shared enthusiasm and commitment towards their vision.

This isn't just a fleeting excitement; it's a deep-rooted passion that is intertwined with their very sense of purpose. For these entrepreneurs, their work is not just a means to an end but a calling. They are driven by the belief that what they are creating has the potential to make a real difference in the world. This conviction becomes the fuel for their persistence, empowering them to push boundaries, surmount obstacles, and forge new paths.

In moments of doubt or failure, when the odds seem insurmountable, it's their passion that acts as a beacon of hope, guiding them back on track. It's the inner flame that reminds them why they started in the first place and the reason they continue to persevere. Their passion is their compass, pointing them towards their north star, keeping them focused and steadfast on their entrepreneurial journey.

Thus, passion in entrepreneurship is more than just a trait; it's a fundamental element of their identity. It's the driving force that enables them to keep striving for excellence, to never settle for mediocrity, and to continually aspire for more. Let this narrative of passionate persistence serve as an inspiration, reminding us that with true passion, we can overcome any hurdle, break any barrier, and achieve our loftiest goals. The story of entrepreneurship is, at its core, a story of passion fueling persistence, a testament to the power of a driven heart and a determined mind.

✧ Determination and Tenacity

In the exhilarating odyssey of entrepreneurship, determination and tenacity are the twin beacons that guide every visionary on their path. These qualities are not just attributes; they are the very essence of the entrepreneurial spirit. Imagine an entrepreneur navigating the uncharted waters of business. They face not only the unknown but often the improbable. It is their unwavering determination that serves as their compass, steering them through these unexplored territories, be they markets, technologies, or innovative business models.

This determination is a relentless force, a kind of inner fire that burns with the conviction of their vision. It fuels the countless hours of hard work, the persistence in the face of setbacks, and the resilience in the throes of challenges. Entrepreneurs possess a tenacity that is formidable, a steadfast resolve that drives them to push boundaries, to continuously learn, adapt, and grow. They view each day as an opportunity to edge closer to their goals, each failure as a lesson to be learned, and each success as a milestone to be surpassed.

This tenacity is what enables entrepreneurs to transform obstacles into stepping stones. Where others might see a roadblock, they see a puzzle to be solved, a challenge to be overcome. Their determination is the force that propels them to keep moving forward, to innovate, to iterate, and to persevere, even when the end goal seems like a distant mirage on the horizon. It's this quality that helps them navigate the complex maze of entrepreneurship, turning what may appear as insurmountable hurdles into opportunities for growth and innovation.

Moreover, this determination and tenacity are contagious, inspiring teams, attracting supporters, and compelling investors. It's a magnetic force that draws others to their cause, galvanizing collective efforts to turn a vision into reality. Entrepreneurs lead by example, showing that with enough grit, resilience, and tenacity, even the loftiest goals can be achieved.

In essence, the story of every successful entrepreneur is underpinned by an unwavering determination and an indomitable tenacity. These qualities are the lifeblood of their journey, fueling their pursuit and enabling them to carve paths where none existed. Let this narrative remind us that with determination and tenacity, we too can chart our course, overcome our challenges, and reach the destinations we set for ourselves. In the world of entrepreneurship, these qualities are not just desirable; they are essential for navigating the voyage from vision to achievement.

- ✧ Adaptability and Flexibility

In the dynamic and ever-shifting landscape of business, adaptability and flexibility stand as the twin pillars that uphold the entrepreneurial spirit. These traits are more than mere buzzwords; they are the lifeblood of a successful entrepreneur's journey. Imagine an entrepreneur navigating the unpredictable tides of the market – they are akin to a skilled sailor, adjusting their sails to the changing winds, always ready to chart a new course. This agility is not just about surviving; it's about thriving in a world where change is the only constant.

Entrepreneurs with this adaptive mindset view each shift in the market, each new technological advancement, and each emerging trend not as hurdles, but as opportunities to evolve. They are the masters of reinvention, constantly learning from their environment and experiences, and applying this knowledge to pivot their strategies when necessary. This flexibility is their superpower, allowing them to stay nimble and responsive in a competitive landscape. It's this ability to adapt that enables them to seize opportunities that others might miss and to navigate their way through challenges that might derail others.

The essence of adaptability in entrepreneurship is beautifully encapsulated in their ability to embrace change. Where others may see change as a threat, these visionaries see it as a catalyst for growth and innovation. They understand that to remain relevant and successful, one must be willing to continually evolve. This evolution is not just about business models or products; it's about an overarching mindset that embraces change, learns from it, and uses it as a stepping stone towards greater achievements.

The psychology of the entrepreneur, rich in adaptability and flexibility, offers a window into the minds of some of the most successful and influential figures in the business world. It's a fascinating blend of creativity, resilience, passion, determination, and an unwavering willingness to adapt. These traits do not solely define their business acumen; they encapsulate their approach to life. As we delve deeper into understanding these entrepreneurial minds, we uncover a wellspring of inspiration.

Let the stories of these adaptable entrepreneurs invigorate us, reminding us that with the right mindset, we too can navigate the complexities of our ambitions. They encourage us to embrace our entrepreneurial spirit, to think differently, and to approach the unpredictable journey of business and life with adaptability and resilience. These narratives are not just tales of business prowess; they are guides that show us how, with flexibility and adaptability, we can turn the uncertain terrain of our dreams into the solid ground of reality.

Societal Impact and the Role of the Entrepreneur

In the vibrant tapestry of society, entrepreneurs emerge as pivotal artisans, weaving threads of innovation, progress, and change into the fabric of our communities. Their role transcends the boundaries of mere business creation; they are catalysts for societal transformation. As we explore the societal impact of entrepreneurs, we uncover a narrative that is as inspiring as it is impactful. Entrepreneurs are not just builders of companies; they are architects of societal change, driving advancements that reshape how we live, work, and interact.

Imagine the entrepreneur as a visionary, seeing not only the potential for profit but also the opportunity for positive societal impact. They recognize that with every innovative product, service, or business model, there is a chance to improve lives, uplift communities, and address pressing societal challenges. Whether it's through creating jobs, fostering economic growth, or pioneering sustainable practices, their endeavors ripple outwards, touching lives and shaping societies. Their work often sparks a chain reaction of progress, inspiring others to innovate and push boundaries, creating a cycle of growth and development that benefits the broader community.

Entrepreneurs also play a crucial role in setting new standards and norms within society. Through their innovative approaches and ethical business practices, they can influence industries to adopt more responsible and sustainable methods. They often lead by example, showing that success can be achieved without compromising on values or the well-being of the community. In doing so, they not only contribute to the economic health of their societies but also to the moral and ethical compass of the business world.

Moreover, the impact of entrepreneurs often extends into the realms of culture and identity. They can be powerful agents of cultural preservation and promotion, using their platforms to celebrate and disseminate cultural heritage and values. Through their products and services, they can bring attention to local crafts, traditions, and stories, fostering a sense of pride and identity within communities.

In essence, the societal impact of entrepreneurs is profound and far-reaching. Their role in shaping and influencing society is as crucial as their role in business. As we delve into the stories of these entrepreneurs, let their journey inspire us to think beyond the confines of individual success. Let us be motivated by their example to consider the broader impact of our actions and to strive for ventures that not only achieve business success but also contribute positively to the world around us. The narrative of the entrepreneur is not just a tale of business acumen; it is a story of societal progress, a testament to the power of visionary thinking and responsible leadership in creating a better world for all.

Key Traits of Successful Entrepreneurs

In the captivating journey of entrepreneurship, certain key traits stand out, defining the essence of successful entrepreneurs. These characteristics form the backbone of their success, acting as guiding stars in their ventures. As we unravel these traits, we find a consistent theme – a blend of personal qualities that combine to create the dynamic and effective entrepreneur.

Firstly, there's the unwavering resilience that entrepreneurs possess. This isn't just about bouncing back from setbacks; it's about viewing failures as stepping stones to success. Imagine them as navigators in the vast ocean of business, where resilience is their compass, steering them through storms towards their destination. This trait enables them to face challenges head-on, learn from their mistakes, and emerge stronger with each hurdle they overcome.

Then, there's the inexhaustible passion that fuels their journey. This passion goes beyond mere enthusiasm; it's a deep-seated drive that propels them to pursue their vision with relentless vigor. It's the fire that keeps them going through long workdays and the spark that ignites innovation. This passion is infectious, spreading to their teams, investors, and customers, creating a shared belief in their vision.

Creativity and innovation are also pivotal traits. Successful entrepreneurs have the unique ability to think outside the box, to see possibilities where others see dead-ends. They are the trailblazers who venture off the beaten path, bringing new ideas to life. Their creativity isn't confined to product development; it permeates every aspect of their business, from problem-solving to marketing strategies.

Moreover, adaptability is a crucial trait in the ever-changing business landscape. Successful entrepreneurs are agile, able to pivot their strategies in response to market shifts. They understand that flexibility and the willingness to evolve are key to staying relevant and competitive. This adaptability is what allows them to ride the waves of change, rather than being swept away by them.

Lastly, effective communication skills are essential. The ability to articulate ideas clearly, persuade stakeholders, and inspire teams is crucial for any successful entrepreneur. They are storytellers, narrating their vision in a way that resonates with others, turning listeners into allies in their entrepreneurial journey.

In summary, the key traits of successful entrepreneurs - resilience, passion, creativity, adaptability, and effective communication - are the cornerstones of their success. These traits interweave to form the fabric of the entrepreneurial spirit. As we delve into the stories of successful entrepreneurs, let their qualities inspire us to cultivate these traits within ourselves. Their journeys illustrate that with the right combination of qualities, the path of entrepreneurship can lead to remarkable achievements and lasting impacts in the world of business and beyond.

As we conclude this first chapter of our journey into 'The Foundations of Entrepreneurship', we stand at the threshold of a deeper understanding and appreciation of what drives this dynamic and impactful field. Throughout this chapter, we have navigated the rich historical tapestry of entrepreneurship, delving into the evolution of trade and commerce from ancient civilizations to the industrial revolutions. This exploration has not only highlighted key historical milestones but also revealed the enduring spirit of human ingenuity and the relentless pursuit of progress that defines entrepreneurship.

We have also ventured into the psychological realm, unraveling the motivations, fears, and mindsets that fuel the entrepreneurial spirit. This introspection has offered us valuable insights into the heart of ambition and resilience, uncovering the inner workings of the entrepreneurial mind and the driving forces behind their risk-taking and innovation.

Furthermore, we have examined the significant impact entrepreneurs have on society, shaping economies, altering societal norms, and influencing cultural trends. This section has underscored the symbiotic relationship between entrepreneurship and societal development, highlighting the role of entrepreneurs as change agents, innovators, and visionary leaders.

As we wrap up this chapter, we reflect on the relevance and importance of entrepreneurial traits in today's rapidly changing business landscape. In a world marked by technological advancements and globalization, the foundational qualities of entrepreneurship – innovation, resilience, adaptability, and visionary thinking – continue to be essential for success. These traits are the guiding stars for aspiring entrepreneurs, illuminating the path to achievement in the modern business world.

This chapter has been more than just an introductory exploration; it has been an invitation to view the world through the entrepreneurial lens. It has encouraged us to understand the deep roots and significant impact of entrepreneurship on our world. As we progress through this journey, let us carry forward the curiosity, eagerness to learn, and openness to be inspired by the countless stories of determination, innovation, and success.

Now, as we turn the page to the next chapter of our journey, we are better equipped with the foundational knowledge that will guide us through the multifaceted world of entrepreneurship. Let us dive deeper into this fascinating field, ready to uncover more secrets, embrace more insights, and be inspired by the endless possibilities that entrepreneurship holds. Get ready to continue this enlightening journey, as we further explore and understand the vast and vibrant world of entrepreneurship.

Chapter 2: Cultivating an Entrepreneurial Mindset

Welcome to Chapter 2: "Cultivating an Entrepreneurial Mindset," a journey into the core of what makes entrepreneurs tick and thrive. In this chapter, we dive deep into the psychological landscape of entrepreneurship, exploring the crucial mental frameworks and attitudes that differentiate the successful entrepreneur from the rest. This journey is not just about acquiring skills or knowledge; it's about nurturing a mindset that empowers you to embrace challenges, learn continuously, and evolve incessantly.

Growth Mindset vs. Fixed Mindset

Our exploration begins with the fundamental dichotomy between a growth mindset and a fixed mindset. Picture two entrepreneurs, each facing the same setback. One sees it as a dead end, a confirmation of their limitations. The other views it as a challenge, an opportunity to learn and grow. This is the essence of the growth mindset – the belief that abilities and intelligence can be developed, that potential is nurtured through perseverance and effort. In this chapter, we'll delve into how cultivating a growth mindset fuels innovation, resilience, and ultimately, success.

Embracing Risk and Failure

Next, we turn to the entrepreneur's relationship with risk and failure. The journey of entrepreneurship is inherently risky, and failure is an inevitable companion. Yet, it's in the crucible of risk and failure that the entrepreneurial spirit is tempered and strengthened. We'll explore how embracing risk is not about recklessness but about calculated courage, and how failure, far from being a setback, is a valuable teacher. It's about shifting perspectives, where risks become opportunities for groundbreaking innovations and failures become stepping stones to success.

Continuous Learning and Adaptability

The final pillar of cultivating an entrepreneurial mindset is the commitment to continuous learning and adaptability. In a world that's constantly changing, the ability to adapt and learn is not just an asset; it's a necessity. We'll examine how successful entrepreneurs are lifelong learners, constantly seeking new knowledge, skills, and experiences. They are agile, ready to pivot their strategies in response to new information or changing market conditions. This section will not only inspire you to embrace a philosophy of lifelong learning but will also provide practical strategies to integrate continuous learning and adaptability into your entrepreneurial journey.

As we embark on this chapter, remember that cultivating an entrepreneurial mindset is a journey, not a destination. It's about embracing growth, learning from every experience, and being flexible enough to adapt to the ever-changing business landscape. Let this chapter be your guide in developing the mindset that will empower you to navigate the challenges of entrepreneurship and turn your visions into realities. Get ready to be inspired, to challenge your perceptions, and to embrace the mindset that will set you on the path to lasting success and growth.

Growth Mindset vs. Fixed Mindset

In the vibrant tapestry of entrepreneurship, the dichotomy between a Growth Mindset and a Fixed Mindset serves as a defining thread, weaving the narrative of success and resilience. Picture two entrepreneurs, both confronted with challenges and setbacks. The one with a Growth Mindset sees these moments not as roadblocks but as opportunities for growth and learning. This mindset is akin to a fertile soil where abilities and intelligence can be cultivated and expanded through dedication and effort.

✦ The Growth Mindset: Cultivating Potential

The Growth Mindset, a transformative philosophy embraced by visionary entrepreneurs, heralds a profound shift in the way challenges and setbacks are perceived. At its core, this mindset champions the belief that abilities and intelligence are not fixed traits but malleable qualities that can be honed and expanded through dedication and effort. Let's delve into the essence of the Growth Mindset, unveiling the mindset's profound impact on entrepreneurial journeys.

> ➢ Cultivating a Dynamic Perspective

Entrepreneurs embracing a Growth Mindset approach their endeavors with an unwavering belief in their capacity to evolve and adapt. Challenges are not viewed as insurmountable obstacles but rather as integral components of the entrepreneurial journey, presenting opportunities for growth and refinement. This dynamic perspective sets the stage for a continuous cycle of improvement and learning.

In the landscape of the Growth Mindset, challenges cease to be daunting impediments; rather, they are embraced as opportunities for personal and professional development. Entrepreneurs recognize that each hurdle encountered presents a chance to grow, refine their skills, and deepen their understanding of the intricacies of their chosen endeavors. This perspective fosters an environment where challenges become catalysts for improvement rather than hindrances to success.

The dynamic perspective ingrained in the Growth Mindset becomes the driving force behind a perpetual cycle of improvement. Entrepreneurs, fueled by the belief in their ability to adapt, constantly seek ways to enhance their skills, innovate, and refine their approaches. This mindset propels them forward, ensuring that every experience, whether a triumph or a setback, becomes a stepping stone toward mastery and continuous improvement.

A Growth Mindset transforms the entrepreneurial journey into an evolution, a dynamic process where adaptation and growth are embraced as fundamental principles. Entrepreneurs with this mindset understand that the path to success is not a linear trajectory but a winding road full of twists and turns. Each twist in the journey is met with curiosity and the firm conviction that it presents an opportunity for evolution and advancement.

In essence, cultivating a dynamic perspective within the Growth Mindset represents a paradigm shift in how entrepreneurs perceive challenges. Rather than being daunted by difficulties, they welcome them as essential components of the entrepreneurial landscape. This shift not only reframes obstacles but also instills a sense of resilience and optimism, making the entrepreneurial journey a continuous quest for growth, refinement, and the pursuit of excellence.

> Stepping Stones Toward Mastery

In the realm of the Growth Mindset, challenges cease to be roadblocks; instead, they transform into stepping stones toward mastery. Entrepreneurs with this mindset perceive difficulties not as deterrents but as essential components of the entrepreneurial landscape. Each obstacle becomes a chance to enhance skills, deepen understanding, and fortify resilience.

A crucial aspect of viewing challenges as stepping stones toward mastery is the shift in perspective from adversity to opportunity. Entrepreneurs understand that each hurdle, whether large or small, offers a unique chance for growth and improvement. Rather than fearing challenges, they welcome them as integral to the learning process, recognizing that overcoming difficulties is a fundamental aspect of mastering their craft.

Moreover, the Growth Mindset instills a sense of curiosity and a hunger for continuous improvement. Entrepreneurs are not content with maintaining the status quo; instead, they actively seek out challenges that push the boundaries of their skills and knowledge. This proactive approach to learning turns each obstacle encountered into a deliberate choice to advance along the path of mastery.

The journey toward mastery is marked by a commitment to adaptability. Entrepreneurs with a Growth Mindset understand that the entrepreneurial landscape is dynamic, requiring constant evolution. By perceiving challenges as opportunities for growth, they cultivate a mindset that thrives on change and innovation. This adaptability becomes a defining trait as they navigate the complexities of entrepreneurship, turning challenges into catalysts for personal and professional development.

Furthermore, the notion of stepping stones toward mastery underscores the iterative nature of the entrepreneurial journey. Entrepreneurs recognize that mastery is not a destination but a continuous process of refinement. Each challenge surmounted becomes a foundation for the next, propelling them forward on a trajectory of perpetual improvement. This iterative mindset ensures that the entrepreneurial path is not a linear progression but a cyclical process of learning, adapting, and advancing.

In essence, perceiving challenges as stepping stones toward mastery is a mindset that transforms the entrepreneurial journey. It shifts the narrative from overcoming difficulties to embracing them as essential elements of growth. Entrepreneurs who embody this mindset not only navigate challenges with resilience but actively leverage them as opportunities for advancement on the journey toward mastery.

> Relishing in the Joy of Learning

A defining characteristic of the Growth Mindset is the genuine joy derived from the process of learning. These entrepreneurs relish the acquisition of new knowledge and skills, recognizing that every experience contributes to their personal and professional development.

Learning is not merely a means to an end; it's an intrinsic part of the entrepreneurial journey.

For entrepreneurs with a Growth Mindset, the joy of learning is rooted in a deep curiosity about the world and an eagerness to explore uncharted territories. They approach each new challenge with enthusiasm, seeing it as an opportunity to expand their understanding and refine their abilities. This innate curiosity fuels a continuous cycle of learning, where every experience, whether successful or challenging, becomes a source of valuable insights.

Furthermore, the joy of learning is intertwined with the resilience to embrace failures as valuable lessons. Entrepreneurs with a Growth Mindset understand that setbacks are not indicators of incompetence but stepping stones toward improvement. In the face of difficulties, they maintain a positive outlook, viewing challenges as platforms for learning and growth. This resilience allows them to navigate the complexities of entrepreneurship with an unwavering commitment to continuous improvement.

The joy of learning is also evident in the proactive pursuit of knowledge. Entrepreneurs actively seek out opportunities for learning, whether through formal education, mentorship, or hands-on experiences. This proactive approach transforms the entrepreneurial journey into a dynamic quest for knowledge, where each piece of information gained contributes to their overall expertise and adaptability.

Moreover, the joy of learning extends beyond individual development to the cultivation of a collaborative and innovative mindset. Entrepreneurs with a Growth Mindset value the insights of others and actively engage in knowledge-sharing environments. They recognize that learning is not a solitary endeavor but a communal experience that fosters creativity and collective advancement.

In essence, relishing in the joy of learning is a cornerstone of the Growth Mindset. It transforms the entrepreneurial journey from a series of tasks to an exhilarating exploration of possibilities. Entrepreneurs who embody this mindset not only find fulfillment in their continuous learning but also inspire those around them with the infectious enthusiasm for growth and knowledge.

> ➢ Failures as Valuable Lessons

In the Growth Mindset paradigm, failures are not stigmatized but embraced as invaluable lessons. Entrepreneurs who encounter setbacks perceive them as opportunities for introspection and refinement. Rather than dwelling on the perceived failure of a product launch, for example, they analyze what went wrong, extract meaningful insights, and use this knowledge to recalibrate their strategies.

One of the fundamental aspects of viewing failures as valuable lessons is the recognition that entrepreneurship is inherently challenging, and setbacks are a natural part of the journey. Entrepreneurs with a Growth Mindset understand that taking risks inherently involves the possibility of failure. Rather than fearing failure, they see it as an integral aspect of the learning process, an opportunity to gain insights that can lead to future success.

Moreover, failures are seen as indicators of areas for improvement. Entrepreneurs with a Growth Mindset don't perceive a setback as a definitive endpoint but as a pivot point for growth. They use the experience to identify weaknesses in their approach, be it in product development, marketing strategies, or operational processes. This introspective analysis enables them to iterate on their methods, enhancing their capabilities and increasing the likelihood of success in subsequent endeavors.

The process of turning failures into valuable lessons involves a proactive and solution-oriented mindset. Instead of succumbing to discouragement, entrepreneurs with a Growth Mindset actively seek ways to overcome challenges. They collaborate with their teams, seek mentorship, and explore innovative solutions. This approach transforms the aftermath of a failure into a period of intense learning and adaptation.

Furthermore, the perspective on failures extends beyond the individual to contribute to a resilient organizational culture. Entrepreneurs with a Growth Mindset instill in their teams the idea that setbacks are not reasons to abandon ship but opportunities to evolve. This culture of embracing failures as valuable lessons creates a positive and forward-thinking atmosphere, where each challenge becomes a stepping stone toward greater achievements.

In conclusion, the Growth Mindset redefines failures as indispensable components of the entrepreneurial journey. Entrepreneurs who cultivate this mindset not only bounce back stronger from setbacks but leverage them as catalysts for continuous improvement and future success. This transformative approach to failure contributes to a culture of resilience, adaptability, and perpetual growth within the entrepreneurial ecosystem.

> A Beacon of Optimism, Innovation, and Resilience

The Growth Mindset stands as a beacon of optimism, illuminating the entrepreneurial path with innovation and resilience. Entrepreneurs guided by this mindset are not deterred by setbacks; instead, they view them as catalysts for improvement. The optimism inherent in the Growth Mindset fuels a continuous cycle of innovation and an unwavering commitment to overcoming challenges.

Optimism is a cornerstone of the Growth Mindset, shaping the way entrepreneurs perceive difficulties. Rather than seeing challenges as insurmountable obstacles, they view them as opportunities for growth and refinement. This optimistic outlook allows them to approach obstacles with a proactive mindset, seeking creative solutions and innovative approaches to navigate through difficulties.

Innovation is a natural byproduct of the Growth Mindset's optimistic perspective. Entrepreneurs with this mindset embrace challenges as chances to explore new ideas, experiment with novel strategies, and push the boundaries of what's possible. The belief that abilities and intelligence can be developed fosters a culture of continuous improvement, encouraging entrepreneurs to think outside the box and pursue groundbreaking solutions.

Resilience is a key characteristic cultivated by the Growth Mindset's optimistic approach. Entrepreneurs who view setbacks as temporary hurdles rather than insurmountable roadblocks are more resilient in the face of adversity. This resilience enables them to bounce back from failures, learn from the experience, and apply those lessons to future endeavors.

Moreover, the optimism embedded in the Growth Mindset acts as a motivating force. Entrepreneurs guided by this mindset maintain a positive outlook even in challenging times, inspiring themselves and their teams to persevere. This positive energy becomes a driving force for sustained effort, propelling them forward with determination and enthusiasm.

The unwavering commitment to overcoming challenges is a defining trait of entrepreneurs with a Growth Mindset. Setbacks are not viewed as reasons to give up but as opportunities to learn, adapt, and come back stronger. The Growth Mindset's optimism and resilience create a mindset that thrives on the belief that success is not only achievable but a result of continuous learning, adaptation, and innovation.

In conclusion, the Growth Mindset serves as a beacon of optimism, lighting the entrepreneurial path with innovation and resilience. Entrepreneurs who embrace this mindset cultivate a proactive approach to challenges, foster a culture of continuous improvement, and exhibit unwavering determination in the face of adversity. This optimistic perspective not only shapes individual journeys but contributes to a dynamic and innovative entrepreneurial ecosystem.

Example:

Consider a visionary entrepreneur who faced a significant setback during the launch of a new product. Rather than succumbing to defeat, they embraced the challenge, meticulously analyzed the factors contributing to the setback, and used this experience as a catalyst for refining their strategy. This adaptive and resilient approach not only resulted in a successful relaunch but also became a driving force for continuous improvement, shaping the trajectory of their entrepreneurial journey.

In the vibrant tapestry of entrepreneurship, the Growth Mindset emerges as a guiding philosophy, propelling individuals toward continuous improvement, innovation, and enduring success. It serves as a testament to the transformative power of embracing challenges with a dynamic and optimistic mindset.

✧ The Fixed Mindset: Stagnation in the Face of Challenges

On the other side of the spectrum, a Fixed Mindset constrains potential, acting as a barrier to growth and innovation. Entrepreneurs with this mindset may perceive challenges as immutable barriers, a reflection of their intrinsic limitations. The fear of failure becomes paralyzing, hindering growth and innovation. This mindset traps individuals in a static state, reluctant to step out of their comfort zones.

A Fixed Mindset is characterized by a belief that one's abilities and intelligence are fixed traits, unchangeable and predetermined. This perspective can lead entrepreneurs to view challenges not as opportunities for growth but as indicators of personal shortcomings. The fear of failure, ingrained in the Fixed Mindset, becomes a significant obstacle, preventing individuals from taking risks and exploring new avenues.

In the context of a Fixed Mindset, setbacks are often perceived as personal failures rather than learning experiences. Entrepreneurs with this mindset may internalize failures, viewing them as evidence of their limitations rather than as stepping stones toward improvement. This fear of failure can paralyze decision-making, hindering the ability to adapt strategies and embrace change.

Consider an entrepreneur who, after facing a setback, views it through the lens of a Fixed Mindset. In this scenario, the setback is not seen as a challenge to overcome but as a confirmation of personal limitations. The fear of failure may prevent them from exploring new strategies, taking calculated risks, or venturing outside their comfort zones. This reluctance to adapt and embrace change becomes a significant hindrance to their entrepreneurial journey.

The Fixed Mindset fosters a static state where individuals resist challenges and avoid situations that might lead to failure. The belief in fixed abilities limits the willingness to take risks, experiment with new ideas, and pursue innovation. Entrepreneurs with a Fixed Mindset may find themselves stuck in routines and practices that offer a sense of security but hinder their potential for growth and success.

In essence, the Fixed Mindset represents a mindset of stagnation in the face of challenges. Entrepreneurs guided by this mindset may struggle to adapt, innovate, and navigate the dynamic landscape of entrepreneurship. Overcoming the limitations imposed by a Fixed Mindset requires a shift in perspective, an openness to learning and embracing challenges, and a recognition that failures are not reflections of inherent inadequacies but opportunities for growth and improvement.

Example:

Imagine an entrepreneur who, after facing a setback, views it as a personal failure, a confirmation of their limitations. This Fixed Mindset may prevent them from exploring new strategies or taking calculated risks, hindering their ability to adapt and grow.

✧ Cultivating a Growth Mindset: Practical Strategies

The journey toward a Growth Mindset is transformative and liberating, offering entrepreneurs a dynamic approach to challenges and continuous improvement. Cultivating this mindset involves adopting practical strategies that reshape perspectives and foster a belief in boundless potential.

1. Embrace Challenges:

Entrepreneurs can actively cultivate a Growth Mindset by embracing challenges as opportunities for learning and growth. Rather than viewing obstacles as insurmountable barriers, consider them as stepping stones toward mastery. Approach challenges with curiosity and a belief that each hurdle presents a chance to refine skills and deepen understanding.

2. Seek Feedback:

Feedback is a valuable tool on the path to a Growth Mindset. Entrepreneurs should actively seek feedback on their endeavors, recognizing it as a constructive guide for improvement. Constructive criticism becomes a catalyst for growth, providing insights into areas for development and refining strategies. Embrace feedback as a means to iterate and enhance your entrepreneurial journey.

3. View Effort as a Path to Mastery:

In the Growth Mindset paradigm, effort is not a sign of inadequacy but a deliberate path toward mastery. Entrepreneurs should shift their perspective on effort, seeing it as an investment in personal and professional development. Recognize that sustained effort, coupled with a willingness to learn, is a powerful combination that propels individuals forward on their journey.

4. Celebrate Others' Success:

A Growth Mindset extends beyond personal achievements; it involves celebrating the successes of others. Entrepreneurs can foster this mindset by acknowledging and learning from the accomplishments of peers and industry leaders. Instead of viewing others' success as a threat, see it as inspiration and motivation. Learning from the journeys of successful individuals contributes to a culture of continuous improvement.

5. Learn from Experiences:

Experiences, whether successes or setbacks, are valuable teachers on the road to a Growth Mindset. Entrepreneurs should reflect on their experiences, extracting lessons that contribute to personal and professional growth. Every venture, regardless of the outcome, offers insights that can inform future endeavors. Embrace the notion that learning is an ongoing process woven into the fabric of the entrepreneurial journey.

6. Recognize the Potential for Boundless Growth:

At the core of the Growth Mindset is the belief that one's potential is boundless. Entrepreneurs should cultivate a mindset that goes beyond fixed notions of capabilities. Recognize that skills and intelligence can be developed over time with dedication and learning. This perspective opens doors to new possibilities and encourages an ongoing pursuit of excellence.

As entrepreneurs embark on their entrepreneurial journey, it's crucial to understand that the Growth Mindset is not a static trait but a mindset that can be actively cultivated and developed. By embracing challenges, seeking feedback, viewing effort as a path to mastery, celebrating others' success, learning from experiences, and recognizing the potential for boundless growth, entrepreneurs can unlock their full potential. In the dynamic world of entrepreneurship, the Growth Mindset serves as the key to navigating challenges with resilience and optimism, fostering continuous improvement and enduring success..

Embracing Risk and Failure

In the thrilling saga of entrepreneurship, the chapter on embracing risk and failure unfolds as a gripping tale of resilience and triumph. Entrepreneurs, much like intrepid adventurers, navigate uncharted waters where risk is not a deterrent but a gateway to unparalleled growth and innovation.

Imagine a visionary entrepreneur standing at the edge of the unknown, fueled by the audacity to take risks. In this narrative, risk is not a formidable adversary; it's a daring companion on the entrepreneurial journey. The willingness to step into uncertainty becomes the catalyst for groundbreaking ideas and revolutionary ventures.

Consider the tale of a bold entrepreneur who, in pursuit of an innovative concept, faced the possibility of failure. Instead of succumbing to fear, they embraced the uncertainty, recognizing that failure is not a verdict but a pivotal moment of transformation. In the face of adversity, they discovered resilience and a reservoir of untapped potential.

Entrepreneurs who embrace risk understand that it's not about avoiding failure but about leveraging it as a stepping stone toward success. Failure becomes a mentor, offering invaluable lessons that propel them forward. Picture the entrepreneur as a seasoned storyteller, recounting tales of challenges overcome and failures transcended, each chapter adding depth to their narrative of triumph.

In this riveting exploration of risk and failure, entrepreneurs emerge not as gamblers but as calculated risk-takers. They understand that without venturing into the unknown, there can be no discovery, no innovation. Risk becomes a language they speak fluently, a dialect of opportunity that leads to unforeseen heights of achievement.

The entrepreneurial landscape is dotted with stories of those who embraced risk, faced failure, and emerged stronger and more resilient. It's a testament to the indomitable spirit that propels entrepreneurs to turn setbacks into comebacks, transforming failures into stepping stones toward success.

As you embark on your entrepreneurial odyssey, remember that risk and failure are not adversaries to be feared but allies guiding you toward greatness. Embrace the uncertainty, learn from failures, and let each risk taken be a beacon illuminating the path to triumph. In the grand tapestry of entrepreneurship, it's those who dare to embrace risk and failure that etch their stories into the annals of success.

Continuous Learning and Adaptability

In the dynamic realm of entrepreneurship, the chapter on continuous learning and adaptability unfolds as an enthralling odyssey of growth and evolution. Imagine the entrepreneur as a perpetual student, eagerly navigating the corridors of knowledge, and adapting to the ever-changing landscapes of the business world.

Envision a scenario where learning is not a mere means to an end but a profound and intrinsic part of the entrepreneurial journey. Entrepreneurs with an insatiable thirst for knowledge are akin to explorers charting new territories. They understand that the business landscape is a living organism, constantly evolving, and adapting is not a choice but a survival strategy.

Consider the story of a visionary entrepreneur who, faced with the rapid advancements in technology, embraced continuous learning as a strategic imperative. Instead of being daunted by the pace of change, they transformed it into an opportunity for innovation. Through constant learning, they not only stayed relevant but also became pioneers in integrating cutting-edge technologies into their ventures.

In this narrative, adaptability becomes the entrepreneur's secret weapon. Picture them as agile acrobats, gracefully navigating the twists and turns of market dynamics. The ability to pivot, shift strategies, and embrace change is not a response to challenges; it's a proactive stance toward an ever-shifting business landscape.

Entrepreneurs who prioritize continuous learning are not confined by the boundaries of their current knowledge; instead, they view each challenge as a chance to expand their expertise. The entrepreneurial odyssey is a perpetual cycle of learning, unlearning, and relearning – a symphony of growth that resonates with the dynamic beats of the business world.

As you embark on your own entrepreneurial journey, recognize that the pursuit of knowledge and adaptability is not a destination but a lifelong expedition. Embrace change, cultivate a hunger for learning, and let adaptability be your compass in the uncharted waters of business. In the saga of entrepreneurship, those who weave continuous learning and adaptability into their narratives emerge not just as entrepreneurs but as architects of enduring success.

In the fast-paced changes in their industry, embraced continuous learning as a strategic imperative. In this narrative, learning becomes a compass guiding them through the complexities of market dynamics, technological advancements, and shifting consumer behaviors. The entrepreneur, like a masterful conductor, orchestrates a symphony of adaptability and knowledge acquisition, ensuring that their business stays ahead of the curve.

Continuous learning is not confined to formal education but extends to a mindset of perpetual curiosity. Entrepreneurs actively seek new knowledge, skills, and experiences, transcending the boundaries of conventional wisdom. They immerse themselves in a culture of learning, where each interaction, success, or failure becomes a source of valuable insights.

Adaptability, the symbiotic companion of continuous learning, is the entrepreneur's ability to pivot in response to new information and changing circumstances. Picture the entrepreneur as a skilled navigator, adept at adjusting the sails to catch the winds of opportunity. In a world where change is the only constant, adaptability becomes the entrepreneur's armor, shielding them from obsolescence and propelling them toward innovation.

In this captivating exploration of continuous learning and adaptability, entrepreneurs emerge as architects of their own evolution. They recognize that standing still is not an option and that success is not found in stagnation but in the dynamic dance of adaptation and growth.

As you traverse the terrain of entrepreneurship, let continuous learning be your compass, guiding you through the seas of knowledge. Embrace adaptability as your ally, ensuring that every pivot is a step toward mastery. In the grand narrative of entrepreneurship, it's those who embark on the quest for continuous learning and adaptability that carve a legacy of enduring success and innovation.

In conclusion, Chapter 2 of our entrepreneurial journey delves into the profound nuances of cultivating an entrepreneurial mindset. The dichotomy between a Growth Mindset and a Fixed Mindset serves as the defining thread, weaving the narrative of success and resilience. Entrepreneurs embracing a Growth Mindset approach challenges with a dynamic perspective, viewing them as opportunities for growth and refinement. Challenges cease to be daunting impediments; rather, they become stepping stones toward mastery.

The Growth Mindset transforms failures into valuable lessons, fostering resilience, adaptability, and continuous improvement. Challenges are relished as essential components of the entrepreneurial landscape, opportunities for personal and professional development. Entrepreneurs view setbacks not as roadblocks but as stepping stones toward mastery, actively leveraging failures as catalysts for advancement.

The chapter unfolds as a saga of optimism, innovation, and resilience. The Growth Mindset becomes a beacon illuminating the entrepreneurial path, shaping individual journeys and contributing to a dynamic and innovative entrepreneurial ecosystem. Entrepreneurs who embrace this mindset cultivate a proactive approach to challenges, foster a culture of continuous improvement, and exhibit unwavering determination in the face of adversity.

As we conclude this chapter, let the lessons of a Growth Mindset resonate in your entrepreneurial journey. Embrace challenges with curiosity, view failures as stepping stones toward mastery, and let continuous learning and adaptability be your guiding principles. In the grand tapestry of entrepreneurship, it's the cultivation of an entrepreneurial mindset that sets the stage for lasting success, growth, and innovation. Get ready to embark on the next chapter, where we delve into the strategic intricacies of entrepreneurial decision-making and risk management.

Chapter 3: Vision and Goal Setting

In the labyrinth of entrepreneurship, the compass that guides us through uncertainty is crafted from two essential elements: Vision and Goal Setting. These pillars not only define the trajectory of our ventures but also shape the very essence of our entrepreneurial journey.

Navigating the Entrepreneurial Horizon: The Power of Vision in Entrepreneurship

The Quintessence of Visionary Thinking in Entrepreneurship

Vision in entrepreneurship acts as more than just a goal or a destination; it is the very heartbeat of entrepreneurial endeavor—the pulsating force that propels entrepreneurs forward, fueling their passion and guiding their journeys. This section aims to delve deeply into the essence of visionary thinking, exploring how it shapes and drives the entrepreneurial spirit.

Exploring the Stories of Trailblazers Across Industries

To truly grasp the impact of vision in entrepreneurship, we journey through the stories of trailblazers across various industries. These narratives provide a rich tapestry of insights into how visionaries have harnessed their dreams and aspirations to create impactful and enduring enterprises. From tech innovators who envisioned a digitally connected world to social entrepreneurs who sought to address pressing societal issues, each story offers unique lessons in the transformative power of vision.

By dissecting the anatomy of their visions, we aim to understand the components that make a vision compelling and effective. This exploration includes examining the clarity of purpose, the boldness of ambition, and the capacity to inspire and mobilize others. These stories not only serve as inspiration but also as practical case studies in the art of crafting and realizing a vision.

Understanding the Transformative Power of a Well-Crafted Vision

A well-crafted vision is a powerful tool for transformation. It serves as a north star, guiding entrepreneurs through the tumultuous journey of building and growing a business. A strong vision helps in aligning teams, attracting investment, and resonating with customers. It is the foundation upon which strategies are built and decisions are made.

However, the creation of a vision is not a static process; it is dynamic and evolving. As we examine the lives of successful entrepreneurs, we observe how their visions adapted to changing circumstances without losing their core essence. This adaptability is crucial in the ever-changing landscape of business, where new challenges and opportunities constantly arise.

Navigating the Entrepreneurial Horizon with Purpose and Foresight

Equipped with an understanding of the transformative power of vision, entrepreneurs can navigate the entrepreneurial horizon with greater purpose and foresight. This section aims to provide the tools and perspectives necessary to cultivate a visionary mindset, one that sees beyond immediate challenges and focuses on long-term impact.

A strong vision fosters a sense of purpose, instills resilience, and ignites innovation. It is the compass that guides entrepreneurs through uncertainty and complexity. As we dissect and learn from the visions of past and present entrepreneurs, we prepare ourselves to create our own visionary paths, embarking on journeys that not only lead to business success but also contribute to shaping a better world.

In conclusion, understanding and harnessing the power of vision is fundamental for any aspiring or established entrepreneur. It is the catalyst for change, the source of inspiration, and the guiding light in the entrepreneurial journey. Through exploring the stories of visionary leaders and understanding the dynamics of crafting a compelling vision, we can better equip ourselves to face the challenges and seize the opportunities that lie on the entrepreneurial horizon.

Charting the Course: Mastering Effective Goal Setting Techniques in Entrepreneurship

In the realm of entrepreneurship, goals act as the tangible milestones that chart our journey towards realizing a vision. They are the stepping stones that translate visionary thinking into actionable steps. This section is dedicated to dissecting the art and science of effective goal setting, an essential skill for any entrepreneur looking to navigate the complex waters of business success.

The Intricacies of SMART Goal Setting

The SMART criteria—Specific, Measurable, Achievable, Relevant, and Time-bound—is a fundamental framework for effective goal setting, providing a structured approach that ensures goals are clear and attainable. Specific goals, the first element of this framework, are well-defined targets that clarify exactly what needs to be achieved, making it easier to focus efforts and resources. The second aspect, Measurable goals, allows for the tracking of progress and the quantification of success, enabling adjustments in strategies as needed. Achievable goals ensure that objectives are realistic and within reach, considering available resources and constraints, while Relevant goals align with the broader vision and mission of the enterprise, ensuring that each goal matters and contributes to overall objectives. Finally, Time-bound goals introduce a sense of urgency and a timeline for achievement, fostering a disciplined approach to goal completion. This comprehensive approach, encompassing all five aspects of the SMART criteria, provides a solid foundation for setting and pursuing goals effectively, ensuring alignment with broader visions and encouraging consistent progress..

Beyond SMART: The Artistry of Aspirational Goal Setting

While the SMART framework provides a structured and practical approach to goal setting, the importance of aspirational goal setting in the entrepreneurial journey should not be underestimated. Aspirational goals go beyond the conventional boundaries of practicality and realism, challenging entrepreneurs to stretch their imagination and ambition to new heights. These goals are not just about incremental progress; they are about envisioning significant changes and breakthroughs that can redefine the scope of what's possible in a business.

Aspirational goals are characterized by their ability to inspire and motivate. They encapsulate a vision that is bold and ambitious, often seeming unreachable at first glance. However, it is this very nature of aspirational goals that makes them powerful. They serve as beacons that keep entrepreneurs aligned with a higher purpose and drive them to exceed their limits. When entrepreneurs set aspirational goals, they commit to a journey of transformation, innovation, and growth.

These goals also play a crucial role in driving innovation. By setting targets that seem beyond the current capabilities or understanding, entrepreneurs are forced to think creatively and explore new avenues. This can lead to the development of new products, services, or business models that can revolutionize industries. Aspirational goals often require entrepreneurs to venture into uncharted territories, requiring them to learn, adapt, and develop new skills and perspectives.

Moreover, aspirational goals can have a magnetic effect, attracting talent, investors, and partners who are drawn to the ambitious vision and the challenge it presents. They can help in building a culture of excellence within the organization, where the pursuit of these lofty goals becomes a shared endeavor that galvanizes the team.

However, it's important to balance aspirational goals with a sense of realism. While they should push the boundaries of what's currently feasible, they should not venture into the realm of the impossible. The key is to find the sweet spot where goals are challenging enough to stimulate progress and innovation but still grounded in a level of possibility that prevents discouragement and burnout.

In conclusion, while the SMART framework lays a solid foundation for effective goal setting, the art of aspirational goal setting is equally vital in the entrepreneurial landscape. Aspirational goals act as catalysts for innovation, growth, and transformation, pushing entrepreneurs and their teams to explore the full extent of their potential and achieve remarkable advancements in their ventures. They are essential for entrepreneurs who aim not just to succeed but to redefine the parameters of success in their respective fields.

Assembling a Comprehensive Toolkit for Entrepreneurs

To empower entrepreneurs in their goal-setting journey, a comprehensive toolkit is crafted, merging the structured precision of the SMART criteria with the visionary scope of aspirational goals. This toolkit is thoughtfully designed to support various facets of goal setting, encompassing everything from the inception of ideas to their execution and ongoing evaluation. At its core, it aids in transforming overarching visions into tangible, actionable objectives.

The initial phase of the toolkit focuses on conception and vision setting, equipping entrepreneurs with tools for defining their long-term objectives and identifying key milestones. Techniques such as vision boarding and brainstorming sessions are included to foster creative thinking and expansive goal formulation. Following this, the toolkit guides entrepreneurs through refining these goals using the SMART criteria, ensuring each goal is Specific, Measurable, Achievable, Relevant, and Time-bound. Templates and checklists are provided to streamline this process, aligning goals effectively with the broader vision.

Acknowledging the complexity of some goals, the toolkit offers strategies to deconstruct these into smaller, manageable tasks. This breakdown is vital for maintaining progress and avoiding overwhelm, with frameworks for task delegation and milestone setting included. Additionally, the toolkit addresses goal prioritization and resource allocation, helping entrepreneurs decide where to focus their efforts for maximum efficiency.

A critical aspect of the toolkit is its emphasis on sustaining focus and motivation. It includes resources for building resilience, motivational tools, and strategies for maintaining a positive mindset, crucial for navigating the often challenging path toward goal realization. This is complemented by tools for monitoring progress and adjusting strategies. It incorporates methods for tracking achievements and conducting regular reviews, ensuring flexibility and responsiveness to the ever-evolving business landscape.

In summary, this toolkit serves as a dynamic guide for entrepreneurs, balancing the practicality of SMART goals with the ambition of aspirational targets. It's not just a collection of tools but a comprehensive roadmap, guiding entrepreneurs through the complexities of setting and achieving goals, turning visions into attainable successes. This toolkit stands as a testament to the idea that with the right approach, even the most ambitious goals can be systematically pursued and realized.

Illuminating the Path with Real-World Examples and Case Studies

Case Study: Zephyr Technologies - Revolutionizing Renewable Energy
Background

Zephyr Technologies, a startup founded in 2018, embarked on a mission to revolutionize the renewable energy sector. With a focus on developing innovative solar panel technologies, their goal was to make renewable energy more accessible and efficient. The company was born from a vision to combat climate change by tapping into the vast potential of solar energy.

Initial Goal Setting and Challenges

Zephyr Technologies' initial goal was to increase the efficiency of solar panels by 25% within three years. This goal was ambitious, considering the average annual efficiency improvement in the industry was around 3-5%. The challenge was not only technical but also involved securing sufficient funding, navigating regulatory landscapes, and establishing a foothold in a competitive market.

Strategy and Execution
To achieve their goal, Zephyr Technologies employed a multifaceted strategy:

1. Innovation and Research: They invested heavily in research and development, hiring leading experts in solar energy and materials science. Collaborations with academic institutions were also initiated for cutting-edge research.

2. Funding and Investment: The startup actively sought venture capital and government grants. They pitched their innovative approach and potential market impact to secure necessary funding.

3. Market Analysis and Adaptation: Understanding the market dynamics was crucial. They conducted thorough market research to identify potential customers and adapt their technology to meet market needs.

4. Regulatory Compliance and Partnerships: Navigating the complex regulatory environment of renewable energy, Zephyr Technologies formed partnerships with regulatory consultants and other renewable energy firms to advocate for favorable policies.

Results and Impact

By the end of the three-year period, Zephyr Technologies had achieved a 22% increase in solar panel efficiency, slightly below their target but still a remarkable achievement in the industry. This breakthrough led to:

1. Increased Investment: The company attracted more investors, including larger industry players, leading to a significant funding round.

2. Market Expansion: With improved technology, Zephyr Technologies expanded its market reach, supplying to both residential and commercial sectors.

3. Policy Influence: Their success and advocacy led to more favorable government policies towards renewable energy technologies.

4. Environmental Impact: The improved technology contributed to greater adoption of solar energy, aiding in the reduction of carbon emissions.

Lessons Learned

The case study of Zephyr Technologies illustrates several key lessons:

1. Ambitious Goals Drive Innovation: Setting high benchmarks can propel a company to achieve remarkable results.

2. Adaptability is Crucial: The ability to adapt strategies in response to funding challenges, market feedback, and regulatory changes is vital.

3. Collaboration and Networking: Forming the right partnerships can be instrumental in overcoming technical and regulatory hurdles.

4. Impact Beyond Business: Entrepreneurial ventures can have significant impacts on industry standards and environmental sustainability.

Conclusion

Zephyr Technologies' journey exemplifies how a startup, with a clear vision and well-defined goals, can not only achieve remarkable success in a competitive industry but also contribute to broader societal and environmental change. Their story serves as an inspiration for entrepreneurs, highlighting the importance of setting ambitious goals, remaining adaptable, and maintaining a focus on the wider impact of their business endeavors.

The effectiveness of goal setting in entrepreneurship is best understood not just through theory but by examining real-world examples and case studies that embody strategic goal formulation and achievement. Exploring a variety of scenarios across multiple industries provides invaluable insights into how successful entrepreneurs and business leaders utilize goal setting as a key driver of their success.

Real-world examples offer concrete illustrations of practical goal setting. These include stories of startup founders who have ambitiously set and achieved revenue targets through detailed planning and execution. Such narratives often highlight the importance of setting specific financial goals to focus a company's growth efforts on critical performance indicators and market opportunities. They also underscore the necessity of adaptability, illustrating how entrepreneurs recalibrate their goals in response to market feedback and evolving business landscapes.

Case studies of social entrepreneurs are equally enlightening. They often demonstrate how setting goals centered on social impact metrics, like the number of individuals positively affected or the degree of environmental improvement, can turn a clear vision for change into actionable and quantifiable objectives. This approach propels social ventures towards significant, measurable impacts.

The toolkit also delves into narratives from established corporations that have successfully maneuvered through major transitions or disruptions by strategically setting and pursuing their goals. These include objectives related to digital transformation, market expansion, or sustainability initiatives, showing how clear, strategic goals can guide large organizations through intricate changes and align various departments and stakeholders under a unified vision.

Moreover, this toolkit incorporates examples from diverse sectors such as technology, healthcare, education, and non-profits, showcasing goal setting's universal applicability as a success tool. Each sector has unique challenges and opportunities, and these case studies offer insights into customizing goals to suit different industry dynamics and organizational frameworks.

Carefully selected, each example and case study aims to inspire and impart practical lessons. Common themes emerge, emphasizing the importance of setting realistic yet ambitious goals, the need for ongoing monitoring and adjustment, and the effectiveness of aligning team efforts towards a collective aim.

In summary, examining these real-world examples and case studies brings the process of goal setting to life in a practical, relatable way. This exploration not only offers entrepreneurs and business leaders a wealth of inspiration and practical advice but also demonstrates how well-conceived goals can serve as catalysts for success in various fields. This comprehensive look at goal setting highlights its transformative potential, providing a guide for those seeking to turn their visions into tangible realities.

The Symbiosis of Aspirations: Aligning Personal and Business Goals

Entrepreneurs stand at the intersection of personal ambition and business objectives, embodying the role of architects not only of their businesses but also of their own destinies. This section explores the symbiotic relationship between personal and business goals, emphasizing the importance of aligning these two critical aspects of an entrepreneur's journey. Understanding and harmonizing personal aspirations with business demands is key to forging a holistic path to success. It involves a delicate balance, where personal goals complement and enhance business objectives, and business achievements contribute to personal fulfillment and growth.

This balance is an art form, requiring entrepreneurs to integrate their personal values, strengths, and life goals with their business strategies. Strategies for this integration include self-assessment tools to identify personal values, goal-setting techniques that align these with business objectives, and methods for regular review and adjustment. This section provides practical steps and insights for entrepreneurs to create a synergistic relationship between their personal and business goals, enhancing both realms.

Additionally, real-life case studies are presented to illustrate successful examples of this integration. These stories offer inspiration and practical examples, showing how entrepreneurs have navigated the challenges of aligning personal and business goals, and the strategies employed to achieve harmony between the two.

In conclusion, the symbiosis of personal and business goals is pivotal for a fulfilling and successful entrepreneurial journey. By aligning these dimensions, entrepreneurs not only drive their businesses forward but also achieve personal satisfaction and development. This comprehensive approach underscores that true entrepreneurial success is measured not just in business achievements, but also in how these accomplishments resonate with and enrich the entrepreneur's personal life and aspirations.

Illuminating Perspectives: Perspectives on Vision and Goal Setting

In the realm of entrepreneurship, the concepts of vision and goal setting are foundational to success. To deepen our understanding and appreciation of these vital components, we engage in a comprehensive exploration that involves inviting thought leaders and experts from various fields to share their perspectives. This initiative provides a rich tapestry of insights, drawing from a wide range of experiences and expertise to examine the complexities, nuances, and challenges associated with vision and goal setting in the entrepreneurial context.

Our journey delves into the heart of what it means to conceptualize and actualize a vision. We explore how visions are born, nurtured, and transformed into tangible realities through effective goal setting. These discussions are not just theoretical but are grounded in practical realities, offering a balanced view that encompasses both the aspirational and the pragmatic aspects of entrepreneurship. We engage with experts who have navigated the challenging waters of setting and achieving ambitious goals, learning from their successes and setbacks.

Furthermore, we broaden the scope of our exploration by incorporating diverse perspectives. This includes insights from seasoned entrepreneurs who have built successful businesses, academics who study the dynamics of business growth and innovation, and consultants who guide companies in strategic planning. Their varied viewpoints provide a holistic understanding of how vision and goal setting operate in different environments and under various circumstances.

This initiative also focuses on the challenges entrepreneurs face in this process, such as aligning personal and business goals, adapting to changing market landscapes, and balancing ambition with feasibility. We discuss strategies to overcome these challenges, sharing practical tools and methodologies that have been proven effective in the real world.

In addition to expert discussions, we facilitate interactive sessions where entrepreneurs can engage with these thought leaders, ask questions, and gain personalized insights. This interactive component ensures that the journey is not just about receiving information but also about applying it in real-life scenarios.

As we embark on this transformative journey through the dimensions of vision and goal setting, we create a platform where profound insights, practical strategies, and diverse perspectives converge. This rich amalgamation of knowledge and experience serves to illuminate the path to entrepreneurial success, providing entrepreneurs with the tools and understanding necessary to navigate the complexities of bringing a vision to life and achieving their goals. This journey is designed to not only inform but also inspire, fostering critical thinking and encouraging entrepreneurs to envision and pursue new heights in their entrepreneurial endeavors.

Navigating the Entrepreneurial Horizon The Power of Vision in Entrepreneurship

In the vast expanse of entrepreneurship, vision stands as the guiding star, illuminating the path to unprecedented success. Let us embark on a captivating journey into the realm of visionary thinking—a realm where dreams are not merely fanciful, but the driving force behind monumental achievements.

✧ Unleashing the Imagination

In the dynamic landscape of entrepreneurship, the capacity to unleash one's imagination is the keystone to visionary thinking. Imagine an entrepreneur not confined by the limitations of conventional strategies but armed with a vivid, compelling image of a future yet to unfold. This is the essence of visionary entrepreneurship—a realm where imagination becomes the catalyst for innovation.

➢ Breaking the Chains of Conventional Thinking

In the annals of entrepreneurship, visionaries like Elon Musk and Oprah Winfrey stand as paragons of breaking the chains of conventional thinking. Their narratives unfold as sagas of liberation, where the constraints of ordinary thought are cast aside to embrace a mindset that propels them into uncharted territories.

Transcending the ordinary, they refuse to be confined by societal expectations and industry norms. It's not merely about defying norms; it's a conscious choice to soar beyond the limitations imposed by well-trodden paths.

At the heart of this paradigm shift is the audacious decision to transcend the ordinary. The power of these visionaries lies not solely in their exceptional business acumen but, more profoundly, in their ability to orchestrate a revolution in mindset. Breaking free from the shackles of the status quo, they usher in a new era of thinking—one that challenges, questions, and redefines the boundaries of what is deemed possible.

Central to this liberation is the unleashing of imagination. Musk envisions a future where humanity inhabits Mars, and Winfrey transforms herself from a talk show host into a media mogul. These feats are not products of linear thinking but are born from the boundless landscapes of imagination, a realm where constraints are mere illusions.

To break the chains of conventional thinking is to willingly confront the unknown. Musk's ventures into space exploration and Winfrey's ascent in the media industry were fraught with risks and uncertainties. Yet, it's precisely in this willingness to embrace the unknown that the seeds of groundbreaking innovation are sown.

While business acumen is undoubtedly a hallmark of their success, it is the courage to challenge the established norms that sets visionaries apart. Musk disrupts traditional notions of space travel, and Winfrey challenges the conventional pathways to media success. In doing so, they exemplify that true innovation often requires a departure from the familiar.

This chapter serves as a call to aspiring visionaries, urging them to recognize that true progress often demands a departure from the familiar. By breaking the chains of conventional thinking, entrepreneurs can tap into the wellspring of creativity, paving the way for transformative ideas and ventures. Through the lens of Musk and Winfrey, we unravel the intricacies of this mindset revolution and illuminate the path to pioneering a new frontier in entrepreneurship.

> ➢ Envisioning the Unseen

Embark on a journey with visionaries Elon Musk and Oprah Winfrey, where the boundaries of the imaginable are shattered, and the unseen becomes a canvas for groundbreaking achievements. In the tapestry of entrepreneurial sagas, Musk's audacious vision to colonize Mars and Winfrey's metamorphosis from a talk show host to a media mogul stand as beacons of individuals who dared to envision the unseen.

Elon Musk, the maverick entrepreneur behind SpaceX, paints a vivid picture of humanity inhabiting Mars. It's a vision that transcends the confines of Earth, a bold leap into the cosmos. Through the lens of Musk's interplanetary ambitions, we unravel the narrative of a mind unbounded by the gravitational pull of conventional thinking.

Oprah Winfrey, the iconic media personality, embarked on a journey that defied the scripted narrative of a talk show host. Her trajectory toward media mogul status is a testament to the transformative power of envisioning the unseen. Winfrey's story unfolds as a saga of self-reinvention, where the invisible threads of imagination weave a narrative that extends far beyond the studio lights.

These tales are not mere narratives; they are chronicles of courage, resilience, and the audacity to dream beyond the visible horizon. Musk's

SpaceX, with its lofty goal of interplanetary colonization, and Winfrey's media empire, a testament to the potency of creative thinking, exemplify how imaginative visions can materialize into tangible realities.

In the realm of entrepreneurship, the capacity to envision the unseen is a superpower. Musk didn't merely dream of reaching Mars; he charted a course to get there. Winfrey didn't just imagine a media empire; she meticulously built one. This chapter serves as a guiding light for aspiring entrepreneurs, encouraging them to look beyond the apparent, to envision the unseen, and to embrace the transformative journey from dreams to reality. Through the lens of Musk and Winfrey, we unravel the secrets of turning imaginative thinking into a force that shapes industries and transcends the ordinary.

> ➤ Revolutionizing Industries through Imagination

In the grand orchestration of entrepreneurial prowess, visionaries Elon Musk and Oprah Winfrey emerge as conductors who didn't just compose individual notes of success but orchestrated entire symphonies of industry revolution. Beyond personal triumphs, their narratives unfold as sagas of reshaping the very fabric of industries, propelled by the boundless power of imagination.

Elon Musk's SpaceX venture is not merely about reaching new heights; it's a paradigm shift in the cosmos. Explore the saga of how Musk, fueled by an unbridled imagination, redefined the possibilities of space exploration. From reusable rockets to interplanetary colonization dreams, Musk's vision extends beyond personal ambition, aiming to transform the way humanity interacts with the cosmos.

Shift the spotlight to Oprah Winfrey, whose journey transcends the confines of talk shows and embraces the vast landscape of media and entertainment. Her media empire becomes the canvas upon which imaginative strokes redefine industry norms. The narrative explores how Winfrey, armed with a visionary spirit, revolutionized the dissemination of information and entertainment, leaving an indelible mark on the media landscape.

At the heart of Musk and Winfrey's impact lies a common thread—the strategic harnessing of imagination as a catalyst for disruptive innovation. Imagination, when wielded with intent, becomes a potent force for challenging the status quo. Musk's SpaceX disrupts the aerospace industry, while Winfrey's media empire transforms conventional notions of entertainment and information consumption.

This chapter invites aspiring entrepreneurs to not only dream big but to recognize the transformative potential of those dreams on a broader scale. Musk and Winfrey illuminate the path where imagination isn't confined to personal aspirations but becomes the engine of change for entire industries. As we navigate through their revolutionary narratives, we uncover the symphony of disruption composed by the harmonious interplay of visionary thinking and strategic execution.

> ➤ Learning from Visionary Pioneers

Standing at the crossroads of entrepreneurial exploration, we find ourselves in the illustrious company of visionary pioneers—Elon Musk and Oprah Winfrey. Their narratives transcend the realm of personal triumphs, unfolding as blueprints for aspiring entrepreneurs eager to embark on their own odyssey of innovation.

Elon Musk, with his audacious pursuits in space exploration through SpaceX and the electrifying revolution brought about by Tesla, beckons us to embrace audacity. His relentless pursuit of colossal goals, from colonizing Mars to transforming the automotive industry, teaches us the transformative potential of bold imagination. Musk's journey serves as a testament to the profound impact that audacious vision can have on industries that were once deemed immutable.

On the other hand, Oprah Winfrey's trajectory from a talk show host to a media mogul unveils the power of resilience and adaptability. Her ability to pivot, diversify, and reshape her career underscores the importance of navigating challenges with unwavering determination. Winfrey's story encourages aspiring entrepreneurs to view obstacles not as roadblocks but as stepping stones to greater heights, where adaptability becomes a cornerstone of sustained success.

As we dissect Musk and Winfrey's journeys, a common thread emerges—the ability to foster creativity through the untethered exploration of imagination. Musk's innovations in space travel and electric vehicles, and Winfrey's redefinition of media and entertainment, showcase the boundless potential of creative thinking. Their stories compel us to break free from conventional molds and approach problem-solving with innovative zeal.

Imagination, as exemplified by these pioneers, becomes a beacon guiding us through the fog of uncertainty. It serves as a compass for envisioning unprecedented solutions to challenges that may seem insurmountable. Musk's vision extends beyond the stratosphere, while Winfrey's influence transcends traditional media boundaries, both pointing to the limitless horizons that imagination can unlock.

In the tapestry of Musk and Winfrey's narratives, we discover not just stories of personal triumph but invaluable lessons for aspiring entrepreneurs. The chapters of their lives offer a curriculum in audacity, resilience, creativity, and the transformative power of imagination. As we delve into these stories, let us not merely observe but actively engage, extracting the gems of wisdom that can illuminate our own path toward entrepreneurial success.

In the subsequent sections of this chapter, we will unravel specific aspects of Musk and Winfrey's journeys, exploring in-depth the nuances of unleashing imagination, breaking free from conventional thinking, and revolutionizing entire industries. Each section serves as a masterclass in entrepreneurial strategy, inviting readers to not only learn from the pioneers but to apply these lessons in shaping their own visionary narratives. As we embark on this intellectual journey, prepare to glean insights that extend beyond the realms of business into the broader landscape of innovation, resilience, and the limitless possibilities that unfold when imagination takes center stage.

> ➤ Imagination as a Renewable Resource

Imagination, often underestimated and confined within the realms of childhood whimsy, emerges as an inexhaustible reservoir of creativity—an untapped wellspring awaiting the discerning entrepreneur's touch. This section serves as a rallying cry, a call to arms for visionary business leaders to recognize the boundless potential residing within the recesses of their own imaginative faculties. Imagination, far from being a finite resource, is a dynamic and renewable force capable of propelling entrepreneurial endeavors to unprecedented heights.

In the crucible of imagination, where the ordinary is transmuted into the extraordinary, visionary entrepreneurs embark on a transformative journey. It is a journey marked by audacious leaps into the unknown, where the status quo is not accepted but challenged, and where the seeds of groundbreaking innovation are sown. Join us in this exploration of the catalytic power of imagination—a force that transcends the boundaries of the known and propels individuals into the avant-garde of entrepreneurial success.

Cultivating and channeling imagination is not a mere suggestion; it is a strategic imperative for those poised to shape the future. As we delve into the intricacies of harnessing this renewable resource, we uncover techniques and methodologies that empower entrepreneurs to awaken and direct their dormant imaginative forces. It is not enough to acknowledge the existence of imagination; one must learn to wield it as a dynamic tool—a force capable of transforming abstract concepts into tangible realities.

In the entrepreneurial landscape, where uncertainty is a constant companion, imagination emerges as a beacon illuminating the path forward. It serves as the driving force behind innovative solutions, disruptive strategies, and the ability to navigate uncharted territories. This section invites entrepreneurs to embark on a transformative journey, one where imagination is not a passive bystander but an active participant, shaping the narrative of success.

As we navigate the contours of imagination as a renewable resource, envision a landscape where creativity knows no bounds and where every challenge becomes an opportunity for innovative expression. The stories of Musk and Winfrey, as we've explored in previous sections, exemplify the transformative potential of imagination when harnessed with strategic intent. Now, it is time to dive deeper, uncovering the nuanced strategies that turn imagination from a dormant force into a dynamic engine driving entrepreneurial pursuits.

Prepare to be inspired, challenged, and equipped with the tools to tap into the infinite reservoir of imagination. The journey ahead is not just a quest for entrepreneurial success but a profound exploration of the limitless possibilities that unfold when imagination becomes an integral and renewable resource in the visionary entrepreneur's arsenal.

✧ **Transformative Impact**

Embarking on a thrilling journey into the heart of transformative impact, this exploration delves into the profound power of vision that transcends the ordinary, propelling individuals into realms of possibility. Vision, often dismissed as an abstract concept, emerges as a dynamic force with the capacity to shape destinies and revolutionize entire industries.

Picture a world seamlessly connected by sleek devices, a vision brought to life by the iconic Steve Jobs. Envision Martin Luther King Jr.'s dream of equality, a vision resonating through history, leaving an indelible mark on the tapestry of human progress.

As we delve into the stories of visionary leaders, the transformative impact of their visions unfolds. Steve Jobs, with unparalleled foresight, not only envisioned but crafted a reality where technology seamlessly integrates into daily lives—the tangible outcomes of a visionary's dream defying conventional boundaries.

Equally powerful is the vision of Martin Luther King Jr., a beacon of hope for equality and justice. His dream transcends time, inspiring generations to strive for a world where individuals are judged not by the color of their skin but by the content of their character. The transformative impact of King's vision extends far beyond the civil rights movement; it permeates the fabric of societal progress.

These stories are not mere historical anecdotes; they are invitations to dream beyond conventional boundaries. The transformative impact of vision lies not just in realizing dreams but in the ripple effect they create—a cascade of inspiration sparking innovation, igniting change, and shaping the course of history.

So, buckle up for a captivating exploration of visionary tales that not only entertain but also ignite the spark of imagination within. Discover how seemingly abstract concepts have the power to transform industries, leaving an enduring legacy resonating across time. It's not just a journey through history; it's an exhilarating ride into the transformative impact of vision, where dreams become catalysts for unprecedented change. Get ready to be inspired, uplifted, and propelled into a world where visionary leaders shape destinies, redefining the very fabric of our existence.

Case Study: The Visionary Odyssey of Tesla, Inc.

In the annals of visionary leadership, Tesla, Inc. stands as a testament to the transformative impact of a bold and imaginative vision. Buckle up for a captivating exploration of Tesla's journey, a narrative that not only entertains but also ignites the spark of imagination within.

The Genesis of a Vision:

In the early 2000s, Elon Musk, a visionary entrepreneur with a penchant for transformative ventures, set his sights on revolutionizing the automotive industry. His mission was to disrupt the conventional landscape and propel the world towards sustainable energy solutions. Musk's visionary narrative began with the seemingly abstract concept of introducing electric vehicles that seamlessly blended performance, elegance, and environmental consciousness.

Elon Musk, often characterized as a modern-day innovator, saw beyond the limitations of traditional combustion engine vehicles. His vision was not just about creating cars; it was about fundamentally altering the way society perceived and interacted with transportation. The genesis of Musk's vision was rooted in the belief that technology could be harnessed to address pressing environmental concerns while delivering unparalleled automotive experiences.

Transforming Industries with Electric Dreams:

As Musk embarked on this audacious journey, Tesla's foray into electric vehicles became a groundbreaking chapter in the automotive sector's history. Musk's vision challenged the status quo, pushing the boundaries of what was deemed possible. The introduction of electric cars was not merely a technological innovation; it was a paradigm shift that extended beyond conventional boundaries.

Tesla's electric vehicles were designed to be more than an eco-friendly alternative; they were envisioned as high-performance, elegant machines that would captivate car enthusiasts worldwide. Musk's audacious dream of clean energy-powered cars dominating the market became the catalyst for unprecedented change. This vision did not only transform Tesla into a prominent player in the automotive industry but also reshaped the entire trajectory of how societies perceive and adopt sustainable transportation.

The electric dreams of Tesla extended beyond the manufacturing of vehicles. Musk's vision encompassed creating an entire ecosystem of sustainable energy solutions, including solar power and energy storage. This holistic approach aimed not only to revolutionize the automotive sector but to redefine the relationship between technology, energy, and the environment.

In essence, Elon Musk's visionary leadership and the genesis of Tesla's vision were instrumental in pushing the automotive industry towards a more sustainable and innovative future. The audacity to challenge conventional norms and the commitment to a cleaner, more efficient future exemplify how visionary thinking can transform industries, leaving an indelible mark on the entrepreneurial and environmental landscape.

Leaving an Enduring Legacy:

As Tesla's electric vehicles gracefully navigated the roads, the transformative impact of Elon Musk's visionary pursuit unfolded, leaving an enduring legacy that extends far beyond the automotive realm. The legacy of Tesla is not confined to the sleek designs and innovative features of its cars; it resonates as a pioneer in the realm of sustainable energy solutions.

Tesla's foray into electric vehicles marked a paradigm shift in the automotive industry, but its enduring legacy lies in the comprehensive ecosystem of sustainable energy solutions it pioneered. The introduction of the Powerwall, solar products, and energy storage systems showcased Musk's commitment to creating a holistic approach towards addressing environmental challenges. This legacy exemplifies how seemingly abstract concepts can evolve into a multifaceted and sustainable business model.

Inspiring Innovation Across Time:

The journey of Tesla stands as a beacon of inspiration for entrepreneurs across generations. Elon Musk's visionary leadership not only steered Tesla to remarkable success but also ignited a wave of innovation across the automotive and renewable energy sectors. The ripple effect of Tesla's vision transcends time, influencing how businesses approach sustainability and innovation.

Musk's audacious dream of electric vehicles was not merely about creating a new mode of transportation; it was a catalyst for sparking innovation and redefining industry standards. The enduring legacy of Tesla serves as a testament to the power of visionary thinking in inspiring lasting change. Entrepreneurs and businesses worldwide continue to draw inspiration from Tesla's success story, realizing that abstract concepts, when grounded in purpose and innovation, can transform industries and leave a lasting impact on the entrepreneurial landscape.

In essence, the legacy of Tesla is not just about the cars we see on the roads today; it's about the paradigm shift it initiated and the inspiration it continues to provide for future innovators. Elon Musk's vision, embodied in Tesla's sustainable energy solutions, has set a precedent for businesses to follow—a legacy that goes beyond individual success to shape the trajectory of industries and inspire a commitment to a more sustainable future.

The Unveiling of the Future:

Tesla's narrative transcends the boundaries of a traditional historical account; it's a riveting expedition into the transformative impact of visionary thinking. Elon Musk's dreams, once confined to the realm of abstract concepts, materialized into tangible realities, transforming Tesla into more than just a car manufacturer—it became a force propelling change across industries.

As the curtains were drawn back to unveil the future envisioned by Musk, Tesla emerged as a paradigm-shifting entity. The visionary leaders at Tesla, under Musk's guidance, orchestrated a narrative that surpassed the conventional norms of the automotive and energy industries. It wasn't merely about producing electric vehicles; it was about rewriting the script of what was possible in the intersection of sustainability, innovation, and consumer experience.

The destinies shaped by Tesla's visionary leaders reverberate through the very fabric of industries. The automotive landscape, once dominated by conventional fuel vehicles, witnessed a seismic shift propelled by Musk's unwavering commitment to sustainable energy solutions. Tesla's impact extended beyond manufacturing electric cars; it set the stage for redefining how society perceives and adopts clean energy.

In Conclusion:

In drawing the final strokes of this case study, the odyssey of Tesla stands as a testament to the transformative power of visionary thinking. Musk's audacious pursuit became a catalyst for groundbreaking innovation, not only within the automotive sector but across the broader landscape of energy solutions. This case study invites you to be more than a spectator—it encourages you to be inspired, uplifted, and propelled into a world where visionary leaders, epitomized by Elon Musk, shape destinies and redefine the very essence of our existence.

As you navigate through Tesla's transformative impact, envision the possibilities for your own entrepreneurial journey. Let the narrative of Tesla serve as a guiding light, illustrating how abstract concepts, when embraced with passion and determination, have the potential to lead to unprecedented change. Just as Musk reshaped the narrative of the automotive and energy industries, this case study prompts you to consider how your visionary narrative can contribute to shaping the future of your entrepreneurial endeavors. The journey doesn't end here; it continues as an invitation to explore the transformative impact of vision and strive for a legacy that transcends the ordinary.

✧   Crafting Your Visionary Narrative

Embark on an exhilarating journey into the heart of entrepreneurial storytelling, unraveling the secret that sets visionaries apart—the art of crafting a narrative that captivates and resonates with a broader audience. Picture yourself, the aspiring visionary, stepping onto the stage of your entrepreneurial expedition armed not only with a business plan but with a narrative that transforms dreams into reality.

Crafting your visionary narrative is not a mere step in the entrepreneurial process; it's a transformative experience that sets the stage for your entire journey. Envision your narrative as a vibrant tapestry, intricately woven with threads of ambition, passion, and purpose. It transcends the realm of business goals; it's about creating a story that captures the hearts and minds of those who join you on this thrilling adventure.

In this immersive exploration, delve into the intricacies of narrative craftsmanship—it's not just about words on paper; it's about creating a symphony of ideas that resonates with your audience. Learn the art of infusing your narrative with the essence of your vision, making it a magnetic force that attracts supporters, collaborators, and believers in your mission.

As you navigate through the process, envision your narrative as a living entity, evolving and adapting to the dynamic landscape of entrepreneurship. The compelling nature of a visionary narrative lies in the fusion of authenticity, relatability, and a touch of magic that sparks curiosity. Your narrative becomes the compass guiding your entrepreneurial ship, steering it toward success.

Join us in this thrilling escapade where crafting your visionary narrative becomes more than a skill—it's a superpower. Uncover the secrets of narrative alchemy, transforming your ideas into a compelling story that resonates across audiences. Whether you're a budding entrepreneur or an experienced trailblazer, the journey of narrative crafting awaits, promising a ride filled with creativity, inspiration, and the assurance of a narrative that leaves an indelible mark on the entrepreneurial landscape. Get ready to unleash the storyteller within and embark on a narrative adventure that propels your vision into the hearts and minds of those ready to join your entrepreneurial odyssey.

Exercise Component	Description	Example (Sustainable Fashion Venture)
Objective	Develop and refine skills in crafting a visionary narrative that captivates and resonates with your audience.	N/A
Define Your Core Message	Identify the central theme or message of your narrative.	Focus on transforming the fashion industry through eco-friendly practices.
Identify Key Elements	Pinpoint key elements, events, or experiences that have shaped your journey.	Highlight the realization for sustainable fashion and the challenges faced in initiating this journey.
Embrace Authenticity	Share personal insights, challenges, and triumphs to add authenticity.	Narrate personal experiences with sustainable practices and commitment to changing the fashion landscape.
Appeal to Emotions	Evoke emotions in your audience, such as inspiration, empathy, or excitement.	Share anecdotes of how your initiative positively impacts communities and the environment.
Create a Compelling Opening	Craft an engaging opening to capture attention.	Start with a statement like, "In a world overrun by fast fashion, I envisioned a revolution—a sustainable fashion movement..."
Build a Narrative Arc	Structure your narrative with a clear beginning, middle, and end.	Begin with the inception of your idea, delve into challenges during implementation, and conclude with the impact achieved.
Incorporate Visual Imagery	Use descriptive language and imagery to paint a vivid picture.	Describe vibrant colors, textures, and eco-friendly materials of your fashion products.
Conclude with a Call to Action	Conclude by inspiring action, such as supporting your venture or spreading awareness.	Urge the audience to embrace sustainable fashion choices and join the transformative movement.

Note: Tailor the exercise to suit your specific entrepreneurial journey and vision. Crafting a compelling narrative is an ongoing process, so revisit and refine your story as your venture evolves.

✧ Overcoming Challenges with Vision

Embark on a riveting exploration into the heart of entrepreneurship, where challenges become the forge for visionary resilience. Picture yourself navigating the unpredictable terrain of the entrepreneurial landscape, encountering obstacles that may seem insurmountable. Yet, in the world of visionaries, challenges are not roadblocks; they are opportunities for transformation.

Join us on a rollercoaster of anecdotes, where setbacks are transformed into stepping stones. The entrepreneurial journey, akin to a thrilling adventure, is laden with unexpected twists and turns. Through the lens of visionary thinking, witness how challenges become catalysts for growth, and setbacks evolve into strategic advantages.

In this exhilarating narrative, we uncover the art of overcoming obstacles with a clarity of vision that acts as a guiding light. Visionaries possess a unique resilience—an ability to navigate storms with unwavering determination, emerging stronger on the other side. It's not about avoiding challenges; it's about transforming them into fuel for your entrepreneurial journey.

As we delve into real-life stories of visionary leaders who turned adversity into triumph, discover the secrets of leveraging setbacks as opportunities for innovation. It's a mindset shift, a paradigm where challenges become the raw material for crafting success stories. Learn the art of maintaining focus and clarity amidst chaos, emerging not just unscathed but fortified by the challenges you encounter.

Whether you're a seasoned entrepreneur or embarking on your maiden voyage, this exploration into overcoming challenges with vision is a roadmap to navigate the entrepreneurial wilderness. Brace yourself for a journey where setbacks become the spice that flavors your success story. Get ready to embrace challenges with a visionary mindset, turning each obstacle into a stepping stone towards your entrepreneurial summit.

As we navigate the tumultuous seas of entrepreneurship, the transformative power of vision emerges as a beacon guiding us through the storm. Visionaries don't merely face challenges; they seize them as opportunities to innovate and evolve. Imagine the story of Steve Jobs, envisioning a world connected by sleek devices, or Martin Luther King Jr., dreaming of a society built on equality. These visionary leaders left an indelible mark on history, showcasing the profound and transformative impact of their visions.

Crafting your visionary narrative is a pivotal step in this entrepreneurial odyssey. What sets visionaries apart is their ability to weave a compelling story that resonates not only with their business goals but also with the hearts and minds of those joining them on the expedition. It's about creating a narrative that captivates, inspires, and aligns a community around a shared vision.

In the crucible of challenges, visionaries don't crumble; they rise. Every setback becomes an opportunity to showcase the resilience inherent in visionary thinking. Learn from the anecdotes of those who turned adversity into triumph, where challenges were not stumbling blocks but stepping stones. Navigating storms with unwavering clarity of vision, visionaries emerge from challenges not just intact but fortified.

This exhilarating journey into overcoming challenges with vision is a call to arms. It's an invitation to transform obstacles into fuel for innovation, setbacks into strategic advantages. As you embark on your entrepreneurial adventure, remember that challenges are an integral part of the narrative. Embrace them with a visionary mindset, turning each obstacle into a stepping stone towards your summit.

So, whether you're a seasoned entrepreneur weathering storms or a novice setting sail on uncharted waters, this exploration is your compass. Vision becomes the guiding light, and resilience the steadfast companion, as you chart a course through the unpredictable waves of entrepreneurship. Let the transformative impact of vision be the driving force that propels you forward, shaping destinies and transforming industries. The adventure continues, and it's time to navigate challenges with the clarity and fortitude of a true visionary.

✧ Empowering the Entrepreneurial Spirit

In the vast expanse of the entrepreneurial landscape, a beacon of inspiration beckons—a call to action that transcends mere theoretical discourse. This is not a passive exploration but an impassioned journey, igniting the flames of the entrepreneurial spirit. Let the power of vision be the driving force, propelling you into the realms of possibility and empowering your aspirations.

➢ The Entrepreneurial Odyssey Unveiled

Prepare to embark on a thrilling expedition into the heart of visionary entrepreneurship, where the ordinary gives way to the extraordinary. In this exploration, we break free from the shackles of convention and venture into uncharted territory—a realm where dreams are not confined by the limitations of the status quo. This is not a passive observation but a resounding call to action, urging you to summon the audacity to dream big and think boldly.

The entrepreneurial odyssey, unlike many predefined journeys, is not a prescribed path but a vast canvas awaiting the strokes of your visionary brush. Envision this terrain as a blank canvas, devoid of preconceived notions and limitations. It is a tabula rasa, a clean slate upon which you have the privilege to craft your narrative.

As you step onto this transformative terrain, take a moment to imagine the canvas before you. It's expansive, stretching beyond the horizons of conventionality. It's blank, free from the constraints of past endeavors. It's a canvas, ready to be painted with the vibrant hues of your aspirations. Every brushstroke represents an idea, an action, a decision—each contributing to the masterpiece that is your entrepreneurial journey.

In the realm of visionary entrepreneurship, liberation from conventional boundaries is paramount. The entrepreneurial spirit thrives on breaking molds and challenging norms. It's about daring to venture where others haven't dared, envisioning a future that transcends the present, and creating opportunities where none seem to exist.

Consider the likes of Elon Musk, who dared to envision a world where sustainable energy powers our lives. His audacious dream shattered the conventional boundaries of the automotive and energy industries. Think of Steve Jobs, whose bold vision brought us sleek, seamlessly integrated devices. Their journeys were not confined to the beaten path; they forged new trails.

As you navigate this transformative terrain, your imagination becomes your greatest asset. It knows no bounds, and it thrives in the realm of visionary entrepreneurship. Imagine your canvas as a space where creativity, innovation, and audacity converge. It's here that your ideas take shape, where your dreams become tangible.

In this uncharted territory, you have the creative freedom to explore, experiment, and innovate. Every idea you conceive, every strategy you formulate, and every decision you make is a brushstroke on your canvas. Your vision guides the composition, but your imagination adds the colors and textures that make it come alive.

In essence, the entrepreneurial odyssey begins as you step onto this transformative terrain. It's an exhilarating adventure where the rules are not set in stone, and the possibilities are as vast as your imagination. This is a call to arms, urging you to embrace the transformative potential within your visionary aspirations.

So, dream big—let your ambitions soar beyond the confines of convention. Think boldly—challenge the norms and dare to be different. Your journey is not about adhering to a predefined path; it's about forging your own. Envision your canvas as a work of art in progress, with each stroke of brilliance contributing to the vibrant tapestry of your entrepreneurial story.

As you embark on this expedition, remember that the entrepreneurial odyssey is not a destination; it's a transformative journey. It's a canvas awaiting the bold strokes of your visionary brush, and it's an adventure where dreams are not confined by conventional boundaries but given the freedom to soar.

> Vision as the North Star

As we delve deeper into this exploration of visionary entrepreneurship, the concept of vision emerges as the North Star that will illuminate your path through the labyrinthine twists and turns of entrepreneurial endeavors. This is not a mere abstract notion; it is a practical and indispensable tool—an unwavering compass that aligns your actions with your loftiest aspirations.

Picture your vision as a magnetic force, a powerful pull that beckons you toward unprecedented heights. It is not a distant and unattainable goal but a dynamic and ever-present force that actively shapes destinies. Your entrepreneurial journey commences here, in this realm where imagination knows no bounds.

True vision defies the constraints of the ordinary and shatters the limits of the conventional. It is the audacious belief that compels you to push past the boundaries of what is considered achievable and strive for the extraordinary. In this exhilarating terrain, your vision is not just a passive destination; it is an active catalyst that transforms challenges into opportunities and setbacks into stepping stones.

Imagine yourself at the helm of a ship, navigating through the unpredictable waters of entrepreneurship. The waves may be turbulent, and the horizon uncertain, but your North Star—your vision—remains a constant and unwavering guide. It provides the clarity needed to chart a course through the stormiest of seas.

In the world of visionary entrepreneurship, your vision serves as your North Star in several profound ways:

1. Alignment: Your vision aligns your actions and decisions with your ultimate goals. It acts as a litmus test, ensuring that every choice you make contributes to the realization of your visionary dream.

2. Inspiration: Vision is the wellspring of inspiration. It fuels your passion, drives your determination, and ignites the creative fire within. It is the force that propels you forward even when faced with adversity.

3. Resilience: Challenges and setbacks are inevitable in the entrepreneurial journey. However, your vision empowers you to view these obstacles not as roadblocks but as opportunities for growth and innovation. It instills the resilience needed to persevere through the toughest of times.

4. Magnetism: Like a magnet, your vision attracts like-minded individuals who share your passion and belief in your mission. It draws collaborators, supporters, and allies who contribute to the collective pursuit of your visionary goals.

5. Focus: In the midst of the chaos and noise of the entrepreneurial landscape, your vision serves as a focal point—a beacon of clarity that guides your decisions and actions. It helps you prioritize and stay on course.

Transformation: Your vision is a transformative force. It has the power to transform not only your own life but also the lives of those your entrepreneurial endeavors touch. It creates ripples of change that extend far beyond your immediate sphere of influence.

In essence, your vision is not a passive destination but an active force. It is the dynamic North Star that leads you through uncharted territory, guiding you toward the realization of your entrepreneurial aspirations. It is the audacious belief that propels you beyond the ordinary, urging you to reach for the extraordinary.

As you navigate the entrepreneurial horizon, remember that your vision is not an abstract concept but a tangible and powerful force. It is the compass that keeps you on course, the source of inspiration that fuels your journey, and the catalyst that transforms challenges into opportunities. Embrace your vision as the North Star that will illuminate your path, and let it be the driving force that propels you toward unprecedented heights in your entrepreneurial odyssey.

> Dream Big, Think Boldly

In the realm of entrepreneurship, audacity is the fuel that propels the entrepreneurial spirit forward—an audacity to dream big and think boldly. This section serves as a resounding call to action, urging you to not only harbor visionary aspirations but also to fully embrace the transformative potential within them.

Consider the visionary architects of our time—Elon Musk, Steve Jobs, and others who dared to dream beyond the confines of the ordinary. Their audacious visions were not constrained by the status quo; instead, they envisioned futures that transcended the present realities. These visionaries serve as luminous examples of what can be achieved when one dares to dream big and think boldly.

1. Elon Musk: A Pioneer of Sustainable Energy

Musk's audacious dream was to transform the energy landscape of the world. He envisioned a future where sustainable energy sources would power our lives, and he set out to make it a reality through companies like Tesla and SpaceX. His vision was not merely to build electric cars but to revolutionize the entire automotive industry and lead humanity towards a more sustainable future.

2. Steve Jobs: The Seamless Integration of Technology

Steve Jobs envisioned a world where technology seamlessly integrated into our daily lives, where sleek and user-friendly devices would become extensions of ourselves. His audacious thinking led to the creation of iconic products like the iPhone, which not only transformed Apple but also redefined the way we interact with technology.

These visionary leaders did not merely follow the trends or play it safe. They dared to dream beyond the ordinary, envisioning futures that were often considered impossible by others. Their audacious dreams were the driving force behind their transformative impact on industries and society as a whole.

As you embark on your own entrepreneurial journey, let these stories serve as beacons of inspiration. They remind us that audacity is not a trait reserved for a select few but a quality that can be cultivated within each of us. Here's how you can apply the spirit of dreaming big and thinking boldly to your own entrepreneurial aspirations:

1. Dream Beyond the Ordinary:

Challenge the status quo and question the limits of what is considered possible. Don't confine your dreams to the boundaries of current conventions. Instead, envision a future that transcends the present and dares to be extraordinary.

2. Envision Impact:

Think beyond personal gain and consider the broader impact of your entrepreneurial endeavors. How can your vision create positive change in the lives of individuals, communities, or even the world? Your audacious thinking can be a force for greater good.

3. Active Engagement:

Audacity is not a passive trait. It requires active engagement with your visionary potential. Act on your audacious dreams, take calculated risks, and push the boundaries of what you believe is achievable. Bold thinking requires bold action.

4. Embrace Transformation:

Understand that audacious dreams are not just about achieving personal success; they are about catalyzing transformation. Embrace the idea that your visionary aspirations have the power to reshape industries, inspire innovation, and leave a lasting legacy.

5. Persistence and Resilience:

Audacious dreams may encounter resistance and setbacks. However, the audacity to dream big also includes the resilience to persevere in the face of challenges. Stay determined, adapt when necessary, and keep moving forward with unwavering faith in your vision.

In conclusion, the entrepreneurial spirit thrives on audacity—the audacity to dream big and think boldly. The stories of visionary leaders like Elon Musk and Steve Jobs remind us that audacious thinking can lead to transformative impact. As you embark on your entrepreneurial journey, dare to dream beyond the ordinary, envision a future that transcends the present, and actively engage with the audacious potential within you. Embrace audacity as a driving force, and let it propel you toward unprecedented heights in your pursuit of visionary entrepreneurship.

> The Compass of Entrepreneurial Greatness

Your vision is more than just a distant destination; it serves as the compass guiding you toward entrepreneurial greatness. In this section, we delve into the profound significance of vision as the guiding force throughout your entrepreneurial journey. It's not solely about reaching a goal; it's about embracing the entire voyage—the process of transforming your visionary aspirations into tangible reality.

1. The Journey of Vision:

Your entrepreneurial journey is akin to sailing through uncharted waters, where your vision acts as a luminous beacon illuminating the path forward. Envision yourself as the captain of your entrepreneurial ship, embarking on a thrilling expedition with the unwavering clarity provided by your vision. Just as sailors rely on the North Star to navigate, your vision becomes the guiding light amidst the uncertainties of entrepreneurship.

2. Challenges as Catalysts:

In the entrepreneurial odyssey, challenges are not mere hindrances; they are invaluable opportunities for growth and innovation. Your vision serves as the anchor that keeps you grounded during the storms of adversity. With your vision as a constant reference point, you can navigate with resilience, determination, and a keen sense of purpose. It's a transformative experience where setbacks are not setbacks at all; they become the raw material for innovation and the stepping stones to progress.

3. Vision and Adaptability:

While your vision provides clarity and direction, it's important to embrace adaptability along the way. The entrepreneurial landscape is dynamic, and unforeseen circumstances may require adjustments to your course. However, your vision remains the constant that guides your decision-making process. It allows you to adapt without losing sight of your ultimate destination.

4. Turning Obstacles into Advantages:

Entrepreneurs who possess a clear vision have the remarkable ability to turn obstacles into strategic advantages. Instead of seeing challenges as insurmountable barriers, visionaries view them as opportunities to differentiate themselves and innovate. By leveraging your vision, you can transform adversity into a catalyst for creative problem-solving.

5. Resilience and Determination:

Your vision infuses you with the resilience and determination needed to weather the entrepreneurial storms. It's the unwavering belief in your vision that keeps you going when faced with setbacks or uncertainties. Your commitment to the journey is bolstered by the profound impact your vision can have on the world.

6. The Power of Long-Term Focus:

Visionary entrepreneurs possess the ability to maintain a long-term focus. While short-term gains and losses may occur, your vision reminds you of the bigger picture and the enduring impact you aim to create. This long-term perspective can help you make decisions that align with your ultimate goals.

In conclusion, your vision serves as the compass that leads you toward entrepreneurial greatness. It not only defines your destination but also shapes the entire journey. Challenges are not roadblocks but opportunities for growth, and setbacks are transformed into strategic advantages. With your vision as your constant reference point, you navigate the entrepreneurial terrain with resilience, adaptability, and an unwavering determination to turn your aspirations into reality. Embrace the transformative power of your vision as you set sail on your entrepreneurial voyage, and let it be the guiding force that propels you to unprecedented heights.

Imagination Unleashed: A Blank Canvas Awaits

As you traverse this transformative landscape, recognize that your imagination knows no bounds. This is a canvas awaiting the strokes of your visionary brush. Immerse yourself in the artistry of entrepreneurship, where creativity and innovation are the brushstrokes that bring your vision to life. Think of your entrepreneurial journey as a masterpiece in the making, with each decision, action, and innovation contributing to the vibrant tapestry of your success.

Conclusion: A Call to Entrepreneurial Arms

In conclusion, this section is not a mere discourse; it's a call to entrepreneurial arms. The power of vision is not a passive force; it's an active catalyst for change. Dream big, think boldly, and let the transformative potential within your visionary aspirations empower your entrepreneurial spirit. Your journey begins now, where the entrepreneurial odyssey unfolds, and the canvas of imagination awaits the strokes of your visionary brush. Let vision be your guiding light, propelling you into the realms of unprecedented entrepreneurial greatness.

Charting the Course: Goal Setting Techniques Effective Goal Setting Techniques

Embarking on the entrepreneurial journey is akin to setting sail on a vast and uncharted sea. To navigate this challenging terrain successfully, one must possess a clear map—a set of goals that serve as guiding stars. In this section, we will delve into the art of goal setting, exploring techniques that will not only chart your course but also keep you on track, motivated, and inspired throughout your entrepreneurial odyssey.

1. Clarify Your Vision:

Before setting goals, it's crucial to have a crystal-clear vision of where you want to go. Your vision serves as the North Star guiding your entrepreneurial ship. Take the time to envision your long-term objectives and the impact you wish to make. What is the ultimate destination of your entrepreneurial journey?

2. Setting SMART Goals:

SMART (Specific, Measurable, Achievable, Relevant, Time-Bound) goals are the cornerstone of effective goal setting. Each goal should be specific and well-defined, allowing you to measure your progress. Ensure that your goals are achievable and relevant to your overarching vision. Set realistic deadlines to keep yourself accountable.

3. Break Down Big Goals:

Large, audacious goals can be overwhelming. Break them down into smaller, actionable steps. These bite-sized tasks become milestones on your journey, making your grand vision feel more achievable. Celebrate each milestone as you progress toward your larger goals.

4. Prioritize Your Goals:

Not all goals are created equal. Prioritize them based on their importance and impact. What goals are critical for your business's growth and success? Focus your energy and resources on these high-priority objectives.

5. Create a Vision Board:

A vision board is a visual representation of your goals and aspirations. It can be a powerful tool for keeping your vision alive. Use images, quotes, and symbols that resonate with your goals. Place your vision board where you can see it daily, reminding you of your objectives.

6. Develop an Action Plan:

Setting goals is just the beginning; you need a clear plan of action to achieve them. Break down each goal into specific steps and tasks. Assign responsibilities if you have a team. Having a well-structured plan will keep you on track and organized.

7. Embrace Accountability:

Share your goals with someone who can hold you accountable—a mentor, coach, or a trusted colleague. Regular check-ins and discussions about your progress can provide valuable insights and motivation.

8. Stay Adaptable:

Entrepreneurship is dynamic, and unforeseen challenges may arise. Be prepared to adapt your goals as needed while staying true to your vision. Flexibility is a key trait of successful entrepreneurs.

9. Celebrate Achievements:

Don't forget to celebrate your accomplishments, no matter how small they may seem. Recognize the progress you've made and use it as motivation to continue pushing toward your goals.

10. Stay Inspired:

Entrepreneurship can be a long and challenging journey. Keep your motivation and inspiration alive by revisiting your vision, reminding yourself why you started this journey in the first place. Surround yourself with like-minded individuals who share your passion and drive.

In conclusion, effective goal setting is the compass that will guide you through the entrepreneurial landscape. It provides direction, motivation, and a sense of purpose. By clarifying your vision, setting SMART goals, and developing a strategic plan, you can chart a course that leads to success. Embrace accountability, adaptability, and the joy of celebrating achievements along the way. Stay inspired and never lose sight of your vision. Your goals are the milestones on your entrepreneurial journey, and with effective goal setting techniques, you can navigate the seas of entrepreneurship with confidence and purpose.

The Symbiosis of Aspirations Aligning Personal and Business Goals

Embarking on the entrepreneurial journey is not merely a professional endeavor—it's a holistic pursuit that intertwines personal and business aspirations. In this section, we will explore the symbiotic relationship between your personal and business goals, revealing how aligning these aspirations can be a transformative force in your entrepreneurial odyssey.

1. The Fusion of Passions:

Successful entrepreneurs often find their greatest achievements at the intersection of personal and business passions. Consider the story of a fitness enthusiast who starts a health-focused business or an avid traveler who creates a travel-related venture. When your personal passions align with your business endeavors, work becomes a labor of love.

2. The Power of Purpose:

Your personal values and beliefs can profoundly impact your business decisions. Aligning your business with your personal purpose gives your entrepreneurial journey a deeper sense of meaning. It's not just about profit; it's about making a difference in alignment with your values.

3. Balancing Act:

Balancing personal and business goals can be challenging, but it's a critical aspect of a fulfilling entrepreneurial life. Strive for harmony between the two by setting clear boundaries, prioritizing self-care, and maintaining a healthy work-life balance.

4. Authenticity in Action:

Authenticity is a cornerstone of success in today's business world. When your personal values and beliefs align with your business practices, authenticity shines through. Customers and clients are drawn to businesses that operate with integrity and a genuine sense of purpose.

5. Personal Growth Catalyst:

Entrepreneurship is a journey of personal growth and self-discovery. Aligning personal and business goals can accelerate your personal development. As you overcome challenges and achieve milestones, you'll not only grow as an entrepreneur but also as an individual.

6. Passion-Driven Innovation:

Passion fuels innovation. When your personal passions drive your business pursuits, you're more likely to innovate and come up with creative solutions to industry challenges. Your passion becomes the driving force behind your entrepreneurial creativity.

7. Visionary Alignment:

Aligning personal and business visions is essential for long-term success. Your vision for your life should seamlessly integrate with your vision for your business. This alignment creates a powerful sense of direction and purpose.

8. The Ripple Effect:

The positive impact of aligning personal and business goals extends beyond your own life. It ripples out to your team, customers, and even society. A business driven by aligned aspirations can inspire others and create a ripple effect of positive change.

9. Celebrating Achievements Together:

Achieving personal and business goals in tandem is a cause for celebration. Recognize and celebrate your successes with your team, family, and community. These shared victories strengthen your bonds and fuel your drive to reach new heights.

10. A Fulfilling Journey:

In the end, the entrepreneurial journey is not just about reaching a destination—it's about the fulfillment you find along the way. Aligning personal and business goals can make this journey deeply satisfying, as you live a life that resonates with your truest aspirations.

In conclusion, the symbiosis of personal and business goals is a powerful force in the entrepreneurial world. It allows you to infuse your business with purpose, authenticity, and innovation. It propels you toward personal growth and fulfillment while positively impacting those around you. Embrace this alignment as you embark on your entrepreneurial odyssey, and watch as your aspirations flourish in harmony, creating a life and business that are truly extraordinary.

Illuminating Perspectives
Perspectives on Vision and Goal Setting

In the grand tapestry of entrepreneurship, vision and goal setting are the threads that weave the narrative of success. As we delve into this enlightening section, we'll explore a spectrum of perspectives on vision and goal setting that illuminate the path to entrepreneurial greatness. These insights are not just theoretical musings; they are beacons guiding you toward your own unique path to success.

1. The Dreamer's Lens:

Imagine the entrepreneur as a dreamer, gazing upon the horizon with boundless optimism. For the dreamer, vision is the North Star—a guiding light that illuminates the way through the darkness of uncertainty. Goals are the constellations, each representing a milestone on the journey to turn dreams into reality.

2. The Pragmatic Planner:

On the opposite end of the spectrum, we find the pragmatic planner. This entrepreneur sees vision as a blueprint, a detailed map of where the business should go. Goals are the waypoints, meticulously planned and executed to ensure steady progress.

3. The Adaptive Navigator:

Some entrepreneurs embrace adaptability as their guiding principle. They view vision as a compass rather than a fixed destination. Goals, in this perspective, are flexible markers that may shift with changing circumstances. The focus is on navigating the ever-changing entrepreneurial landscape.

4. The Purpose-Driven Visionary:

For the purpose-driven visionary, vision is not solely about business success. It's a higher calling—a mission to make a positive impact on the world. Goals are stepping stones toward a greater purpose, each contributing to a larger, meaningful narrative.

5. The Collaborative Creator:

Entrepreneurship is not a solitary journey for the collaborative creator. In this perspective, vision is a shared vision, co-created with a team of like-minded individuals. Goals are collective milestones, and success is measured not just in personal achievements but in the growth and success of the entire team.

6. The Risk-Taking Maverick:

Some entrepreneurs thrive on taking risks. They see vision as a daring adventure into the unknown, and goals are the thrilling challenges along the way. Success is not just about achieving goals; it's about conquering the next uncharted territory.

7. The Legacy Builder:

Legacy builders envision their businesses as lasting legacies that will outlive them. Vision, in this perspective, is about creating a timeless impact. Goals are milestones on the path to leaving a lasting imprint on the entrepreneurial landscape.

8. The Resilient Optimist:

In the face of adversity, the resilient optimist sees vision as a source of resilience. Goals are the beacons of hope that keep the entrepreneurial spirit alive. This perspective emphasizes the power of determination in achieving even the loftiest of goals.

9. The Lifelong Learner:

Lifelong learners view entrepreneurship as a continuous journey of growth and discovery. Vision is not a fixed point but a dynamic force that evolves with knowledge and experience. Goals are the markers of progress on the never-ending path of learning and improvement.

10. The Visionary Philanthropist:

Some entrepreneurs are driven by a vision of giving back to society. Their vision extends beyond business success to creating positive social change. Goals are the means to achieve both financial success and social impact.

In conclusion, the diverse perspectives on vision and goal setting in entrepreneurship are a testament to the richness of this field. As you embark on your own entrepreneurial journey, consider these various viewpoints and find the one that resonates most with your values and aspirations. Whether you're a dreamer, a planner, a risk-taker, or a collaborator, your unique perspective will shape your path to success. Illuminate your entrepreneurial journey with the wisdom of these perspectives and let them guide you toward your vision's brilliant realization.

Chapter 4: Innovation and Creativity

Welcome to Chapter 4 of our transformative journey, where we delve into the exhilarating realms of innovation and creativity. This chapter is not just a collection of ideas; it's a dynamic exploration that invites you to unlock the doors of your creative genius.

Imagine this chapter as a treasure chest filled with the gems of innovation waiting to be discovered. As we embark on this adventure, you'll find that innovation is not reserved for the few; it's a wellspring of potential that flows within each of us. Creativity, the beacon of innovation, lights the way, guiding you to forge new paths and redefine the status quo.

Let's embark on this journey together, where the canvas is blank, and the possibilities are boundless. Whether you're an aspiring entrepreneur or a seasoned trailblazer, the principles of innovation and creativity are the keys to unlocking your full potential.

In the pages that follow, you'll uncover the secrets of innovative thinking, explore the art of ideation, and learn how to foster a culture of creativity within your entrepreneurial endeavors. From problem-solving to disruptive innovation, we'll traverse the landscape of creativity with enthusiasm and vigor.

Remember, innovation is not just about groundbreaking products or services; it's a mindset, a way of approaching challenges, and a commitment to continuous improvement. It's about taking risks, embracing failure as a stepping stone to success, and letting your imagination soar.

So, let's dive in, shall we? Together, we'll embark on a journey to unleash the creative genius within you. Chapter 4 awaits, promising an engaging, informative, and enthusiastic exploration of innovation and creativity that will leave you inspired and ready to take on the world with fresh, innovative perspectives.

Fostering Creativity in Business

In the ever-evolving landscape of entrepreneurship, creativity isn't just a desirable trait; it's a powerful catalyst for success. This section is your guide to nurturing and harnessing the creative spirit within your business endeavors.

Imagine a world where your business isn't bound by the confines of convention. Instead, it's a playground where innovation knows no bounds. Creativity becomes your trusted companion, leading the way to groundbreaking ideas, fresh perspectives, and, ultimately, unparalleled growth.

Let's embark on this journey together, where we'll uncover the secrets to fostering creativity in business. Whether you're a startup founder or a seasoned executive, the principles we explore here will transform the way you approach challenges and opportunities.

Throughout this section, we'll share captivating stories of businesses that thrived by embracing creativity as their guiding force. From Apple's revolutionary product designs to Airbnb's disruptive approach to travel accommodations, these tales serve as beacons of inspiration, demonstrating the transformative impact of creativity in the business world.

But fostering creativity isn't just about inspiration; it's a structured process that can be cultivated and nurtured. We'll provide you with actionable techniques and strategies to infuse creativity into your business culture. You'll learn how to create an environment that encourages innovative thinking, empowers your team, and sparks the kind of creative magic that leads to game-changing solutions.

Creativity isn't a luxury; it's a necessity in today's competitive business landscape. As we dive deeper into this section, remember that your unique perspective, your ability to think outside the box, and your willingness to embrace the unknown are your greatest assets.

So, let's embark on this thrilling exploration of fostering creativity in business. Together, we'll unlock the door to a world where innovation is the norm, and where creativity becomes the driving force behind your business's success. Get ready to unleash your creative potential and take your entrepreneurial journey to new heights.

In the dynamic realm of entrepreneurship, our journey into fostering creativity in business reaches its zenith. As we conclude this section, it's not merely an ending; it's an invitation to a new beginning—a beginning where creativity becomes the lifeblood of your entrepreneurial endeavors.

Picture this: Your business is no longer confined by the boundaries of tradition and routine. It's a realm where innovation flows freely, where creative sparks ignite groundbreaking ideas, and where the status quo is merely a stepping stone to higher heights.

Our voyage together has been one of exploration, revelation, and transformation. We've witnessed the stories of businesses that transcended mediocrity by embracing creativity as their guiding star. From the ingenious designs of Apple's products to the disruptive innovations of Airbnb's travel accommodations, we've seen how creativity reshapes industries and defines success.

But beyond inspiration, this section has equipped you with practical tools and strategies. You've learned to cultivate a culture of creativity, empower your team to think innovatively, and navigate the challenges that accompany the creative process.

Now, as you move forward in your entrepreneurial journey, remember that creativity isn't an elusive muse; it's a skill that can be honed and mastered. Your unique perspective, your willingness to take risks, and your ability to see opportunities where others see obstacles are your superpowers.

In the ever-evolving landscape of entrepreneurship, creativity isn't just a choice; it's a necessity. As you embrace the creative spirit within you and within your business, you'll discover that it's not a destination but a continuous journey of growth and transformation.

So, let's conclude this section by embracing the creative potential that resides within each of us. As you continue your entrepreneurial odyssey, may creativity be your constant companion, guiding you to uncharted territories and unprecedented success. Your creative spirit is the beacon that will illuminate your path forward, and your journey has only just begun.

The Process of Innovation

In the realm of entrepreneurship, innovation isn't just a buzzword; it's the lifeblood of progress and success. This section is your gateway to understanding the intricacies of the innovation process—the journey from the inception of an idea to its real-world impact.

Picture this: You're seated at the helm of your business, surrounded by a team brimming with ideas, and you're on the brink of creating something truly groundbreaking. Innovation is the driving force that propels your business forward, setting you apart in a crowded marketplace.

As we embark on this illuminating journey, let's explore the various stages of innovation, from idea generation to implementation. This isn't just theory; it's a practical guide that equips you with the tools to turn your innovative aspirations into tangible results.

We'll traverse the landscape of innovation together, drawing inspiration from the stories of visionary entrepreneurs who dared to think differently. Consider the tale of Jeff Bezos and the inception of Amazon, a company that redefined the way we shop. Or think about the transformative impact of Elon Musk's SpaceX, which revolutionized space travel. These stories serve as beacons, illuminating the path to innovation.

But innovation isn't reserved for tech giants; it's a mindset that can be cultivated in any business, regardless of size or industry. Throughout this section, we'll provide you with practical strategies and techniques to foster a culture of innovation within your organization. You'll learn how to encourage creative thinking, embrace risk, and navigate the challenges that come with innovation.

Innovation isn't a solitary endeavor; it thrives in a collaborative ecosystem. We'll delve into the importance of teamwork, cross-disciplinary collaboration, and the power of diverse perspectives in driving innovation forward.

As we navigate the intricacies of the innovation process, remember that innovation is not about perfection; it's about progress. It's the willingness to experiment, adapt, and learn from both successes and failures. It's about staying curious and open to new possibilities.

So, let's embark on this thrilling journey into the heart of innovation. Together, we'll uncover the secrets to fostering a culture of creativity and transforming ideas into impactful innovations. Get ready to unleash your entrepreneurial spirit and make your mark on the world through the power of innovation.

In the ever-evolving landscape of entrepreneurship, innovation isn't just a buzzword; it's the very essence of progress and success. As we delve deeper into the process of innovation, our voyage continues, charting a course through the uncharted waters of creativity and ingenuity.

Imagine yourself at the helm of your business, surrounded by a team fueled by boundless ideas, standing on the precipice of creating something truly revolutionary. Innovation isn't a mere tool; it's the driving force that propels your business forward, setting you apart in a sea of competitors.

Our journey through this illuminating section takes us on a tour of the various stages of innovation, from the spark of an idea to its real-world impact. But this isn't a theoretical exploration; it's a practical guide, providing you with the tools and insights to transform your innovative dreams into tangible realities.

Together, we'll traverse the innovation landscape, drawing inspiration from the stories of visionary entrepreneurs who dared to challenge the status quo. Consider Jeff Bezos and the inception of Amazon, a company that reshaped the way we shop. Reflect on Elon Musk's SpaceX, a trailblazer in revolutionizing space travel. These tales illuminate the path to innovation, demonstrating that groundbreaking ideas can come to life.

However, innovation isn't reserved for tech giants alone; it's a mindset that can flourish in any business, regardless of its size or industry. Throughout this section, we'll equip you with practical strategies to cultivate a culture of innovation within your organization. You'll learn how to foster creative thinking, embrace calculated risks, and navigate the inevitable challenges that accompany the innovation journey.

Innovation isn't a solitary endeavor; it thrives in a collaborative ecosystem. We'll delve into the significance of teamwork, cross-disciplinary collaboration, and the transformative power of diverse perspectives. Together, we'll explore how these elements can drive innovation forward and open doors to unimagined possibilities.

In the world of innovation, perfection isn't the goal; progress is. It's about the willingness to experiment, adapt, and learn from both successes and failures. It's about maintaining a perpetual curiosity and remaining open to the ever-unfolding landscape of possibilities.

As we continue this thrilling journey into the heart of innovation, remember that you possess the power to unleash your entrepreneurial spirit and leave an indelible mark on the world. Through the creative forces of innovation, you have the potential to transform ideas into impactful innovations that shape the future. So, brace yourself for this exhilarating adventure and prepare to make your entrepreneurial vision a reality through the power of innovation.

Case Studies of Innovative Entrepreneurs

In the captivating world of entrepreneurship, the stories of innovative visionaries serve as beacons of inspiration, illuminating the path to success. As we delve into the lives and achievements of these remarkable individuals, prepare to embark on a journey of discovery, learning, and limitless possibilities.

The Story of Jeff Bezos: Amazon's Evolutionary Pioneer

Our first case study introduces us to the relentless innovator, Jeff Bezos, the driving force behind Amazon's meteoric rise. Imagine a time when online shopping was a novel concept, and books were just the beginning. Bezos had a vision, one that extended far beyond the pages of books. He envisioned a digital marketplace where customers could find virtually anything they desired.

As you dive into Bezos's journey, witness how his audacious dream transformed the retail landscape. Amazon became the world's largest online marketplace, a platform offering everything from A to Z. Through relentless innovation, from the introduction of Amazon Prime to the pioneering of voice-activated shopping with Alexa, Bezos demonstrated the power of innovation to redefine industries.

But it wasn't just about products; it was about the customer experience. Bezos prioritized customer satisfaction above all else, pioneering innovations like one-click shopping and same-day delivery. His commitment to customer-centricity became a blueprint for businesses worldwide, emphasizing the importance of continuous improvement and adaptation.

The Visionary Ventures of Elon Musk: From PayPal to SpaceX
Our next case study transports us into the realm of Elon Musk, a true visionary whose endeavors have transcended multiple industries. Musk's

journey began with the co-founding of PayPal, revolutionizing online payments. Yet, his aspirations reached far beyond the digital realm.

With SpaceX, Musk set his sights on the cosmos, envisioning a future where humanity could become an interplanetary species. The audacity of this vision spurred SpaceX's relentless pursuit of innovations in rocket technology, paving the way for more affordable space travel and redefining the possibilities of human exploration.

But Musk's ventures didn't stop there. He ventured into electric vehicles with Tesla, challenging the automotive industry's status quo and accelerating the transition to sustainable transportation. His commitment to renewable energy with SolarCity and the development of the Hyperloop further exemplify his dedication to transformative innovation.

Airbnb: Redefining Travel Accommodations

Our final case study immerses us in the world of Airbnb, a disruptor in the travel and hospitality industry. Founded by Brian Chesky, Joe Gebbia, and Nathan Blecharczyk, Airbnb began as a simple idea—to provide travelers with unique and authentic accommodation experiences. Little did they know that their vision would lead to a global phenomenon.

As you explore the Airbnb story, witness how a simple concept evolved into a platform with millions of listings worldwide. The founders' commitment to innovation and user experience led to innovations like online booking, secure payments, and host-guest reviews that transformed the way people travel and book accommodations.

But Airbnb's innovation wasn't limited to lodging; it extended to the concept of community and belonging. By fostering connections between hosts and guests, Airbnb redefined travel as a personal and cultural experience. It's a testament to how innovation can reshape entire industries by addressing unmet needs and enhancing the customer journey.

Lessons from Visionaries

These case studies offer valuable insights into the entrepreneurial mindset of innovative leaders. They demonstrate that innovation isn't confined to a specific industry; it's a mindset, a relentless pursuit of improvement, and a commitment to delivering exceptional value to customers. Whether you're in e-commerce, space exploration, or travel accommodations, the principles of innovation remain universal.

As you dive into these stories, envision how their lessons can be applied to your own entrepreneurial journey. Embrace the audacity to dream big, prioritize customer-centricity, and be open to disruption. These visionary entrepreneurs have shown that innovation isn't a solitary endeavor but a collaborative effort that can reshape industries and leave an indelible mark on the world.

So, as we explore these case studies of innovative entrepreneurs, remember that their journeys are more than stories; they are blueprints for achieving transformative success. Get ready to be inspired, encouraged, and equipped with the tools to infuse innovation into your own entrepreneurial endeavors.

Chapter 5: Decision-Making and Problem-Solving

Welcome to a pivotal chapter in our entrepreneurial journey, where we delve into the art and science of decision-making and problem-solving. Picture this: you, as the captain of your entrepreneurial ship, navigating through uncharted waters, facing a sea of choices and challenges. It's a journey where every decision shapes your course, and every problem is an opportunity waiting to be seized.

In this chapter, we embark on an exploration of the decision-making and problem-solving processes, not as isolated concepts but as intertwined forces that drive entrepreneurial success. Decision-making is the compass that guides you through the labyrinth of possibilities, while problem-solving is the toolkit that empowers you to overcome obstacles and seize opportunities.

As we journey together through the entrepreneurial maze, you'll discover that decision-making is not merely about making choices; it's about making informed, strategic choices. It's about understanding the risks and rewards, analyzing data, and embracing both intuition and logic. It's about the art of balancing calculated risk with bold ambition.

Problem-solving, on the other hand, is the entrepreneurial superpower that transforms challenges into stepping stones. It's about seeing problems as puzzles to be solved, not as roadblocks. It's about creativity, adaptability, and resilience in the face of adversity. It's about turning setbacks into catalysts for growth.

Throughout this chapter, we'll draw inspiration from real-world entrepreneurs who navigated complex decisions and tackled formidable problems. Their stories will serve as guiding lights, illustrating the transformative power of effective decision-making and problem-solving. From Elon Musk's daring ventures to Jeff Bezos's strategic choices, we'll uncover the strategies and mindset that set them apart.

But decision-making and problem-solving are not reserved for industry titans; they are skills that can be honed and mastered by entrepreneurs at every stage of their journey. Whether you're a startup founder facing critical choices or a seasoned executive leading a team through turbulent times, the principles we explore here are universally applicable.

So, as we set sail into the world of decision-making and problem-solving, remember that each chapter of your entrepreneurial story is defined by the choices you make and the solutions you craft. Together, we'll unravel the mysteries of effective decision-making and problem-solving, equipping you with the tools and insights to navigate the entrepreneurial maze with confidence and clarity. Get ready to embrace the challenges and choices that lie ahead, for they are the building blocks of your entrepreneurial legacy.

Strategies for Effective Decision-Making

> ❖ The Tale of Two Paths: A Decision-Making Odyssey

Envision yourself as the master of a formidable ship, the S.S. Enterprise, steering a path through the business world's vast and ever-shifting ocean. This sea, with its fluctuating currents and winds, is a vivid metaphor for the business landscape, constantly evolving and presenting new challenges and opportunities. Each wave symbolizes a decision to be made; each breeze, a potential prospect or hazard. Your role as the captain involves scanning the horizon with discerning eyes, ready to confront the unfolding mysteries. As the fog clears, two islands emerge, each embodying a distinct approach to decision-making: the Isle of Analysis, with its focus on data and logic, and the Realm of Intuition, where instinct and gut feelings reign supreme.

Maneuvering Through Business Currents

In the ever-evolving journey of entrepreneurship, navigating through the business landscape can be likened to maneuvering a ship through the vast and unpredictable ocean. Just as the ocean's behavior is dynamic and ever-changing, so is the nature of the business environment. There are moments of calm seas, symbolizing stable market conditions where business operations run smoothly and predictably. However, these tranquil periods may abruptly give way to turbulent storms, akin to the unforeseen challenges and market disruptions that businesses often encounter. These storms represent economic downturns, technological disruptions, competitive pressures, or changes in consumer behavior, each capable of testing the resilience and adaptability of any business venture.

As the captain of this ship, your role extends beyond mere navigation. Each decision you make, whether it's charting a course through calm waters or steering through a tempest, significantly impacts the journey's outcome. These decisions can lead you to prosperous destinations, where business growth and success await, or into perilous situations fraught with risks and setbacks. The responsibility is immense, as the welfare and success of your venture rest upon your ability to foresee, assess, and navigate through these varying conditions.

Moreover, the crew aboard your ship, representing the diverse departments and perspectives within your organization, plays a crucial role in this journey. They are your team, each member bringing unique skills, insights, and viewpoints that contribute to the overall strength and capability of your business. As their leader, they look to you not only for direction but also for reassurance and motivation, especially during challenging times. Your ability to lead effectively, to communicate your vision and strategy clearly, and to inspire confidence among your team members is pivotal in maintaining morale and fostering a collaborative spirit.

This analogy of maneuvering through business currents underscores the complex and dynamic nature of entrepreneurship. It highlights the need for strategic foresight, effective decision-making, and strong leadership. Just as a skilled captain understands the sea's unpredictability and prepares for various scenarios, a successful entrepreneur must be adept at anticipating market trends, adapting strategies, and leading their team through both tranquil and turbulent times. This journey is not just about reaching the destination but also about how effectively you navigate the currents, how well you adapt to changing conditions, and how you lead your team through the myriad challenges and opportunities that the business world presents.

Approaching the Isle of Analysis

As you navigate closer to the Isle of Analysis, the scenery unfolds to reveal an environment that epitomizes the essence of structured and methodical thinking. This island, a metaphor for a systematic and analytical approach to decision-making, presents a landscape where every detail is organized and every process is deliberate. The coastlines of the Isle are lined with impressive institutions that symbolize centers of research and analysis, bustling with experts who are deeply immersed in the study and interpretation of data.

The atmosphere on the Isle is one of intellectual rigor. Here, professionals from various fields – economists, data scientists, market analysts, and strategic planners – are engaged in the meticulous examination of data and statistics. These experts work tirelessly, sifting through vast amounts of information to uncover insights and patterns. In this realm, decisions are not made on hunches or intuition but are deeply rooted in empirical evidence and thorough investigation. The emphasis is on factual precision, ensuring that every conclusion drawn and every strategy formulated is based on solid, verifiable data.

On the Isle of Analysis, the approach to problem-solving is methodical. Complex issues are broken down into smaller, more manageable components, and each aspect is analyzed with precision. This process involves various analytical techniques, from quantitative analysis and statistical modeling to qualitative assessments and comparative studies. The goal is to derive clarity and insights from data, transforming raw information into actionable intelligence.

In this environment, careful deliberation is valued over haste. Decision-making is a process that involves weighing all the evidence, considering multiple perspectives, and evaluating potential outcomes. The culture here is one that fosters critical thinking and encourages a questioning mindset, where assumptions are continuously challenged, and decisions are made with a deep understanding of the underlying factors and implications.

The Isle of Analysis, therefore, represents a critical aspect of strategic decision-making in business. It serves as a reminder of the importance of grounding decisions in solid analysis and research. For any entrepreneur or business leader, a visit to this metaphorical island is a journey into the heart of informed decision-making, where data and evidence provide the compass and map for navigating the complex and often uncertain waters of the business world. It underscores the value of an analytical approach, where thoughtful consideration, rigorous investigation, and a commitment to precision are the keys to making sound, effective decisions.

Venturing Towards the Realm of Intuition

As you venture towards the Realm of Intuition, a distinct shift in atmosphere becomes apparent. This island, bathed in a gentle, mystical glow, stands in stark contrast to the orderly and methodical Isle of Analysis. It represents a less structured, more vibrant and spontaneous environment, embodying the intuitive and instinct-driven aspect of decision-making. Here, in this realm, the rules of conventional logic and structured analysis give way to a world where creativity, emotional intelligence, and the ability to read subtle cues and signals reign supreme.

This mystical island is characterized by its fluidity and dynamism, reflecting the often unpredictable nature of intuitive decision-making. In this space, entrepreneurs and leaders rely on their inner wisdom and gut feelings, making decisions that may seem spontaneous or unorthodox but are deeply rooted in a wealth of experience and a profound connection with their surroundings. The landscape of the Realm of Intuition is rich with abstract concepts and imaginative possibilities, where creative solutions and innovative ideas flourish without the constraints of rigid data or empirical evidence.

In the Realm of Intuition, decisions are frequently made swiftly, guided by an internal compass that is informed by years of experience, insights gleaned from past successes and failures, and an innate understanding of the market and human behavior. This approach values the power of a hunch, the significance of a fleeting thought, and the importance of emotional responses. Here, the ability to sense the undercurrents of a situation, to read between the lines, and to understand the unspoken needs and desires of customers and clients is crucial.

This realm is also a testament to the importance of emotional intelligence in business. It highlights how empathy, understanding, and the ability to connect with others on a deeper level can be powerful tools in decision-making. Leaders who navigate this realm successfully are those who can balance their emotional insights with their rational thoughts, merging the art of intuition with the science of analysis.

In conclusion, the Realm of Intuition offers a vibrant and spontaneous environment that plays a vital role in the decision-making process. It complements the analytical approach by adding depth, creativity, and emotional intelligence to the mix. Navigating this realm requires an open mind, a willingness to trust one's instincts, and the ability to embrace uncertainty. For entrepreneurs and business leaders, understanding and valuing the insights that come from this intuitive space can lead to more holistic and well-rounded decision-making, blending the best of both worlds – the analytical and the intuitive.

Confronting the Decision Dilemma

As you, the captain of your entrepreneurial voyage, approach the pivotal moment of decision-making, you find yourself confronting a decision dilemma at the confluence of two contrasting islands - the Isle of Analysis and the Realm of Intuition. This critical juncture presents a challenging choice, as both islands offer indispensable insights but in fundamentally different ways. The Isle of Analysis, with its structured and methodical layout, provides a solid foundation of data, empirical evidence, and logical frameworks. It represents a world where decisions are grounded in research, quantitative analysis, and factual accuracy, offering a sense of security and predictability.

Conversely, the Realm of Intuition offers a starkly different approach. It is a world where instinctual knowledge, experiential wisdom, and emotional intelligence are paramount. In this realm, decisions are often made swiftly, based on gut feelings, personal experiences, and an intuitive understanding of the market and human behavior. It's a space that values creativity, innovation, and the ability to read and respond to subtle cues and underlying trends that may not be immediately apparent in data sets.

As the captain, your challenge is to navigate between these two worlds, integrating their insights to formulate a comprehensive navigational strategy. This requires a delicate balance, discerning when to anchor firmly in the realm of data and structured analysis and when to set sail on the winds of intuition. It involves recognizing that while data and analysis provide clarity and reduce uncertainty, intuition can often lead to breakthrough innovations and swift decision-making in situations where data may be lacking or inconclusive.

The key to this balance is understanding that neither approach is superior in all situations, and the most effective strategy often lies in combining the strengths of both. When confronting complex business decisions, it may be prudent to start with the solid ground of analysis, using data to inform the initial direction. However, there will be moments when the data is inconclusive or the situation is unprecedented, and here, intuition, borne out of experience and a deep understanding of the business landscape, becomes invaluable.

In summary, as you confront the decision dilemma in your entrepreneurial journey, the ability to adeptly balance the logical rigor of the Isle of Analysis with the instinctual insights of the Realm of Intuition becomes crucial. This balanced approach allows for more nuanced, well-rounded decision-making, leveraging the strengths of both analytical thinking and intuitive insight. It is in navigating this delicate balance that you, as the captain, can steer your venture toward success, adeptly handling the complexities and uncertainties of the business world.

Setting the Strategic Course

As you chart the strategic course for your business journey, the path ahead calls for a nuanced blend of adaptability and flexibility in your decision-making processes. This intricate navigation involves discerning when to rely on a data-centric strategy and when to trust your intuition, based on the unique demands of each situation you encounter.

In scenarios where the waters are clear and the direction is well-defined, a data-centric approach becomes essential. Here, risks can be quantitatively assessed, and decisions are underpinned by solid empirical evidence and thorough analysis. This approach is particularly vital in situations where the stakes are high, and the margin for error is slim. It involves meticulously gathering and analyzing relevant data, using this information to forecast potential outcomes, and formulating plans with precision and caution. In such contexts, leaning heavily on the Isle of Analysis allows you to navigate with confidence, backed by the security of data-driven insights.

However, there are also instances where the seas of business are uncharted, and the path is not illuminated by the light of existing data. In these unprecedented circumstances, your intuition becomes a guiding star. When faced with novel challenges or opportunities where historical data may be limited or inapplicable, trusting your instinctual knowledge and experiential wisdom becomes crucial. This intuitive approach is particularly relevant in rapidly changing markets, during innovative product development, or when responding to unforeseen market disruptions. In such cases, the ability to read between the lines, to sense the undercurrents of the market, and to make swift decisions based on a deep, intuitive understanding of your business and its environment becomes invaluable.

Setting the strategic course, therefore, is not a matter of choosing between data and intuition in a mutually exclusive fashion. Rather, it's about skillfully navigating between these two approaches, understanding that each has its place and time. It requires the agility to switch between a rigorous, data-driven mindset and an intuitive, flexible approach as different situations arise. This balanced strategy empowers you to make informed decisions when clarity and certainty are available and to rely on your entrepreneurial instincts when venturing into the unknown.

In summary, the journey of setting a strategic course in business is about mastering the art of adaptability and flexibility in decision-making. It involves recognizing the value of both data-centric strategies and intuitive judgment, and adeptly applying them based on the demands of each unique business situation. By cultivating this dual approach, you equip yourself with a versatile toolkit for navigating the complex and ever-changing waters of the business world, enhancing your ability to steer your venture towards success and growth.

Embarking on a Continual Learning Journey

Your journey in the realm of decision-making is not a finite endeavor but a continual voyage of balance and growth, a persistent quest to master the delicate harmony between analytical reasoning and intuitive insight. This journey is akin to navigating a vast ocean, where the waters represent the ever-changing dynamics of the business world. As you embark on this journey, it involves integrating the structured, data-driven wisdom of the Isle of Analysis with the fluid, instinctive insights of the

Realm of Intuition. It's a perpetual process of learning, adapting, and refining your approach to decision-making.

This continual learning journey is characterized by an ongoing exploration of new knowledge, strategies, and perspectives. It's about developing an adeptness in interpreting complex signals from the business environment, which often requires a fusion of both analytical and intuitive faculties. You learn to recognize when to delve deep into data, meticulously analyzing trends and statistics, and when to rely on your gut feelings and the subtle nuances that data alone cannot capture.

In this process, your role transcends the traditional boundaries of navigation. You become a mentor and guide to your team, sharing your insights and fostering a culture of learning and adaptability within your organization. Your ability to balance different decision-making approaches becomes a model for your team, encouraging them to develop their analytical and intuitive skills.

Moreover, this journey involves a constant reflection on past decisions, both successes and failures, to glean lessons and insights. It's about building an ever-evolving understanding of your business landscape, your team's dynamics, and your personal decision-making style. This reflective practice helps in fine-tuning your strategies, making you more equipped to handle future challenges.

As you progress, the journey also demands that you stay abreast of emerging trends and technologies that can impact your business. It requires a commitment to continuous education and professional development, ensuring that your decision-making skills remain sharp and relevant in a rapidly evolving business world.

In conclusion, embarking on a continual learning journey in decision-making is about more than just reaching specific business milestones. It's about developing a deep understanding of the interplay between data and intuition, honing the skills to blend these approaches effectively, and guiding your team and enterprise toward ongoing growth and success.

This journey is an unending pursuit of mastery in decision-making, marked by continuous learning, adaptation, and growth.

As you embark upon the Isle of Analysis, you immerse yourself in an environment where data and evidence-based decision-making form the cornerstone of the landscape. This island epitomizes the essence of a systematic, analytical approach, where every corner is pulsating with the rhythm of rigorous analysis and empirical data.

In this realm, the inhabitants are akin to masterful data architects and analysts. They are engrossed in the meticulous collection, interpretation, and application of information, serving as guardians over vast databases, detailed surveys, and insightful market reports. Their expertise in statistical models and predictive analytics equips them to adeptly navigate the intricate and often turbulent seas of business.

The Isle is home to expansive data repositories, akin to grand libraries, where comprehensive collections of market research, consumer behavior trends, and economic forecasts are meticulously maintained. These repositories serve as invaluable treasure troves, offering a wealth of information crucial for informed and strategic decision-making.

Scattered across the island are collaborative hubs, dynamic think tanks where teams of analysts, statisticians, and experts converge. In these spaces, data is not just analyzed but is debated and discussed, leading to the forging of robust strategies and innovative solutions.

Decision-making on the Isle of Analysis is a methodical and structured process:

Data Collection and Aggregation: The journey begins with the gathering of relevant data from diverse sources - market surveys, customer feedback, financial reports, and competitive analyses.

Data Cleaning and Processing: This crucial stage involves refining the raw data, cleansing it of any inaccuracies or inconsistencies, thereby ensuring its reliability and suitability for in-depth analysis.

Analysis and Interpretation: Utilizing advanced analytical tools, the data is thoroughly examined to uncover patterns, trends, and critical insights. Techniques like regression analysis, time-series forecasting, and machine learning algorithms are employed to extract meaningful information from the data.

Scenario Modeling and Simulation: Here, the islanders leverage sophisticated modeling techniques to simulate various business scenarios. This approach aids in visualizing potential outcomes, allowing for a comprehensive assessment of different decision paths.

Risk Analysis and Mitigation: With a wealth of data at their disposal, risks are identified, quantified, and analyzed, providing a clear understanding of potential impacts. This stage is integral to formulating effective contingency plans and mitigation strategies.

Data-Driven Decision-Making: Decisions are ultimately made based on this rigorous analytical process, grounded in empirical evidence and logical reasoning. These decisions are often supported by data models and projections, offering a solid justification for the chosen course of action.

In essence, the Isle of Analysis stands as a beacon of structured, data-driven decision-making, where every step is underpinned by detailed analysis and empirical evidence, guiding businesses towards informed, strategic, and successful outcomes.

The Philosophy of the Isle

On the Isle of Analysis, there prevails a steadfast philosophy that positions data as the paramount guide in navigating the often uncertain and tumultuous waters of the business world. In this domain, the inherent belief is that data, with its objective and quantifiable nature, offers a beacon of reliability and clarity amidst the complexities and unpredictabilities of the market. Here, decision-making is not left to the whims of emotions or the vagaries of intuition; instead, it is firmly rooted in the solid ground of careful, reasoned analysis.

The ethos that permeates the Isle of Analysis is grounded in the conviction that, given sufficient data and the appropriate analytical tools, any business obstacle can be dissected, understood, and surmounted. This perspective champions the power of data to illuminate paths forward, believing that even the most daunting of business challenges can be addressed through meticulous data analysis. Decisions on the Isle are thus products of rigorous scrutiny and logical deliberation, where every choice and strategy is backed by empirical evidence and detailed research.

The culture here venerates the role of data as a source of insights and solutions. The residents of the Isle, experts in various analytical disciplines, operate under the guiding principle that data holds the key to unlocking business potential and averting risks. They approach each business question with a methodical mindset, seeking to gather as much relevant information as possible and applying sophisticated analytical techniques to parse this data for actionable insights.

On this Isle, data is more than just numbers and statistics; it's a narrative that, when interpreted correctly, can reveal the underlying dynamics of market trends, customer behaviors, and economic shifts. It is this narrative that informs every business strategy, operational decision, and future planning. The belief is that by diligently applying data analytics, businesses can not only solve existing problems but also anticipate and prepare for future challenges.

In essence, the philosophy of the Isle of Analysis is one of unwavering faith in the power of data and analysis. It's a belief system that sees data as the compass by which to steer the ship of business, providing direction and confidence in decision-making. This philosophy underscores the conviction that with the right data, analytical skills, and tools, any business terrain can be navigated successfully, leading to informed decisions and strategic success.

The Limitations and Challenges

The Isle of Analysis, while embodying the strengths of a data-driven approach to decision-making, also presents certain limitations and challenges that cannot be overlooked. One of the primary issues encountered here is the phenomenon of analysis paralysis, where the sheer volume and complexity of data available can become overwhelming. In such situations, the process of sifting through, interpreting, and making decisions based on this vast array of information can be daunting, sometimes leading to indecision or delayed action.

Additionally, the Isle's heavy reliance on historical data and established patterns poses its own set of challenges, especially in a rapidly evolving business landscape. While historical data provides valuable insights, it may not always be a reliable predictor of future trends or market shifts. This is particularly true in industries that are subject to swift technological changes, evolving consumer behaviors, or unpredictable economic conditions. In such dynamic environments, the patterns and trends inferred from historical data may lose relevance, rendering decisions based on such data less effective or even misguided.

These limitations highlight the importance of recognizing that data, though immensely powerful, is not an all-encompassing solution. It underscores the need for a more holistic approach to decision-making that incorporates, but is not solely reliant on, data analysis. The Isle of Analysis, therefore, serves as both a beacon of guidance and a reminder of the intricacies involved in navigating the business landscape. It emphasizes that while data provides a critical foundation for informed decision-making, it should be complemented by other perspectives and approaches.

In summary, the Isle of Analysis stands as a testament to the critical role of data in shaping strategic business decisions, offering a structured, logical framework for navigating the complexities of the business world.

However, it also brings to light the inherent limitations of a purely data-driven approach, advocating for a balanced strategy that combines the rigor of analysis with the agility of other decision-making methodologies. This balanced approach acknowledges the power of data while also recognizing the need for flexibility, adaptiveness, and, at times, the integration of intuitive insights to navigate the ever-changing tides of the business environment effectively.

> ✧ Key Strategy: Embrace Data-Driven Decisions

Collecting Insights: The Foundation of Informed Choices

Gathering Data: The first step in embracing data-driven decisions is the meticulous collection of relevant data. This includes internal data like sales figures, customer feedback, and operational metrics, as well as external data such as market trends, industry reports, and competitive analysis.

Analyzing Trends: Once data is collected, the next crucial phase is analyzing it to identify trends and patterns. This involves using statistical tools and techniques to interpret the data, looking for correlations, fluctuations, and emerging tendencies that could influence decision-making.

Utilizing SWOT Analysis: A key tool in this process is the SWOT analysis. By identifying Strengths, Weaknesses, Opportunities, and Threats, businesses can gain a comprehensive view of their position in the market. This analysis helps in understanding the internal and external factors that can impact decision-making.

Scenario Planning: Anticipating Future Possibilities
Imagining Different Futures: Scenario planning involves envisaging various future states and preparing for these potential outcomes. This practice helps businesses anticipate changes and adapt to different market conditions.

Strategic Flexibility: By considering a range of possible futures, organizations can develop flexible strategies that are resilient to change. This prepares them to swiftly adapt to unforeseen circumstances.

Risk Assessment: Balancing Opportunities and Threats

Quantitative Risk Analysis: This involves using statistical methods to understand and quantify risks. By assigning probabilities to different outcomes, businesses can make more informed decisions.

Pros and Cons Evaluation: A thorough risk assessment includes weighing the advantages and disadvantages of potential decisions. This balanced approach ensures that decisions are not just data-informed but also consider the broader implications for the business.

Exercise: Reflecting on Past Decisions

Consider a recent significant decision made in your business. Reflect on the following:

Data Utilization: How was data used in making this decision? Were there gaps in the data collected?

Outcome Analysis: Could additional or different data have led to a different outcome?

Learning Opportunity: What can be learned from this decision-making process? How can data collection and analysis be improved in the future?

2. The Realm of Intuition: Navigating with Instinct

As the journey progresses from the structured shores of the Isle of Analysis, the sails are set towards the ethereal Realm of Intuition. This shift from the tangible to the intangible represents a crucial aspect of decision-making – the power of instinct and intuition.

Embracing the Intuitive Approach

In the Realm of Intuition, decisions are not solely grounded in data and analysis but are also influenced by the innate understanding and gut feelings of decision-makers. This realm acknowledges that not all decisions can be quantified and that human instinct plays a vital role in navigating complex situations.

Trusting the Inner Voice: Here, business leaders learn to trust their instincts, drawing upon their experiences and internal cues. This trust is built over time, as leaders become more attuned to their intuitive insights.

Valuing Emotional Intelligence: Emotional intelligence is paramount in the Realm of Intuition. Understanding and managing emotions, both one's own and others', can significantly influence decision-making.

Leveraging Experience and Knowledge: Intuition is often a subconscious synthesis of past experiences and accumulated knowledge. Leaders in this realm learn to tap into this reservoir of subconscious understanding when making decisions.

In conclusion, the journey of decision-making encompasses both the analytical rigor of the Isle of Analysis and the instinctual wisdom of the Realm of Intuition. Mastering decision-making requires a harmonious balance of these two realms, where data-driven insights are blended with intuitive understanding to navigate the multifaceted landscape of business challenges.

✧ Key Strategy: Trusting Your Instincts

Developing Emotional Intelligence

Embracing the concept of emotional intelligence is pivotal when it comes to trusting your instincts in decision-making. This form of intelligence begins with developing a deep, acute awareness of your own emotions and understanding how these emotions influence your decision-making processes. It's about being introspective, recognizing your emotional responses, and discerning how they impact your thoughts and actions. This self-awareness is the first step in harnessing the power of your instincts effectively.

But understanding emotional impact goes beyond self-awareness. It also involves a keen perception of others' emotions and an ability to empathize with them. This aspect of emotional intelligence is particularly crucial in leadership and team dynamics. As a leader, the ability to understand and relate to the emotions of your team members can significantly enhance communication, morale, and overall team cohesion. It allows for a more empathetic and effective leadership style, where team members feel understood and valued, fostering a positive and productive work environment.

Additionally, your 'gut feeling' or intuition is often a reflection of your cumulative experiences and the wisdom you have gained over time. It's important to recognize that this instinctual feeling is not random or baseless but is instead a subconscious integration of your entire knowledge base. Your past experiences, the lessons you have learned, and the knowledge you have acquired all contribute to this internal guidance system. When you have a gut feeling, it's your brain drawing on patterns and insights that have been ingrained through past experiences, even if you're not consciously aware of it.

This instinctual wisdom can provide invaluable insights that might not be immediately apparent through logical analysis alone. In situations where data is scarce or when you're faced with unprecedented scenarios, relying on this distilled wisdom can guide you towards effective solutions. Your experiences act as a compass, guiding your decisions in subtle yet powerful ways.

In essence, by understanding and developing your emotional intelligence and recognizing the value of your experiences, you create a powerful toolset for decision-making. This combination of emotional awareness, empathy, and instinctual wisdom based on experiences forms a comprehensive approach, enabling you to navigate complex decisions with a deeper understanding and insight. It underscores the importance of balancing logical analysis with emotional and experiential knowledge, leading to more holistic and effective decision-making.

Practicing Mindful Reflection

Attuning to Instincts: Mindful reflection involves taking a pause to listen to what your instincts are communicating. It's about creating a space where you can tune in to your subconscious mind, which can be particularly adept at noticing anomalies or red flags that your conscious mind might overlook.

Deciphering Subconscious Signals: Often, your intuition can offer valuable signals, especially in complex or ambiguous situations. Reflecting mindfully allows you to decode these signals and use them to inform your decision-making process.

Achieving a Balanced Approach

Harmonizing Intuition and Data: While intuition is powerful, it's important to balance it with empirical evidence. The key is not to let intuition completely overshadow hard facts. Instead, use it as a complementary tool that adds depth and perspective to the data-driven insights.

Navigating Uncertainties: In situations where data is incomplete or ambiguous, your intuition can be a guiding force, helping to fill in the gaps and navigate through uncertainties.

Exercise: Analyzing an Instinct-Led Decision
Reflect on a recent decision where you primarily relied on your instinct. Consider the following aspects:

Context and Intuition: What was the situation, and what did your instincts tell you?

Decision Outcome: How did the decision play out? Was your instinct accurate?

Learning Points: What can be learned from this experience? How did relying on your intuition impact the decision-making process?

3. Navigating the Storm: Overcoming Decision Paralysis

The Challenge of Overchoice
In the vast sea of decision-making, a common obstacle is the storm of overchoice - having too many options can lead to decision paralysis, where making any choice becomes daunting.

Strategies to Weather the Storm

Prioritizing Decisions: Not all decisions hold the same level of importance. Identifying which decisions are crucial and which are less critical can help in focusing your energies appropriately.

Simplifying Choices: Break down complex decisions into smaller, more manageable parts. This approach makes the decision-making process less overwhelming and more structured.

Setting Deadlines: Imposing time limits for making decisions can be an effective way to combat paralysis. This creates a sense of urgency that can help in cutting through indecision.

Seeking External Input: Sometimes, consulting with others can provide new perspectives and help in clarifying thoughts. External input, especially from those with different experiences or expertise, can be invaluable.

Accepting Imperfection: Recognize that not every decision will be perfect. Being comfortable with 'good enough' can often be more beneficial than seeking an unattainable perfection.

Learning from Experience: Every decision, regardless of its outcome, is an opportunity to learn. This mindset can reduce the fear of making 'wrong' choices and encourage more decisive action in the future.

Reflecting on Past Decisions

Think back to a time when you faced decision paralysis. Reflect on what caused the paralysis and how you eventually overcame it. What strategies worked for you, and what would you do differently next time?

In summary, navigating the realms of intuition and analysis in decision-making involves a delicate balance. Developing emotional intelligence and mindful reflection aids in harnessing the power of instincts, while strategies like prioritizing decisions and simplifying choices help overcome decision paralysis. The goal is to integrate these approaches, utilizing both the analytical and intuitive faculties to make informed, balanced, and timely decisions.

✧ Key Strategy: Simplifying Complex Decisions

Identifying Key Decisions: The first step in simplifying complex decisions is to prioritize. Not every decision demands the same level of attention and resources. Identifying which decisions are pivotal and which are less consequential can greatly streamline the decision-making process.

Impact Analysis: Evaluate the potential impact of each decision. Decisions that have a significant effect on the organization's direction, resources, or values should be given higher priority.

Breaking It Down: Decomposing Complex Decisions
Dividing Into Smaller Components: Complex decisions can often be overwhelming due to their scope and the number of variables involved. Breaking them down into smaller, more manageable parts makes them less daunting and more approachable.

Sequential Decision-Making: Tackle each smaller component one at a time. This sequential approach helps in maintaining focus and clarity, ensuring that each aspect of the decision is thoroughly considered.

Seeking Diverse Perspectives: Enriching Decision-Making
Consulting with Others: Involving others in the decision-making process can provide valuable insights. Different people bring different perspectives, experiences, and expertise, which can contribute to a more well-rounded view of the situation.

Avoiding Tunnel Vision: Consulting with a diverse group helps in avoiding tunnel vision, where you might become too focused on one aspect of the decision or one particular outcome. It encourages open-mindedness and consideration of alternatives.

Exercise: Reflecting on Decision Overwhelm
Think back to a time when you were overwhelmed by a complex decision. Reflect on the following aspects:

Nature of the Decision: What made the decision complex? Was it the number of options, the stakes involved, or the lack of information?
Breaking Down the Decision: How could the decision have been broken down into smaller parts? Identify the components that could have been tackled individually.
Impact of Simplification: Consider how breaking the decision into smaller parts could have eased the decision-making process. Would it have made the decision more manageable? Would it have changed the outcome?
Conclusion: Mastering the Art of Decision-Making
The journey of decision-making is indeed an intricate blend of analytical precision and intuitive insight. As a decision-maker, akin to a skilled navigator, you must adeptly discern when to rely on the compass of data and when to chart your course by the stars of your intuition.

Harmonizing Data and Intuition: The key is not to exclusively depend on one approach but to harmonize both. Data provides a solid foundation, while intuition can fill in the gaps where data is lacking or ambiguous.

Adaptability and Flexibility: Being adaptable and flexible is crucial. The business landscape is ever-changing, and so should be your decision-making approach. What works in one scenario may not work in another.

Continuous Learning and Growth: Each decision, whether successful or not, is an opportunity for learning and growth. Embrace both the successes and the challenges as part of your developmental journey.

Confidence and Clarity: Approach each decision with confidence and clarity. Confidence stems from your preparation, analysis, and intuition, while clarity is achieved through simplifying complex decisions and seeking diverse perspectives.

Remember, each decision you make shapes the trajectory of your journey. Be bold in your choices, wise in your deliberations, and sail forth into the sea of possibilities with a sense of purpose and determination. The art of decision-making is not just about reaching destinations but also about the wisdom gained and the growth experienced during the voyage.

Overcoming Cognitive Biases

Let us embark on a journey into the labyrinthine world of our minds. Picture yourself as a navigator, charting a course through a sea fraught with invisible currents and deceptive mirages. These are the cognitive biases, the subconscious distortions that sway our thinking and decision-making.

Imagine navigating a ship through the mythical Sirens' waters, where biases are the songs that lure sailors off course. Recognizing these songs – these biases – is the first step in steering clear of their beguiling influence.

1. The Echoes of Confirmation Bias

In a cove lies the Echo Chamber, where the sounds of confirmation bias resonate. Here, sailors hear only what they wish to hear, ignoring the whispers of contrary winds.

Key Strategy: Seek Contradictory Voices

Challenge Your Assumptions: Actively seek information that challenges your beliefs. It's like setting a course against the wind to test the strength of your sails.
Diverse Perspectives: Consult a crew of diverse thinkers. Just as a ship benefits from the varied skills of its sailors, decisions benefit from diverse viewpoints.
Exercise: Reflect on a recent decision. Did you seek out differing opinions, or did you navigate solely by the stars of your existing beliefs?

2. The Mirage of Overconfidence

Further along, the sea presents a deceptive calm, the realm of overconfidence. Here, sailors overestimate their knowledge and underestimate the treacherous waters.

Key Strategy: Embrace Humility and Continuous Learning

Question Your Knowledge: Regularly assess your skills and knowledge as a captain questions the integrity of his vessel.
Embrace Learning: Adopt a mindset of continuous learning. The sea is ever-changing; so too should be your understanding.
Exercise: Think of a time when overconfidence steered you wrong. How could a more humble approach have altered the course?

3. The Whirlpool of Anchoring Bias

Beware the Whirlpool of Anchoring, where initial information grips like a mighty vortex, pulling subsequent thoughts towards it.

Key Strategy: Weigh All Information Evenly

Broaden Your Horizon: Actively seek varied information, like a captain who consults different charts and navigational tools.

Delay Judgement: Allow time to process information, as a wise sailor waits for the fog to lift before setting course.

Exercise: Recall a decision influenced by the first piece of information you received. How might waiting for more data have changed your direction?

In Conclusion: Charting a Course Beyond Bias

In the odyssey of decision-making, recognizing and overcoming cognitive biases is akin to navigating through a sea of illusions. Your mind, the vessel, must be steered with awareness and deliberate effort.

Vigilance and Awareness: Always be on the lookout for the signs of biases, as a vigilant sailor watches for signs of a storm.

Continuous Self-Reflection: Regularly reflect on your decision-making process. Are you sailing true, or are you being swayed by the siren songs of biases?

Embrace the Journey of Learning: See each decision as an opportunity to learn and grow, to become a more skilled navigator of your mind.

So, dear navigator, embark on this journey with enthusiasm and curiosity. Chart a course beyond the biases, and sail forth into the vast sea of clear, critical thinking. Your mind is your compass, and with it, you can steer towards the horizons of sound judgment and enlightened decisions.

Problem-Solving Techniques in Business

Embark on a captivating journey into the world of business problem-solving. Imagine yourself as an intrepid explorer, venturing into uncharted territories where each challenge is a hidden treasure waiting to be unearthed. Just as an explorer uses a map, a compass, and intuition to navigate through unknown lands, you too will learn to employ various problem-solving techniques to navigate the complex landscape of business challenges.

1. The Map of Logical Reasoning

In the heart of the dense jungle of business complexities lies the Map of Logical Reasoning. This tool guides you to dissect problems methodically, much like how an explorer interprets a map to find the best path forward.

Key Strategy: Structured Analysis

Identify the Problem: Clearly define the problem, just as an explorer pinpoints their destination on a map.
Gather Information: Collect relevant data, akin to gathering necessary supplies before a journey.
Analyze the Data: Just as an explorer studies the terrain, analyze the data to understand the problem's nuances.
Exercise: Reflect on a recent business challenge. How did you identify and analyze the problem? Could a more structured approach have led to a different solution?

2. The Compass of Creative Thinking

As you delve deeper, you discover the Compass of Creative Thinking. This tool encourages you to think outside the conventional paths, exploring new territories of thought and possibilities.

Key Strategy: Foster Innovation

Brainstorming Sessions: Conduct brainstorming sessions, inviting ideas as wild as the unexplored territories of the jungle.

Encourage Divergent Thinking: Just as there are many paths in a forest, encourage thinking in multiple directions to find innovative solutions.

Adopt a 'What If' Mindset: Like an explorer asking, "What lies beyond the river?" constantly ask "What if" to explore various scenarios.

Exercise: Think of a problem where a conventional solution was inadequate. How could creative thinking have provided a better outcome?

3. The Binoculars of Perspective Shift

In the maze of business challenges, the Binoculars of Perspective Shift allow you to view problems from different angles, revealing hidden paths and solutions.

Key Strategy: Change Your Viewpoint

Seek Different Viewpoints: Just as binoculars provide a broader view, seek perspectives from various stakeholders.

Reframe the Problem: Sometimes, changing how you view the problem can reveal new solutions, much like observing a landscape from a different vantage point.

Empathize with Others: Understand the problem from others' perspectives, as an explorer learns from the local inhabitants.

Exercise: Recall a complex problem. How might viewing it from a different perspective have influenced the outcome?

In Conclusion: Embracing the Problem-Solving Journey

In the world of business, problem-solving is an exciting and rewarding journey. Each challenge is an opportunity to grow, learn, and innovate.

Embrace Challenges with Enthusiasm: Approach each problem with the eagerness of an explorer embarking on a new adventure.

Develop a Toolkit of Techniques: Just as an explorer carries a range of tools, equip yourself with various problem-solving techniques.

Learn from Each Expedition: Every problem you encounter and solve adds to your experience, making you a more adept business explorer.

So, arm yourself with the Map of Logical Reasoning, the Compass of Creative Thinking, and the Binoculars of Perspective Shift, and set forth on your problem-solving quest. With these tools, you are well-equipped to uncover the treasures of effective solutions and chart a successful course through the ever-evolving landscape of business challenges.

Chapter 6: Financial Acumen

Welcome to the thrilling odyssey of financial acumen, an essential voyage for every intrepid business adventurer. Picture yourself as the captain of a ship sailing the vast and sometimes tumultuous seas of finance. Your mission? To master the art of financial navigation, steering your enterprise through the swirling currents of fiscal challenges and opportunities.

In this chapter, we embark on an exhilarating journey to discover the secrets of financial wisdom. It's a tale not just of numbers and spreadsheets, but of strategic insights and savvy decision-making. Like an expert navigator reading the stars and the winds, you will learn to read market trends, balance sheets, and profit and loss statements to chart your course toward financial success.

1. Unraveling the Mysteries of Financial Statements

The first leg of our journey delves into the heart of financial statements. These documents are not mere collections of numbers, but maps that reveal the hidden treasures and potential pitfalls in your business landscape. We will decode these cryptic scrolls, turning complex jargon into clear, actionable insights.

2. Steering Through Budgeting and Forecasting

As we sail further, we encounter the crucial process of budgeting and forecasting. Here, you'll learn to forecast future financial climates and allocate your resources wisely. It's akin to predicting weather patterns and planning your route accordingly, ensuring that your business ship remains buoyant and on course.

3. Mastering the Art of Investment and Risk Management

No financial journey is complete without venturing into the realms of investment and risk management. This chapter will equip you with the tools to assess investment opportunities and manage risks. It's about making calculated bets, like a seasoned gambler who knows when to take risks and when to play it safe.

4. Deciphering the Language of Finance

Finally, we will delve into the language of finance. Understanding this language is key to communicating effectively with stakeholders, investors, and your own team. It's like learning the local dialects of the various ports you visit, allowing you to navigate financial discussions with confidence and clarity.

Conclusion: Setting Sail with Confidence
As we set sail on this chapter, remember that financial acumen is not just for the accountants and finance professionals. It's an essential skill for every business leader, entrepreneur, and visionary. So, hoist your sails, set your compass, and prepare for a journey that will empower you with the knowledge and skills to navigate the financial seas with expertise and confidence.

Welcome aboard the adventure of financial acumen. Let's chart a course to success, wealth, and fiscal mastery!

Basic Financial Concepts for Entrepreneurs

Embark on a captivating journey into the world of basic financial concepts, tailored for the aspiring entrepreneur. Picture yourself as an intrepid explorer in the realm of business, where understanding the language of finance is key to uncovering treasures and navigating challenges.

1. The Map of Income Statements

Our adventure begins with unraveling the mysteries of the Income Statement. Think of this statement as a treasure map, revealing the paths of revenue and the caverns of expenses your business traverses over time.

Unlocking Revenue Secrets: Discover how to track and analyze your business's revenue streams, the lifeblood of your enterprise. It's about understanding not just the 'how much', but the 'how' and 'why' of money coming in.

Navigating the Expense Trails: Learn to identify and categorize different types of expenses. Just as an explorer needs to manage resources, you need to understand where your funds are going to maintain a healthy business.

2. The Compass of Balance Sheets

Next, we delve into the Balance Sheet, a compass guiding you through your company's financial position at a specific point in time.

Assets – The Tools for Success: Assets are like your equipment on this journey – they're what you have to work with. Understand how to categorize and value them, from cash to equipment to intellectual property.

Liabilities and Equity – Balancing the Scales: Grasp the concept of liabilities (what you owe) and equity (what's left for the owners). It's about ensuring your financial ship is balanced and seaworthy.

3. The Telescope of Cash Flow Analysis

The Cash Flow Statement is your telescope, allowing you to gaze into the future and past of your business's cash movements.

Forecasting Future Tides: Learn how to predict your cash flow, ensuring you have the funds to seize opportunities and weather storms.

Tracking the Currents of Cash: Understand where your cash is coming from and where it's going – crucial for maintaining the liquidity to navigate your business journey.

4. The Anchor of Budgeting

Finally, we explore the vital practice of budgeting – the anchor that keeps your financial ship stable and on course.

Setting a Course with Budgets: Develop skills to create effective budgets that align with your business goals, acting as a guide to where you allocate your resources.
Navigating with Financial Forecasts: Use forecasting to anticipate future financial scenarios, preparing you for both the calm seas and the turbulent waters of business.
Conclusion: Charting the Path to Financial Acumen
As we conclude this chapter, remember that mastering basic financial concepts is not just about crunching numbers; it's about gaining the insights and knowledge to make informed decisions. It's about understanding the story your financials are telling and using that story to guide your business towards growth and success.

So, gear up, dear entrepreneur, for this journey through the land of finance. With each concept you master, you'll be better equipped to steer your business venture towards prosperity and adventure. Let's set sail into the world of finance with enthusiasm and a thirst for knowledge!

Funding Your Venture: Sources and Strategies

Welcome to the exhilarating journey of funding your venture, a pivotal chapter in your entrepreneurial saga. Imagine yourself as an adventurer seeking the fabled treasures of capital to bring your business vision to life. This chapter is your guide through the dense jungle of funding options, each path laden with its own challenges and rewards.

1. The Landscape of Funding Sources

Our adventure begins by exploring the diverse terrain of funding sources. Think of these sources as various ancient cities, each holding its own unique form of wealth.

Venture Capital: The City of High-Stakes: Venture capital is like an elusive, wealthy city, where investors are willing to fund high-potential ventures in exchange for equity. It's a path suited for those with ambitious plans and the potential for rapid growth.

Angel Investors: The Benefactors' Realm: Angel investors are like benevolent benefactors in your journey. These individuals offer funding and guidance in the early stages, often in exchange for equity or convertible debt.

Crowdfunding: The Village of Collective Support: Crowdfunding is akin to rallying a village for support. It involves presenting your idea to the public and garnering small contributions from a large number of people, often in exchange for early access or rewards.

2. Navigating Loan Territories

Sometimes the journey requires traversing the territories of loans – a more traditional path laden with its own rules and rituals.

Bank Loans: The Traditional Route: Securing a loan from a bank is like following a well-trodden path. It requires a solid business plan, creditworthiness, and often collateral, but it offers a straightforward way to fund your venture without giving up equity.

Microloans: The Path for the Underserved: For adventurers who may not have access to traditional banking routes, microloans offer a beacon of hope. These are typically smaller loans aimed at startups or entrepreneurs in developing regions.

3. The Art of Bootstrapping

Bootstrapping is the art of self-funding your journey. It's about using your resources, reinvesting earnings, and maintaining stringent financial discipline.

Resourcefulness and Frugality: Like a skilled survivor in the wilderness, bootstrapping requires you to be resourceful and frugal, stretching every dollar to its maximum potential.

Growth at Your Own Pace: This path allows you to retain full control over your venture, growing at a pace that you set, free from external pressures.

4. Strategic Alliances: The Path of Partnerships

Sometimes, the key to funding lies in forming strategic alliances or partnerships. These can provide not just capital but also valuable resources, expertise, and market access.

Finding Synergy: Seek out partners whose goals align with yours, where both parties can benefit from the success of your venture.

Negotiating Terms: Like forging alliances in days of old, the key lies in negotiating terms that are favorable yet fair to all involved.

Conclusion: Charting Your Course to Funding

As we conclude this chapter, remember that securing funding is not just about obtaining capital; it's about understanding the landscape, choosing the right path, and preparing for the journey ahead. Whether you choose the high-risk, high-reward path of venture capital, the community-driven route of crowdfunding, the disciplined approach of bootstrapping, or the collaborative road of strategic alliances, each avenue offers unique opportunities and challenges.

So, arm yourself with knowledge, prepare your pitch, and set forth on this quest with determination and optimism. The journey of funding your venture is not just a financial expedition but a test of your vision, perseverance, and entrepreneurial spirit. Let's embark on this adventure with the goal of not just funding a venture, but realizing a dream.

Financial Planning and Management

Embark on an enlightening journey through the world of financial planning and management, a crucial expedition for every entrepreneur. Picture yourself as the captain of a ship, not just any ship, but a vessel of dreams and aspirations. Your cargo? The resources and finances of your venture. Your mission? To navigate through the unpredictable seas of the business world with a clear financial plan and robust management strategies.

1. Crafting the Map: Developing a Financial Plan

The first step in your journey is to craft a detailed map – your financial plan. This map is not drawn on parchment but is a dynamic document that outlines your financial goals and the routes to achieve them.

Setting Financial Goals: Like choosing destinations on a nautical map, setting clear, achievable financial goals is vital. These goals could range from short-term objectives like launching a new product, to long-term aspirations like expanding to new markets.

Creating a Budget: Budgeting is akin to planning your provisions for a long voyage. It involves allocating resources efficiently and planning for both expected and unexpected expenses.

Forecasting: Just as a captain forecasts weather conditions, financial forecasting involves predicting future revenue, expenses, and cash flow. This helps in anticipating financial needs and preparing for various scenarios.

2. Navigating with Financial Statements

Understanding and utilizing financial statements is like using navigational tools to steer your ship. These tools – income statements, balance sheets, and cash flow statements – provide real-time insights into your financial health.

Income Statement Analysis: Learn to read and interpret income statements, understanding what your revenues and expenses are telling you about your business performance.

Balance Sheet Insights: The balance sheet offers a snapshot of your financial position at any given time – assets, liabilities, and equity.

Cash Flow Management: Effective cash flow management ensures that you have enough liquidity to meet your obligations and invest in growth opportunities.

3. Steering Through Financial Risks and Opportunities

A crucial part of financial planning and management is navigating through risks and seizing opportunities.

Risk Management: Identify potential financial risks, from market fluctuations to operational hazards, and develop strategies to mitigate them.
Capitalizing on Opportunities: Stay alert to financial opportunities, whether it's an investment, a strategic partnership, or a market expansion, and understand how to leverage them for your venture's benefit.

4. Continual Monitoring and Adjustment

The sea of business is ever-changing, and so must be your financial strategies. Regularly review and adjust your financial plan to ensure it remains aligned with your business goals and the external environment.

Regular Reviews: Conduct periodic reviews of your financial plan, much like a captain regularly checks their course and makes necessary adjustments.
Adaptability: Be prepared to pivot your financial strategies in response to changing market conditions, just as a skilled sailor adjusts their sails to the changing winds.
Conclusion: Mastering the Art of Financial Navigation
As you journey through the chapters of financial planning and management, remember that this is not just a task, but an ongoing adventure. It requires foresight, vigilance, and adaptability. With a solid financial plan and effective management strategies, you will not only safeguard your venture's resources but also steer it towards growth and prosperity.

So, set sail with confidence and enthusiasm. Your financial acumen will not only guide your business through the present but also chart a course for a prosperous future. Let this journey of financial mastery be one of discovery, learning, and triumph.

Conclusion: Navigating Towards Financial Mastery

As we conclude Chapter 6: Financial Acumen, reflect on this remarkable voyage we've embarked upon together. Like a seasoned captain at the helm of their ship, you've navigated the complex and often stormy seas of finance, equipped with newfound knowledge and skills.

From deciphering the cryptic symbols on financial statements to charting a course through budgeting and forecasting, you've gained invaluable insights into the world of finance. You've learned to balance risk with opportunity, weaving through the intricacies of investments and financial management with the precision of a skilled navigator.

The journey has also taken you through the language of finance, empowering you to communicate with confidence and clarity. This skill is like speaking the local dialect in foreign ports, essential for engaging effectively with stakeholders and team members alike.

Remember, the realm of financial acumen is not reserved for a select few. It's a critical domain for every entrepreneur, business leader, and visionary. The skills and knowledge you've acquired here are not just tools for managing numbers; they're instruments of strategic decision-making and business growth.

As we draw this chapter to a close, know that your journey doesn't end here. Each day presents new financial challenges and opportunities. Continue to hone your skills, stay adaptable, and remain curious. Approach each financial decision with the same enthusiasm and diligence as you would in charting a new course on unexplored seas.

You're now set to sail forth with confidence. Armed with financial acumen, you're ready to steer your business towards success, wealth, and prosperity. May your entrepreneurial ship thrive in the vast ocean of business, guided by the stars of financial wisdom and the compass of strategic insight.

Welcome to the world of financial mastery – a world where challenges are opportunities, and knowledge is power. Chart your course, set your sails, and embark on the endless journey of growth and discovery. Here's to your success and the countless adventures that await you in the exciting world of business finance!

Chapter 7: Building and Leading Teams

Welcome to Chapter 7: Building and Leading Teams, a chapter that marks the transition from solitary entrepreneurship to the masterful art of orchestrating a team. Imagine yourself as a conductor standing before an orchestra, each musician poised with their instrument, ready to create a symphony under your guidance. In the world of business, your team is your orchestra, and your leadership is the baton that directs their performance.

This chapter is a journey into the heart of teamwork and leadership, a venture into the dynamics of building, nurturing, and guiding a team towards achieving collective excellence. Here, we unveil the secrets to assembling a star ensemble and leading them to harmonize their talents towards a unified vision.

1. The Art of Assembling Your Ensemble

Just as a conductor selects musicians for their unique talents and how they blend into the orchestra, you will learn how to pick team members not just for their skills but for how they fit into the corporate culture and contribute to team dynamics.

Identifying Talent: Discover how to spot potential stars and hidden gems, understanding that the right team member is not always the one with the most impressive resume, but the one who resonates with your vision and values.
Creating Diversity: Embrace the beauty of diversity in building your team. A mix of backgrounds, skills, and perspectives is like an orchestra with a rich variety of instruments, each adding depth and texture to the music.

2. The Maestro's Strategy: Leading with Vision and Empathy

Leading a team requires a blend of vision and empathy, much like how a maestro leads an orchestra with a clear direction yet remains attuned to each musician's unique style and needs.

Setting the Tempo: Learn how to set the pace and tone for your team, establishing clear goals and expectations while fostering an environment where creativity and innovation flourish.

Harmonizing Differences: Manage conflicts and differences like a maestro who harmonizes diverse musical expressions into a cohesive performance.

3. Cultivating a Symphony of Collaboration

Collaboration is the melody of a successful team. This chapter guides you through fostering a collaborative spirit, ensuring each team member's voice is heard and valued.

Encouraging Teamwork: Instill a sense of unity and collective purpose. Encourage your team to listen to each other, share ideas, and work together towards common goals.

Fostering Communication: Effective communication is the rhythm that keeps the team in sync. Develop channels and practices that ensure open, honest, and constructive communication.

4. Navigating the Crescendos and Diminuendos

Every team faces its high and low points – the crescendos and diminuendos. Learn to navigate these with grace, keeping your team motivated through challenges and celebrating their successes.

Conclusion: Conducting Your Way to Success

As you step into the role of a team builder and leader, embrace the journey with enthusiasm and confidence. Your ability to build and lead a team is not just about managing people; it's about inspiring them, bringing out the best in each individual, and creating harmony within diversity.

In this chapter, we equip you with the tools and insights to become not just a leader but a maestro who brings out the symphony of collaboration in business. Let's raise the baton and begin the captivating journey of building and leading teams to create beautiful music together in the world of business.

The Importance of Team Building in Entrepreneurship

In the grand orchestra of entrepreneurship, team building is not just a function; it's an art. Imagine yourself as a composer, ready to create a masterpiece. Each team member is an instrument, unique in tone and timbre, capable of contributing to an exquisite harmony. This section of our journey explores the profound importance of team building in the entrepreneurial world.

1. The Melody of Diverse Talents

The magic of a great orchestra lies in the diversity of its instruments, each adding a distinct layer to the melody. Similarly, a dynamic entrepreneurial team thrives on the richness of its members' varied skills, experiences, and perspectives.

Harvesting Creativity: Just as different instruments create richer music, diverse teams bring together a spectrum of ideas, fostering innovation and creativity.
Inclusive Leadership: Embrace each team member's unique strengths, just like a maestro who knows the perfect moment for each instrument to shine.

2. The Rhythm of Collaboration

In an orchestra, musicians must listen to and complement each other to create a seamless performance. This collaboration is the heartbeat of any successful team.

Cultivating Team Spirit: Develop a culture where teamwork is celebrated, encouraging members to support and inspire one another, much like musicians playing in perfect sync.
Building Trust and Communication: Like the subtle cues between a conductor and their orchestra, establish clear and open lines of communication to build trust and ensure everyone is aligned with the team's goals.

3. The Harmony of Shared Goals

A symphony is a collective effort towards a shared musical expression. In entrepreneurship, aligning your team around common objectives ensures that every effort contributes to the overall vision of the business.

Vision Alignment: Just as a score guides an orchestra, ensure that every team member understands and is motivated by the company's vision and objectives.
Celebrating Successes Together: Acknowledge and celebrate milestones, fostering a sense of shared achievement and unity.

4. The Crescendo of Growth and Learning

An orchestra grows with each performance, and so does a team. Encourage continuous learning and development, ensuring that your team adapts and evolves together.

Nurturing Talent: Invest in your team's growth, offering opportunities for learning and development, akin to musicians refining their craft.

Adapting to Change: In the ever-changing world of business, equip your team to be agile and adaptable, ready to face new challenges harmoniously.

Conclusion: The Symphony of Success
As we explore the importance of team building in entrepreneurship, remember that the strength of your venture lies in the collective effort of your team. Each member brings a unique note to the symphony, and your role as the leader is to harmonize these notes into a melody of success.

Embrace the journey of building a team that resonates with your vision. Nurture their talents, foster collaboration, align them with your goals, and encourage their growth. In doing so, you create not just a team, but a symphony of skills and talents, playing in unison towards the grand opus of your entrepreneurial dream.

So, let the music begin, and may the symphony of your team resonate with innovation, collaboration, and success in the exciting world of entrepreneurship!

Leadership Styles and Their Impact

Embark on an enlightening journey into the realm of leadership styles, where each style paints a unique hue in the grand tapestry of team dynamics and organizational culture. Imagine leadership as a palette of colors, each style adding its distinct shade and texture to the picture. This section explores the diverse world of leadership styles, illuminating how each impacts and shapes the environment of a team or an organization.

1. The Commanding Leader: The Bold Strokes

First, we encounter the commanding leader, akin to bold strokes on a canvas. This style is characterized by assertiveness and decisiveness, often seen in situations demanding quick action and clear directives.

Strength in Direction: In times of crisis or chaos, this leadership style can bring order and direction, much like a strong brush stroke defines the boundaries in a painting.

Impact on Teams: While effective in specific scenarios, over-reliance on this style can stifle creativity and lower team morale. It's a color used sparingly but effectively.

2. The Visionary Leader: The Inspiring Hue

The visionary leader is like an inspiring hue, illuminating the path forward with enthusiasm and optimism. This style is about inspiring and motivating, painting a compelling picture of the future.

Fostering Innovation: Visionary leaders are like artists who inspire their canvas to come alive with possibilities, encouraging innovation and big-picture thinking.

Empowering Teams: This style can significantly boost team morale and productivity by giving team members a sense of purpose and direction.

3. The Affiliative Leader: The Warm Tones

Affiliative leadership is akin to the warm tones in a painting, fostering harmony and emotional bonds. This style emphasizes teamwork, collaboration, and conflict resolution.

Building Relationships: Just as warm colors create a sense of comfort, affiliative leaders build strong, trusting relationships within their teams.

Impact on Team Dynamics: This approach can create a supportive and collaborative environment but might sometimes require balancing with goal-directed leadership.

4. The Democratic Leader: The Blended Palette

Democratic leadership resembles a blended palette, where multiple colors come together in consensus and collaboration. This style involves team members in decision-making processes, valuing their input and diversity of thought.

Encouraging Participation: Like a collaborative art piece, democratic leadership values each stroke contributed by team members, fostering a sense of ownership and inclusivity.
Balancing Voices: While this approach can lead to innovative solutions and high team satisfaction, it may also require more time to reach decisions and a need for balancing diverse viewpoints.

5. The Coaching Leader: The Guiding Shades

The coaching leader is like the guiding shades in a painting, helping to bring out the best in individuals. This style focuses on developing people for the future, offering guidance and growth opportunities.

Personal Development: Just as an artist guides a novice's hand, coaching leaders develop their team members' skills and competencies.
Long-term Impact: This leadership style can have a profound impact on individual growth and team development, though it requires time and patience.

Conclusion: Painting with Leadership Styles
As we traverse the spectrum of leadership styles, it becomes evident that no single style is superior. Each has its unique impact and suitability depending on the situation, team composition, and organizational goals. The art of effective leadership lies in understanding which style to apply and when, much like an artist chooses the right color and brush to bring a painting to life.

Embrace the diversity of leadership styles, and understand their impacts to become a more versatile and effective leader. Your ability to adapt and blend these styles can transform the canvas of your team or organization into a masterpiece of productivity, innovation, and harmony.

Let's continue to paint with the vibrant colors of leadership, creating environments where teams thrive and organizational goals are achieved with brilliance and flair!

Creating and Sustaining High-Performance Teams

Welcome to the nurturing ground of high-performance teams, a garden where leadership and collaboration bloom together. Imagine yourself as a gardener, where each team is a unique plot of land, rich with potential and waiting to be cultivated into a flourishing ecosystem. In this section, we'll explore the key elements of creating and sustaining teams that don't just grow but thrive.

1. Planting the Seeds of Trust and Respect

In the garden of high-performance, trust and respect are the fundamental seeds from which all else grows. They form the nutritious soil that supports robust growth.

Building a Foundation of Trust: Just as a gardener nurtures the soil, focus on cultivating a culture of trust within your team. It involves consistent, transparent actions and open communication, setting the stage for deep-rooted trust.
Cultivating Respect: Respect is the sunlight that nourishes the team, ensuring each member feels valued and heard. It's about acknowledging diverse viewpoints and appreciating each member's unique contribution.

2. Watering with Clear Communication and Goals

A garden needs regular watering, just as a team needs clear communication and well-defined goals to grow.

Effective Communication: Ensure that lines of communication are always open and clear, like water channels in a garden, allowing information and ideas to flow freely.

Setting Clear, Achievable Goals: Like plotting a garden, set clear, achievable goals for your team. These goals provide direction and focus, guiding your team's efforts towards a common objective.

3. Fertilizing with Continuous Development and Learning

Fertilizers boost a garden's growth; similarly, continuous development and learning enrich a team's performance.

Encouraging Professional Growth: Invest in your team's development through training, workshops, and continuous learning opportunities. It's about adding the nutrients of knowledge and skill to your team's soil.

Promoting a Growth Mindset: Cultivate a mindset that views challenges as opportunities to grow, encouraging innovation and resilience.

4. Pruning and Adjusting: Agile Management

Just as a gardener prunes plants to ensure healthy growth, agile management involves adjusting strategies, roles, and processes to best suit the team's evolving needs.

Being Adaptable: Stay adaptable in your approach, ready to make changes for the betterment of the team's performance.

Addressing Challenges Promptly: Tackle issues and obstacles head-on, just as a gardener would address weeds or pests, ensuring they don't hamper the team's growth.

5. Harvesting Success: Celebrating Achievements

Finally, just as a gardener revels in the harvest, celebrate your team's achievements. Recognizing and celebrating successes fosters a sense of accomplishment and motivates the team to continue striving for excellence.

Conclusion: The Flourishing of High-Performance Teams
As you journey through the process of creating and sustaining high-performance teams, remember that it's a blend of science and art. It requires patience, dedication, and a nurturing hand. Your role as a leader is akin to that of a gardener, cultivating an environment where trust, communication, continuous learning, adaptability, and celebration all come together to create a vibrant, thriving team.

Embrace the challenge and joy of growing high-performance teams. Let's nurture these gardens with care, dedication, and a vision for success, and watch as they bloom into landscapes of achievement and excellence in the world of business!

Chapter 8: Marketing and Branding

Welcome to Chapter 8: Marketing and Branding, a captivating chapter in your entrepreneurial journey where you become an artisan, weaving the vibrant tapestry of your business story. Here, we embark on an adventure into the realm of marketing and branding, where every color thread represents a message, every pattern a perception, and every texture an experience your brand offers to the world.

Crafting Your Unique Brand Identity

Picture your brand as a blank canvas awaiting your creative touch. This chapter guides you in painting this canvas with the unique colors of your business's identity, values, and vision.

Discovering Your Brand's Essence: Like an artist finding their muse, delve into the core of what makes your brand unique. It's a journey of self-discovery for your business, understanding what sets you apart in the marketplace.

Creating a Visual Symphony: Learn how to translate your brand's essence into visual elements – logos, color schemes, and designs that resonate with your audience and become synonymous with your business identity.

The Symphony of Effective Marketing Strategies

Marketing is like composing a symphony, each note carefully chosen to resonate with the audience. This chapter explores the orchestration of various marketing strategies to create a harmonious connection with your customers.

Understanding Your Audience: Just as a composer understands their audience, gain insights into who your customers are, their needs, desires, and what makes them tick.

Crafting Engaging Narratives: Master the art of storytelling, where your marketing campaigns tell captivating tales that engage, inspire, and move your audience to action.

Digital Landscapes and Traditional Pathways

In today's world, marketing is a blend of digital landscapes and traditional pathways. Learn to navigate through social media channels, SEO, content marketing, and also appreciate the power of traditional methods like print media and networking.

Harmonizing Online and Offline Strategies: Find the right mix of digital and traditional marketing strategies, creating a balanced and comprehensive approach that reaches your audience wherever they are.
Measuring Success and Weaving Future Patterns

Finally, understand the importance of measuring the impact of your marketing and branding efforts. Learn to use these insights to refine and evolve your strategies, continually weaving new patterns into your brand's tapestry.

Conclusion: Embarking on Your Marketing Odyssey
As you step into the world of marketing and branding, embrace the role of an artisan and a storyteller. Your brand is more than just a product or a service; it's a story waiting to be told, a tapestry waiting to be woven with the threads of perception, experience, and emotion.

In this chapter, we equip you with the tools, knowledge, and inspiration to bring your brand to life and connect with your audience in meaningful ways. Let's embark on this creative odyssey with enthusiasm, crafting a brand and marketing strategy that not only speaks to the hearts of your customers but also stands as a testament to your entrepreneurial vision.

Welcome to the art and science of marketing and branding – let your business story unfold in the most vibrant and impactful ways!

Crafting Your Unique Brand Identity

Welcome to the vital chapter of crafting your unique brand identity, an adventure akin to uncovering a hidden treasure that's been yours all along. This is not just a process; it's a journey of discovery, of peeling back layers to reveal the core essence of what your brand stands for. It's about creating a distinct identity that resonates deeply with your audience and sets you apart in the bustling marketplace.

1. Unearthing Your Brand's Core: The Quest for Authenticity

Think of your brand as a story waiting to be told, a narrative steeped in authenticity and uniqueness.

Finding Your Brand's Heart: Begin by diving deep into what your brand truly represents. Ask yourself: What are my brand's values? What is its mission? This is like exploring the roots of a tree, understanding what grounds and nourishes your brand.

Telling Your Story: Your brand's story is its heartbeat. It's about more than just what you sell; it's the why and the how. It's the narrative that connects your brand to your audience on an emotional level.

2. The Palette of Visual Identity: Painting Your Brand's Picture

Now, bring your brand to life visually. This is where your brand's essence is translated into tangible elements that people can see and connect with.

Designing Your Logo: Your logo is the flag of your brand's ship. Design a logo that encapsulates your brand's essence and is easily recognizable.

Choosing Your Colors and Fonts: Select colors and fonts that reflect your brand's personality. Are you bold and vibrant, or elegant and understated? Your visual elements should align with your brand's narrative.

3. The Voice and Tone: Singing Your Brand's Song

Your brand's voice and tone are how you communicate with the world. It's the language you use in your marketing materials, on your website, and in your communications.

Developing a Consistent Voice: Ensure your brand's voice is consistent across all platforms. Whether it's professional, friendly, or quirky, it should be unmistakably yours.

Crafting Your Message: Focus on crafting messages that speak directly to your audience's needs and desires. It's like writing a song that your audience wants to hear over and over again.

4. The Experience: Choreographing the Customer Journey

Every interaction with your brand should be an experience, a step in a dance that leads your customers closer to you.

Creating Touchpoints: Identify and refine the touchpoints where customers interact with your brand. From the first website visit to customer service interactions, make each touchpoint memorable and positive.

Encouraging Engagement: Engage with your audience. Listen to their feedback, participate in conversations, and build a community around your brand.

Conclusion: Weaving the Tapestry of Your Brand Identity

As you embark on the journey of crafting your unique brand identity, embrace each step with creativity, passion, and authenticity. Your brand identity is more than a logo or a color scheme; it's the embodiment of your story, values, and vision.

Remember, the strongest brand identities are those that are authentic and resonate with people on a personal level. They are not just seen or heard; they are felt. So, weave the tapestry of your brand with careful hands, infusing it with your passion, vision, and values. Let your brand be a beacon that lights the way to your business, drawing customers into a lasting and meaningful relationship.

Step forth with enthusiasm and confidence, for you are not just building a brand; you are creating an experience, a legacy, and a beacon in the marketplace that is uniquely, authentically yours. Let the world see the brilliance of your brand's identity, and watch as it transforms from a concept into a beloved and enduring symbol of your entrepreneurial journey.

Understanding Your Market

Welcome aboard the voyage of understanding your market, a critical and exhilarating part of your entrepreneurial adventure. Picture yourself as a captain setting sail on the vast ocean of commerce, where understanding the currents, the winds, and the undercurrents of your market is key to navigating towards success. This journey is about exploring, understanding, and adapting to the ever-changing seas of consumer needs, competitors, and industry trends.

1. Mapping the Waters: Market Research as Your Compass

The first step in your voyage is to chart the waters. Market research is your compass, guiding you through the murky depths of consumer behavior and market dynamics.

Gathering Intelligence: Start by collecting data. This can be through surveys, focus groups, or analyzing existing research. It's like casting a wide net to gather as much information as possible about the waters you're navigating.

Understanding Consumer Needs: Dive deep into the psyche of your consumers. What do they want? What do they need? Understanding your consumer is like understanding the currents that can propel your ship forward.

2. Identifying the Landmarks: Recognizing Market Trends

Just as a navigator identifies landmarks to chart their course, you must identify and understand market trends.

Staying Ahead of the Curve: Keep an eye on emerging trends – they are the lighthouses guiding your way. Being ahead of a trend can give you a competitive advantage.

Adapting to Change: The market is like the weather; it can change rapidly. Be prepared to adapt your strategies, just as a skilled sailor adjusts their sails to a changing wind.

3. Knowing the Competitors: Observing Other Ships on the Horizon

Understanding your competition is crucial in charting a successful course.

Analyzing Competitors: Look at what your competitors are doing – their strengths and weaknesses are like hidden reefs and favorable winds in your journey.

Finding Your Unique Position: Use this knowledge to find your unique position in the market. It's like finding the best route that others haven't taken.

4. Continual Navigation: Keeping a Steady Hand on the Helm

Market understanding is not a one-time endeavor; it's an ongoing process.

Keeping a Watchful Eye: Regularly update your market research. Stay vigilant, just as a captain keeps a watchful eye on the horizon for changes in weather or new obstacles.

Adapting and Evolving: Be ready to adapt your strategies based on new information and changing market conditions. It's about steering your ship with agility and precision.

Conclusion: Charting a Successful Course in Your Market

As we conclude this section on understanding your market, remember that this journey requires curiosity, adaptability, and a keen eye for detail. Your market is a living, breathing entity that's constantly evolving, and your ability to understand and adapt to it is crucial for your business's success.

So, keep your compass close, your eyes on the horizon, and your hands steady on the helm. Embrace the challenge of understanding your market, and let this knowledge guide you to new opportunities and uncharted territories of success.

Set sail with confidence and enthusiasm, for the market is your ocean, and understanding it is the key to navigating your business to the shores of success and prosperity. Let the voyage of market discovery begin!

Building a Brand Identity

As you navigate the vast ocean of your market, your next pivotal step is to hoist the flag of your brand identity – a powerful emblem that distinguishes your vessel in the crowded seas of commerce. This stage of your journey is about creating a brand identity that resonates with your audience, embodies your values, and stands as a beacon, drawing customers to your unique offering.

1. Designing Your Flag: The Essence of Your Brand

Think of your brand identity as the flag that tops the mast of your ship. It's the first thing people see, the symbol that represents everything your venture stands for.

Crafting a Memorable Logo: Your logo is the crest on your flag, a visual representation of your brand. Design a logo that captures the essence of your business and sticks in the minds of those who see it, like a memorable landmark on the horizon.

Choosing Your Colors and Fonts: Select colors and fonts that reflect the personality of your brand. Are you a bold adventurer, a reliable trader, or a mysterious explorer? Let your colors and typography speak for your brand's character.

2. Voicing Your Tale: The Narrative of Your Brand

Your brand's voice is the tale you tell as you sail from port to port. It's how you communicate with your audience, from the words on your website to the messages in your advertising.

Crafting Your Story: Every great voyage has its story, and so does every brand. What's yours? Is it one of innovation, tradition, or revolution? Your story should be compelling, authentic, and resonate with your audience.

Consistency in Communication: Maintain a consistent tone and style in all your communications. It's like a familiar song that people recognize and associate with your brand.

3. Building Trust: The Anchor of Your Brand

Trust is the anchor that holds your brand steady in the ever-changing tides of the market. It's built over time and through consistent, positive experiences with your brand.

Delivering on Promises: Just as a reliable captain keeps their word, your brand should deliver on its promises. Whether it's the quality of your products, your customer service, or your after-sales care, make sure you meet or exceed expectations.

Engaging with Your Audience: Engage with your customers like a captain engages with their crew. Listen to their feedback, respond to their needs, and make them feel valued and a part of your brand's journey.

4. Navigating the Tides of Change

The seas of commerce are ever-changing, and so is the world of branding. Stay adaptable, ready to evolve your brand identity as the market and your audience change.

Evolving with the Market: Keep a keen eye on market trends and customer preferences. Your brand should be dynamic, evolving with the times while staying true to its core values.

Refreshing Your Brand: Just as ships need regular maintenance, occasionally refresh your brand to keep it relevant and appealing. This could be a logo update, a revamped website, or a new marketing campaign.

Conclusion: Hoisting Your Brand High

As you build and refine your brand identity, remember that it is more than just a logo or a set of colors. It's the heart and soul of your business, the story you tell, the trust you build, and the flag you proudly hoist as you navigate the seas of entrepreneurship.

So, chart your course with boldness and creativity, infuse your brand with your unique vision, and let it be the flag that guides you to new horizons. Your brand identity is the beacon that lights your way in the marketplace, drawing customers to the unique world you offer.

Embrace the art of branding, for it is an essential compass on your entrepreneurial voyage – one that will lead you to the shores of recognition, loyalty, and success. Let the winds of innovation fill your sails, and set forth on the exciting journey of building a brand identity that stands out in the vast ocean of commerce!

Effective Marketing Strategies for Entrepreneurs

Following the creation of your distinctive brand identity, the next phase of your journey is to navigate the thrilling waters of marketing. This is where you, as an entrepreneurial captain, chart a course to not just reach but engage your audience, using the compass of effective marketing strategies. It's about making waves in the market and ensuring your brand's flag is seen and remembered amidst a sea of competitors.

1. Catching the Wind with Digital Marketing

In the digital age, harnessing the power of online marketing is like catching a favorable wind that propels your ship forward swiftly.

Navigating Social Media Seas: Social media platforms are like bustling ports of call. Identify which platforms your audience frequents and establish your presence there. It's about creating content that resonates and engages, building a community around your brand.

SEO: Charting the Top of Search Engines: Like a lighthouse guiding ships, Search Engine Optimization (SEO) helps guide customers to your website. Invest in strong SEO strategies to ensure that when potential customers search for products or services you offer, they find you first.

2. The Art of Content Creation: Crafting Your Message

Content creation is the art of crafting and sharing your brand's story in a way that captivates and engages your audience.

Blogging and Articles: Share your expertise and insights through blogs and articles. It's like sending out informative missives that build your reputation as a knowledgeable leader in your field.

Video Marketing: Videos are like the captivating tales told by sailors of old. They can be more engaging and memorable, helping to bring your brand to life in the minds of your audience.

3. Email Marketing: The Direct Messenger

Email marketing is a direct line to your audience, like sending a messenger pigeon straight to their hands.

Building a Subscriber List: Gather a list of interested customers and regularly send them updates, offers, and valuable information. It's a way to keep your brand top of mind and build lasting relationships.

Personalization and Segmentation: Tailor your emails to different segments of your audience, ensuring that each message resonates personally, like a letter addressed to their specific needs and interests.

4. Leveraging Traditional Marketing Channels

While sailing the digital seas, don't forget the power of traditional marketing channels. They can be like tried and tested trade routes that still yield valuable connections.

Networking and Events: Attend industry events, trade shows, and networking gatherings. These are like docking at ports where you can meet potential customers, partners, and influencers face-to-face.

Print and Local Media: Utilize print advertising and local media for targeted reach, especially if your business has a strong local presence.

Conclusion: Navigating the Marketing Currents

As you embark on the exciting journey of marketing your business, remember that effective marketing is a blend of art and science. It's about being visible and engaging, about telling your story in a way that resonates with your audience, and about building relationships.

Embrace the ever-evolving landscape of marketing with creativity and adaptability. Keep a keen eye on emerging trends and technologies, but also honor the timeless techniques that continue to hold value.

Your marketing strategies are the sails of your entrepreneurial ship; they catch the wind of customer interest and drive your business forward. So hoist those sails high, set your course with confidence, and embark on a journey to make your mark in the market. May the winds of success carry your brand to new and exciting destinations!

Conclusion: Charting a Successful Voyage in Marketing and Branding

Embarking on Your Marketing Odyssey

As we conclude Chapter 8: Marketing and Branding, we reflect on the journey undertaken, an odyssey that has equipped you with the tools and insights to craft a compelling brand identity and execute effective marketing strategies. You have become both an artisan, weaving the intricate tapestry of your brand, and a skilled captain, navigating the dynamic seas of marketing.

1. The Art of Brand Creation: Your Signature on the World

Your brand identity is more than a mere logo or color scheme; it's the essence of your business's story, values, and mission. It's the flag you raise high on your entrepreneurial ship, signaling your unique presence in the market.

Exercise: Crafting Your Brand Story: Write a narrative that encapsulates your brand's essence. What are its core values? What is its mission? How does it make a difference? This story will be the foundation of all your branding efforts.

2. Navigating the Digital and Traditional Marketing Waters

In the realm of marketing, you've learned to sail both the traditional and digital waters. From the vast ocean of digital marketing, including social media and SEO, to the reliable currents of traditional methods like networking and print media, you have a complete set of tools to reach and engage your audience.

Idea: Marketing Strategy Workshop: Organize a brainstorming session with your team or a group of fellow entrepreneurs. Discuss and map out different marketing strategies that could work for your business. Consider both online and offline approaches and how they can complement each other.

3. Engaging and Retaining Customers through Content and Communication

Content creation and email marketing have emerged as powerful strategies to engage and retain customers. They are the messengers and storytellers of your brand, creating a continuous dialogue with your audience.

Exercise: Email Marketing Campaign Plan: Develop an email marketing campaign. Start with building a subscriber list, segmenting your audience, and planning personalized content that adds value, informs, and entertains your audience.

4. Continuously Adapting and Growing

The final lesson of this chapter is the importance of adaptability and continuous growth. The market is ever-evolving, and so should be your marketing strategies. Keep learning, experimenting, and refining your approaches.

Idea: Monthly Marketing Review: Set up a monthly review of your marketing efforts. Analyze what's working and what isn't. Keep track of emerging trends and technologies, and consider how they can be incorporated into your strategy.

Your Future in Marketing and Branding

As you close this chapter and set sail forward, carry with you the enthusiasm and knowledge you've gained. Your journey in marketing and branding is ongoing, filled with opportunities for creativity, connection, and growth.

Embrace each challenge as an opportunity to reinforce and evolve your brand. Engage with your audience not just as customers but as a community that is part of your brand's story. Remember, in the vast ocean of entrepreneurship, your brand is your beacon, and your marketing strategies are the winds that propel your ship forward.

Raise your sails high, chart your course with confidence, and embark on the continuous journey of making your mark in the world of marketing and branding. May the winds of innovation, creativity, and strategic insight guide you to new horizons of success and fulfillment. Your odyssey in marketing and branding is just beginning, and the possibilities are as vast as the sea itself!

Chapter 9: Navigating Challenges and Setbacks

Welcome to Chapter 9: Navigating Challenges and Setbacks, a crucial chapter in the grand saga of your entrepreneurial journey. As you have skillfully crafted your brand and charted your course in marketing, now prepare to navigate the inevitable storms and turbulent waters of business challenges. This chapter is not about avoiding storms but learning to sail through them with resilience, adaptability, and foresight.

Embracing the Unpredictable Nature of Entrepreneurship

Imagine yourself at the helm of your entrepreneurial ship, sailing through both calm seas and tempestuous waves. Challenges and setbacks are natural elements of this voyage – they test your resolve, hone your skills, and often lead you to new paths of innovation and growth.

Understanding the Landscape of Challenges: Like a seasoned sailor who understands the sea, gain insights into the common challenges entrepreneurs face, from financial hurdles to market shifts and internal team dynamics.

Preparing for the Unexpected: Equip yourself with the knowledge and tools to anticipate and prepare for potential setbacks. It's about having a contingency plan, much like a lifeboat ready for unexpected storms.

2. The Art of Navigating Through Setbacks

Setbacks are not the end of the journey but waypoints that provide lessons and opportunities for growth.

Learning from Failure: View each setback as a learning opportunity. Like a navigator who learns from a wrong turn, use these experiences to refine your strategies and approaches.

Building Resilience: Develop the resilience to bounce back from challenges. It's about cultivating a mindset that sees beyond the storm to the clear skies ahead.

3. Leveraging Resources and Support Networks

No captain sails alone, and in your entrepreneurial journey, having a strong support network is key.

Seeking Guidance and Mentorship: Lean on the wisdom of mentors, advisors, and fellow entrepreneurs. Their experiences and insights can be your guiding stars through difficult times.
Harnessing the Power of Your Team: Empower and rally your team during challenges. Together, you can navigate through any storm with combined strength and creativity.

4. Adapting and Pivoting: The Agile Entrepreneur

In the face of setbacks, the ability to adapt and pivot can be your greatest asset.

Embracing Change: Be open to changing course when necessary. Sometimes the winds of challenge can lead you to new and unexplored territories of opportunity.
Innovative Problem-Solving: Encourage innovative thinking and problem-solving within your team. Challenges often give rise to groundbreaking ideas and solutions.

Setting Sail into the Chapter
As we embark on this chapter, remember that navigating challenges and setbacks is an integral part of the entrepreneurial journey. These experiences, though often tough, are rich with lessons and opportunities for personal and business growth.

Approach each challenge with courage, wisdom, and an open mind. Arm yourself with the tools and strategies discussed in this chapter, and be prepared to face any storm with resilience and adaptability.

Your journey as an entrepreneur is not defined by the challenges you encounter, but by how you navigate through them. So, set your sails, keep your compass close, and steer your ship with confidence and determination. The seas of entrepreneurship are full of challenges, but they are also ripe with opportunities for those brave enough to navigate them.

Welcome to Chapter 9, where you learn to sail through storms and emerge stronger, wiser, and ready for the next leg of your incredible entrepreneurial voyage. Let's embrace the challenges and turn them into stepping stones for success!

Common Challenges Faced by Entrepreneurs

As we journey further into Chapter 9, we navigate into the well-charted but turbulent waters of common challenges faced by entrepreneurs. Just as every seasoned sailor knows the typical storms and obstacles of their routes, understanding these universal challenges prepares you to face them with readiness and strategy.

1. The Gale of Financial Management

Perhaps the most prevailing wind in these waters is the challenge of financial management. Balancing the books, securing funding, and managing cash flow are tasks that can feel as daunting as steering through a gale.

Navigating Cash Flow Currents: Like a ship's captain ensuring there's enough wind in the sails, you must ensure there's enough cash flow to keep your business moving. Learning to forecast and manage cash flow is crucial.

Seeking Safe Harbors of Funding: Finding the right sources of funding, from investors to loans, is akin to seeking safe harbors that can provide the resources for your journey's next leg.

2. The Uncharted Island of Market Competition

Another challenge is the dense fog of market competition. The business sea is crowded with other ships, each vying for their space and destination.

Charting Your Unique Course: Differentiate your business by finding your unique value proposition. It's like charting a course that sets you apart from the rest of the fleet.
Spyglass on Competitors: Keep a watchful eye on your competitors, not to imitate but to understand the waters you're navigating. Learn from their movements – their successes and their mistakes.

3. The Siren Song of Work-Life Balance

For many entrepreneurs, maintaining a healthy work-life balance is like resisting the siren's call. The temptation to pour every waking hour into your venture is strong, but balance is key to long-term success and personal well-being.

Setting Sail with Boundaries: Establish clear boundaries between work and personal life. It's crucial for your mental health and prevents burnout.
Crew Wellness Checks: Just as you would ensure the well-being of your crew, take time to check in with yourself. Prioritize self-care and healthy work habits.

4. Navigating the Storms of Scaling Up
Scaling your business is a challenge akin to navigating through a storm. It involves expanding your team, entering new markets, and increasing your operational capacity.

Preparing for Rough Waters: Scale your business with careful planning. Ensure that your foundations are strong enough to withstand the pressures of growth.

Training Your Crew for Growth: As you scale, invest in training and developing your team. They are your most valuable asset in weathering the storm of scaling up.

Conclusion: Charting a Confident Path Through Challenges
As you sail through the common challenges faced by entrepreneurs, remember that these waters, though challenging, are navigable. Every successful captain has faced these same seas and emerged triumphant.

Embrace these challenges as part of your entrepreneurial journey. They are not just obstacles but opportunities for growth, learning, and innovation. Equip yourself with knowledge, gather a strong and supportive crew, and keep your eyes fixed on your goals.

So, steady your ship, adjust your sails, and face these challenges head-on with confidence and strategy. Remember, the most seasoned sailors were once novices who dared to brave the seas and learn from their voyages. Let these common entrepreneurial challenges be the winds that strengthen your sails and propel you towards success and fulfillment in your business journey.

Resilience and Grit in the Face of Adversity

As we continue our journey through Chapter 9, having charted the common challenges faced by entrepreneurs, we now turn our focus to the crucial virtues of resilience and grit. These qualities are the anchor and rudder that keep your entrepreneurial ship steady and on course, even in the roughest of seas.

1. Building the Foundations of Resilience

Resilience is not just an innate trait; it's a skill that can be developed and strengthened over time. It's about building a ship that can withstand the storms, not just avoid them.

Embracing Challenges as Opportunities: View each challenge as an opportunity to learn and grow. Just as a storm teaches a sailor new navigation skills, each business challenge teaches you something valuable.
Cultivating a Positive Mindset: Keep a positive mindset. It's like keeping your eyes on the stars for guidance, rather than the turbulent waters below.

2. Grit: The Persistent Pursuit of Your Goals

Grit is the steadfast determination to pursue your long-term goals, no matter how distant or difficult they may seem. It's the relentless drive that pushes you forward when the winds are against you.

Setting Long-term Goals: Define clear, long-term goals for your business. They are like distant lighthouses guiding your path through dark waters.
Perseverance in the Face of Setbacks: When faced with setbacks, draw on your inner strength and persevere. Remember, every great entrepreneur has faced and overcome challenges.

3. Learning from Failure: Turning Setbacks into Stepping Stones

Failure is an inevitable part of the entrepreneurial journey. It's not about never failing; it's about learning from each failure and using it as a stepping stone to success.

Analyzing and Learning from Mistakes: After a setback, take time to analyze what went wrong and what can be learned. This reflection is like repairing and improving your ship after a storm.
Bouncing Back with Renewed Vigor: Use your failures as fuel to bounce back with even more determination and clarity.

4. Building a Resilient Team and Support Network

Resilience is also about the company you keep. Surround yourself with a team and a network that bolster your resilience.

Fostering Team Resilience: Encourage a culture of resilience within your team. Like a crew that supports each other in a storm, your team can help each other overcome challenges.
Leaning on Your Support Network: Don't hesitate to seek support from mentors, fellow entrepreneurs, and professional networks. Sometimes, the right advice or encouragement can make all the difference.

Conclusion: Sailing Forward with Resilience and Grit
As you navigate the entrepreneurial seas, remember that resilience and grit are your most valuable companions. They are the qualities that will see you through storms, guide you through uncharted waters, and help you emerge stronger and wiser.

Embrace every challenge with resilience, tackle each obstacle with grit, and keep your eyes firmly on your goals. The journey of entrepreneurship is a test of endurance, adaptability, and strength of spirit. With resilience and grit as your guiding stars, there is no storm too great, no challenge too daunting, and no goal too distant.

So, set your sails with confidence, anchor yourself in resilience, and steer your ship with the grit and determination that define the true spirit of an entrepreneur. The journey ahead is filled with opportunities for growth, success, and fulfillment. Let's sail forward with unwavering resolve and the courage to conquer whatever lies ahead!

Learning from Failure

As we sail further into Chapter 9, having anchored ourselves in resilience and grit, we now delve into the crucial aspect of learning from failure. In the grand voyage of entrepreneurship, failures are not merely setbacks but invaluable lessons – they are the storms that test our ships, only to make us more adept sailors.

1. Recognizing Failure as a Guidepost

Failure, in the world of entrepreneurship, is a guidepost, a beacon that illuminates areas needing improvement and redirection. It's an integral part of the journey, offering insights that calm seas cannot.

Understanding the 'Whys' of Failure: When you encounter failure, take the time to understand why it happened. Like a captain reviewing a navigational error, dissecting the reasons behind a failure helps prevent future mishaps.
Reframing Failure as Opportunity: Change your perspective on failure. See it as an opportunity to grow, an essential step in the evolution of your business.

2. The Art of Constructive Post-Mortem

After experiencing a setback, conducting a constructive post-mortem analysis is key. It's like examining the charts after a storm to understand what went wrong and how to navigate better in the future.

Gathering Insights from the Team: Involve your team in this analysis. Different perspectives can shed light on various aspects of the failure, providing a more comprehensive understanding.
Identifying Lessons and Actionable Steps: From each failure, distill actionable lessons. What can be improved? What strategies need to be changed? These lessons are your takeaways to build a stronger strategy.

3. Cultivating a Culture of Openness and Learning

Creating an environment where failure is openly discussed and learned from is crucial. It encourages innovation and risk-taking, essential components of entrepreneurship.

Encouraging Open Communication: Promote a culture where team members feel safe to discuss failures and learnings. This open communication can lead to invaluable insights and collective growth.

Learning as a Team: Share your learnings with the team. When one member's learning becomes a lesson for all, it strengthens the entire crew.

4. Bouncing Back with Renewed Strategy

Resilience plays a crucial role in bouncing back from failure. It's about taking the lessons learned and applying them to your revised strategies and plans.

Adjusting Sails: Based on your learnings, make the necessary adjustments in your business strategy. It might involve pivoting your approach, exploring new markets, or refining your product or service.

Setting Sail Again with Confidence: Approach your next venture with the confidence that comes from having learned and grown. Each failure equips you with more knowledge and experience.

Conclusion: Charting New Courses with Wisdom Gained

In this chapter, we've explored the transformative power of learning from failure. Remember, every great entrepreneur has faced failures, but what sets them apart is their ability to learn, adapt, and grow from these experiences.

Embrace each failure as a stepping stone to greater success. Let the lessons you learn illuminate your path and guide your decisions. With each challenge overcome, your entrepreneurial journey becomes richer, imbued with the wisdom and experience that only navigating through storms can provide.

So, as you continue to sail the entrepreneurial seas, view each failure not as a setback but as a catalyst for growth and a beacon leading to brighter horizons. The journey ahead is rich with potential and learning, and each failure is a compass that guides you to your ultimate destination:

success. Let's embrace our failures as much as our successes and sail forth with resilience, wisdom, and an unwavering spirit of discovery!

Conclusion: Navigating the Voyage of Entrepreneurial Challenges

As we draw the curtains on Chapter 9: Navigating Challenges and Setbacks, we reflect on the crucial insights and strategies that fortify us for the unpredictable yet exhilarating journey of entrepreneurship. This chapter has equipped you with the navigational tools needed to steer through the often turbulent waters of business challenges, transforming obstacles into opportunities for growth and innovation.

Embracing the Voyage with Preparedness and Positivity

Your journey as an entrepreneur is akin to being the captain of a ship on a vast ocean. The skills you've honed in brand crafting and marketing are your sails and rudders, guiding you forward. But it's your ability to navigate through storms – the challenges and setbacks – that truly tests and proves your mettle.

Adaptability and Foresight: You've learned the importance of being adaptable, of having the foresight to anticipate challenges, and the flexibility to pivot when necessary. These are the traits that will help you navigate through the ever-changing business landscape.
Learning from Every Wave and Wind: Every challenge, every setback you encounter is a lesson in disguise. Embrace these experiences, for they are invaluable in teaching you resilience, strengthening your strategies, and sharpening your entrepreneurial instincts.

The Power of Community and Collective Strength

Remember, no captain sails alone. Your journey is supported by the strength of your team, the wisdom of mentors, and the solidarity of fellow entrepreneurs. Lean on this supportive network, for it is in unity that we find the strength to overcome the toughest of challenges.

Harnessing the Power of Your Team: Your team is your crew, each member bringing their unique strengths to the table. Empower them, learn from them, and together, you'll be able to weather any storm.

Mentorship and Community Support: The guidance of mentors and the support of the entrepreneurial community are like lighthouses guiding you through foggy waters. Don't hesitate to seek advice, share experiences, and draw on the collective wisdom of those who have navigated these waters before you.

Conclusion: Setting Sail with Confidence and Courage

As we conclude this chapter, carry forward the courage, wisdom, and resilience you've garnered. The seas of entrepreneurship are indeed full of challenges, but they are also ripe with opportunities for those brave enough to navigate them.

So, set your sails, keep your compass of resilience close, and steer your entrepreneurial ship with confidence and determination. You are equipped not just to face the storms but to emerge from them stronger, wiser, and ready for the next phase of your incredible entrepreneurial voyage.

Welcome to the end of Chapter 9, where the challenges you've encountered have transformed into stepping stones for success. Now, let's set forth with renewed vigor and vision, ready to embrace the adventures and triumphs that await in your entrepreneurial journey!

Chapter 10: Scaling and Growth

Welcome to Chapter 10: Scaling and Growth, a vital chapter in the entrepreneurial narrative that unfolds the intricate and exhilarating process of expanding your business. This chapter is not just about growth in numbers; it's about maturing in vision, strategy, and execution. It's a journey from the entrepreneurial infancy of a startup to the robust, thriving stages of a scalable enterprise.

The Art of Scaling: Mastering Expansion

Imagine your business as a sapling that you've nurtured from a seed. Scaling your business is akin to guiding this sapling to grow into a towering, resilient tree. It involves more than just pouring resources; it's about strategic nurturing, timely pruning, and robust support systems.

Strategies for Sustainable Growth: Learn how to identify the right time and pace for scaling your business. It's about striking the perfect balance between rapid growth and sustainable development.

Overcoming Scaling Challenges: Every growth phase comes with its own set of challenges - from managing financial resources to maintaining organizational culture. We'll navigate these waters, providing you with the wisdom to overcome these hurdles.

Growth as a Multidimensional Process

Growth in business is not a linear path; it's a multidimensional journey that encompasses various aspects of your enterprise.

Customer Base Expansion: Delve into effective strategies for widening your market reach and deepening customer relationships.

Product and Service Diversification: Explore how diversifying your offerings can open new avenues for growth and revenue.

Building a Scalable Team

Your team is the backbone of your business. As you scale, so must your team's capabilities and size.

Cultivating Leadership: Understand the importance of developing leaders within your team who can shoulder responsibilities and drive growth.

Hiring for Scalability: Learn how to hire individuals not just for current roles but for their potential to grow and adapt as the business expands.

Leveraging Technology and Innovation

In the digital age, leveraging technology is not an option; it's a necessity for scaling.

Technology as a Growth Lever: Incorporate technology to streamline processes, enhance productivity, and open new channels of revenue.

Innovation and Adaptability: Foster a culture of innovation that keeps your business agile and responsive to market changes.

Measuring and Managing Growth

Growth must be measured to be managed effectively. This section focuses on how to track and analyze your growth trajectory.

Key Metrics for Growth: Identify which metrics matter most in measuring your growth and how to use this data to make informed decisions.

Balancing Scale and Core Values: Ensure that your business's core values and mission remain intact as you scale. Growth should not dilute what makes your business unique.

Conclusion: Embracing the Growth Journey

As we embark on Chapter 10, remember that scaling and growth are as much about internal development as they are about external expansion. It's a journey that will test your resolve, challenge your capabilities, and ultimately lead to a phase of transformation and success.

Prepare to embark on this exciting phase of your entrepreneurial story with an open mind, a strategic vision, and an enthusiastic spirit. Let's navigate the complex yet rewarding path of scaling and growth together, turning your business vision into an expansive reality.

Strategies for Scaling Your Business

As we delve deeper into Chapter 10 of "The Entrepreneurial Mindset", we transition to a crucial section: Strategies for Scaling Your Business. This section is the compass guiding you through the often treacherous but rewarding waters of business expansion. It's about charting a course for growth that is as strategic as it is ambitious, ensuring that your business not only grows in size but also in strength and resilience.

The Blueprint for Scaling

Scaling a business requires a well-thought-out blueprint, a strategic plan that considers all facets of growth. This section is dedicated to crafting that blueprint, tailored to your business's unique needs and goals.

Assessing Readiness for Scaling: Before embarking on expansion, it's crucial to assess whether your business is truly ready. This involves evaluating your current resources, market position, and the scalability of your business model.

Defining Clear Objectives: Set clear, measurable objectives for scaling. Whether it's entering new markets, increasing revenue, or enhancing product lines, having defined goals helps in focused growth.

Strategies for Effective Expansion

Once the readiness is established, the next step is to explore various strategies that can effectively take your business to new heights.

Market Penetration and Expansion: Delve into tactics for deeper market penetration and expanding into new markets. It's about understanding where your opportunities lie and how best to seize them.

Diversifying Products and Services: Explore how diversifying your offerings can open doors to new customer segments and revenue streams.

Strategic Partnerships and Alliances: Learn the importance of building strategic partnerships and alliances. Collaborating with the right partners can accelerate growth and provide access to new resources and markets.

The Role of Technology in Scaling

In today's digital age, technology plays a pivotal role in scaling businesses. This section highlights how leveraging the right technology can be a game-changer in your scaling strategy.

Automating for Efficiency: Automation can significantly increase efficiency and reduce costs. We'll explore technologies that can automate various business processes, from customer service to inventory management.

Data-Driven Decision Making: Understand how to use data analytics to drive business decisions. Data can provide valuable insights into customer behavior, market trends, and operational efficiency.

Financial Strategies for Scaling

No scaling strategy is complete without a solid financial plan. This section addresses the financial aspects of scaling your business.

Funding Your Growth: Discuss the different funding options available for scaling, from venture capital to loans and crowdfunding. Understand the pros and cons of each to make informed decisions.

Managing Cash Flow: Learn strategies for managing cash flow during expansion. Effective cash flow management is critical to avoid overextension and maintain financial health.

Managing Risks in Scaling

With growth comes risk. This section is dedicated to understanding and managing the risks associated with scaling a business.

Risk Assessment and Mitigation: Identify potential risks in your scaling plan and learn strategies to mitigate them. This could include market risks, operational risks, or financial risks.

Building a Resilient Business Model: Explore how to build resilience into your business model to withstand the challenges of scaling. It's about creating a business that is adaptable and robust in the face of change.

Conclusion: Embracing the Scaling Journey

As you progress through the "Strategies for Scaling Your Business" section, approach each strategy with a blend of enthusiasm and pragmatism. Scaling is a journey that tests your business acumen, challenges your resourcefulness, and ultimately leads to a phase of significant growth and transformation.

Prepare to navigate this journey with strategic foresight, resilience, and an unwavering commitment to your vision. Here's to scaling new heights and turning your entrepreneurial dreams into expansive realities. Let's embrace the challenge and excitement of scaling your business, guided by the strategies and insights this section offers.

Exercises for Chapter 10: Strategies for Scaling Your Business

To fully grasp and implement the strategies for scaling your business, engaging in practical exercises can be immensely beneficial. These exercises are designed to provide hands-on experience and deeper understanding of the concepts discussed in Chapter 10.

Exercise 1: Readiness Assessment for Scaling

Objective: To evaluate your business's current position and readiness for scaling.

SWOT Analysis: Conduct a SWOT (Strengths, Weaknesses, Opportunities, Threats) analysis of your business. Identify areas where your business excels and areas that need improvement or pose risks.

Resource Evaluation: Make a comprehensive list of your current resources, including staff, technology, capital, and other assets. Assess if these resources are sufficient for scaling or if additional resources are needed.

Market Analysis: Research potential markets for expansion. Analyze market size, competition, customer needs, and market trends.

Exercise 2: Goal Setting for Expansion

Objective: To define clear and achievable goals for scaling your business.

SMART Goals: Set SMART (Specific, Measurable, Achievable, Relevant, Time-bound) goals for your scaling plan. These might include revenue targets, market penetration goals, or product development milestones.

Action Plan: Develop an action plan for each goal. Assign responsibilities, set deadlines, and determine the resources needed.

Exercise 3: Exploring Scaling Strategies

Objective: To explore and select the most suitable scaling strategies for your business.

Strategy Brainstorming: List potential scaling strategies such as market expansion, product diversification, or forming strategic partnerships.

Feasibility Study: For each strategy, conduct a feasibility study assessing the benefits, risks, resource requirements, and potential ROI.

Selection and Planning: Choose the most viable strategies and develop a detailed plan for implementation.

Exercise 4: Technology Integration Plan

Objective: To identify and plan for technology integration that supports scaling.

Technology Audit: Conduct an audit of your current technology stack. Identify areas where technology could enhance efficiency or offer new capabilities.

Research: Research technologies that could aid in scaling, such as automation tools, CRM systems, or data analytics platforms.

Implementation Plan: Create a plan for integrating new technologies, including timelines, budget, training needs, and potential disruptions.

Exercise 5: Financial Planning for Scaling

Objective: To develop a robust financial plan for your scaling efforts.

Budgeting: Create a detailed budget for your scaling initiatives, including expected costs and revenue projections.

Funding Exploration: Explore various funding options for scaling. This could include pitching to investors, applying for loans, or launching a crowdfunding campaign.

Cash Flow Management: Develop a cash flow management plan to ensure financial stability during the scaling process.

Exercise 6: Risk Management Strategy

Objective: To identify and develop strategies to mitigate risks associated with scaling.

Risk Identification: List potential risks that could arise from scaling, such as market risks, operational risks, or financial risks.

Risk Analysis: Analyze each risk in terms of likelihood and potential impact. Prioritize risks based on this analysis.

Mitigation Strategies: Develop strategies to mitigate each identified risk. This could include diversification, insurance, contingency planning, or building a financial buffer.

Exercise 7: Scalability Simulation

Objective: To simulate the process of scaling and identify potential challenges and solutions.

Scaling Scenario Creation: Create hypothetical scenarios of scaling, such as entering a new market or launching a new product line.

Role-Playing: Assign team members different roles within these scenarios (e.g., marketing manager, financial officer, operations lead) and simulate decision-making and problem-solving processes.

Debrief and Analysis: After the simulation, debrief to discuss challenges encountered, solutions proposed, and lessons learned.

Completing these exercises will provide practical insights and prepare you to navigate the complexities of scaling your business. They are designed to be revisited and revised as your business grows and as new opportunities and challenges arise.

Managing Growth Challenges

As businesses embark on their scaling journey, they invariably encounter a variety of growth challenges. Addressing these challenges effectively is crucial to ensure sustainable growth and avoid the pitfalls that can derail scaling efforts. This section of Chapter 10 focuses on identifying common growth challenges and providing strategies to manage them effectively.

Identifying Growth Challenges

Capacity Constraints: Assess your current capacity in terms of resources, staff, and infrastructure. Determine if they are adequate to support growth or if expansion is necessary.

Operational Inefficiencies: Identify areas in your operations that may become bottlenecks as you scale. This could include production, supply chain management, or customer service.

Financial Strain: Understand the financial implications of scaling. Consider the impact on cash flow, expenses, and profitability.

Quality Control: Ensure that the quality of your product or service does not diminish as you scale. Implement quality control measures and systems to maintain high standards.

Cultural Dilution: As your business grows, maintaining your company culture becomes more challenging. Develop strategies to preserve the core values and culture of your organization.

Strategies for Managing Growth Challenges

Capacity Building:

Infrastructure Investment: Plan for infrastructure expansion, such as upgrading technology systems, expanding facilities, or acquiring new tools.

Staff Training and Hiring: Invest in staff training to enhance skills and efficiency. Hire additional personnel as needed to support growth.

Optimizing Operations:

Process Streamlining: Review and streamline operational processes to enhance efficiency and reduce bottlenecks.

Leveraging Technology: Utilize technology solutions for automation and improved operational management.

Financial Management:

Budgeting and Forecasting: Develop detailed budgets and financial forecasts to manage expenses and predict cash flow needs.

Seeking Funding: Explore funding options to support growth, such as loans, investor funding, or government grants.

Quality Assurance:

Implementing Quality Systems: Establish or enhance quality assurance systems to ensure product/service standards are maintained.

Regular Audits and Feedback: Conduct regular quality audits and solicit customer feedback to continually improve your offerings.

Cultural Preservation:

Culture Champions: Assign or hire individuals responsible for maintaining and fostering company culture.

Internal Communication: Strengthen internal communication channels to ensure alignment and shared understanding of company values among all employees.

Managing Change

Change Management Framework: Implement a change management framework to guide your organization through the scaling process.

Stakeholder Engagement: Engage with all stakeholders, including employees, customers, and partners, to manage expectations and gather feedback.

Training and Support: Provide training and support to staff to adapt to new systems, processes, or roles.

Conclusion

Addressing growth challenges is an ongoing process that requires constant attention, adaptability, and strategic planning. By identifying potential challenges early and implementing effective management strategies, businesses can navigate the complexities of scaling while maintaining operational integrity, financial health, and organizational culture. This proactive approach ensures that growth is not just achieved but sustained over the long term, paving the way for a successful and resilient business future.

Planning for Long-Term Success

In the vibrant landscape of entrepreneurship, scaling a business is not just about immediate growth; it's about laying the foundations for long-term success. This section of Chapter 10 focuses on strategic planning and foresight, ensuring that your business not only expands its footprint but also sustains and enhances its impact over time.

Developing a Long-Term Strategic Plan

In the journey of entrepreneurship, laying down a strategic plan for the long-term success of your business is akin to charting a course for an ambitious voyage. This journey requires not only a clear destination but also the foresight to navigate the evolving landscapes of business. Let's delve deeper into the components of developing a long-term strategic plan that can guide your business towards sustained success and innovation.

Crafting a Vision for the Future

A well-defined vision is the north star for your business, illuminating the path ahead and keeping your goals in focus amidst the sea of opportunities and challenges. It's about envisioning where you want your business to be in the next 5, 10, or even 20 years. This vision must be more than a statement; it should be a compelling narrative that encapsulates your aspirations, values, and the impact you wish to make through your business.

Exercise: Crafting Your Vision Statement - Take some time to reflect on what you want your business legacy to be. Consider the impact you desire to have on your industry, community, and the world. Write a vision statement that resonates with these aspirations, making it a beacon for all your strategic decisions.

Setting Strategic Milestones

The journey to your long-term vision is marked by milestones – significant achievements that signify progress. Breaking down your grand vision into attainable, measurable milestones makes the journey more manageable and keeps your team motivated. These milestones act as checkpoints, ensuring that your business stays on course towards its long-term objectives.

Exercise: Milestone Mapping - Identify key milestones that align with your vision. These could include reaching certain revenue targets, expanding to new markets, launching new product lines, or achieving specific impact goals. Map these milestones on a timeline, setting realistic deadlines and identifying the resources required to achieve them.

Conducting Market Analysis and Forecasting

In the fast-paced world of business, staying ahead of market trends and anticipating future shifts is critical. Regular market analysis and forecasting enable you to make informed strategic decisions, adapt to changing market conditions, and identify new opportunities. This continuous analysis ensures that your strategies remain relevant and effective in the evolving marketplace.

Exercise: Trend Analysis and Forecasting - Conduct a thorough analysis of current market trends affecting your industry. Use tools like PESTEL analysis to understand external factors impacting your business. Forecast future market changes and discuss how your business can adapt to these anticipated shifts.

Fostering a Culture of Innovation and Adaptability

In an era of rapid change, fostering a culture of innovation and adaptability within your organization is crucial. It's about creating an environment where creative thinking is encouraged, and flexibility is embedded in the DNA of your business. This culture ensures that your business remains agile, responsive to new trends, and open to transformative ideas.

Exercise: Innovation Workshops - Organize regular innovation workshops where team members can brainstorm new ideas, explore creative solutions to challenges, and propose improvements to current processes or products. Encourage a safe space for out-of-the-box thinking and experimentation.

Conclusion
Developing a long-term strategic plan is a dynamic and ongoing process. It requires a visionary approach, a keen understanding of the market, and a culture that embraces change and innovation. By focusing on these key areas, you can steer your business towards a future that not only meets but exceeds the aspirations set in your vision. Embrace this journey of strategic planning as an essential part of your entrepreneurial growth, leading your business towards new horizons of success and impact.

Ensuring Financial Sustainability

In the realm of entrepreneurial growth, ensuring financial sustainability is akin to securing the keel of your ship – it's foundational to staying buoyant and navigating through the unpredictable waters of business. Let's explore in depth the strategies to fortify your financial stability, diversify revenue streams, and build a resilient financial structure for your business.

Cultivating Diverse Revenue Streams

In the quest for financial stability, diversifying your revenue streams is like casting a wider net – it broadens your financial base, reducing reliance on a single income source and safeguarding against market fluctuations. Diversification can take various forms, such as introducing new products or services, tapping into different markets, or exploring alternative business models.

Exercise: Revenue Diversification Plan - Conduct a brainstorming session to identify potential new revenue streams for your business. Analyze each option for feasibility, market demand, and alignment with your core business. Develop a plan to pilot the most promising ideas, setting clear objectives and success metrics.

Implementing Prudent Financial Management

Effective financial management is the compass that guides your business towards sustainability. It encompasses disciplined budgeting, astute cash flow management, and foresighted financial planning. Regular financial reviews ensure you are on track, helping you make informed decisions and adjust your strategies as needed.

Exercise: Financial Health Checkup - Schedule regular financial review meetings. Analyze your income statements, balance sheets, and cash flow statements. Identify areas for cost reduction, opportunities for improved efficiency, and potential financial risks. Develop action plans to address any issues identified.

Building Robust Financial Reserves

Establishing a financial reserve is akin to having an anchor in turbulent seas – it provides stability and security. Reserves ensure you have the resources to weather unexpected challenges, seize growth opportunities, and invest in long-term strategies without jeopardizing your financial health.

Exercise: Reserve Building Strategy - Determine the ideal size of your financial reserve based on your business's operational needs and growth plans. Develop a strategy for building this reserve, such as allocating a percentage of profits or setting aside funds from specific revenue streams. Monitor and adjust this plan regularly to ensure it aligns with your business's evolving financial situation.

Conclusion

Ensuring financial sustainability is a critical component of long-term business success. By diversifying revenue streams, practicing prudent financial management, and building financial reserves, you create a robust financial foundation for your business. This approach not only safeguards against immediate financial challenges but also positions your business for sustainable growth and resilience in the face of future uncertainties. Embrace these financial strategies as key pillars in your journey of scaling and growth, steering your business towards a future marked by financial stability and enduring success.

Focusing on Customer and Stakeholder Relationships

In the journey of long-term business success, fostering strong relationships with customers and stakeholders is like nurturing a flourishing garden — it requires attention, care, and a commitment to growth. Let's delve into the strategies for building enduring customer relationships and engaging meaningfully with all stakeholders.

Cultivating Enduring Customer Relationships

Building long-term relationships with your customers is more than a business strategy; it's an ongoing commitment to understanding, meeting, and exceeding their expectations. It involves creating a customer experience that's not just satisfactory but memorable and loyalty-inspiring.

Customer Feedback and Engagement: Regularly gather and act on customer feedback. Implement systems for customer engagement that allow you to understand their needs and preferences better.

Personalization and Value Addition: Tailor your offerings to meet the specific needs of your customers. Provide value that goes beyond the transactional — such as educational content, personalized services, or loyalty rewards.

Engaging with Stakeholders

Your stakeholders — employees, suppliers, investors, and the community — are integral to your business's ecosystem. Engaging with them is about creating a dialogue, understanding their perspectives, and incorporating their insights into your business strategies.

Stakeholder Meetings and Surveys: Regularly conduct meetings or surveys with different stakeholder groups to gather their input and discuss how your business can better serve their needs and expectations.

Community and Social Responsibility Initiatives: Engage with the wider community through CSR initiatives. This not only enhances your brand reputation but also builds a sense of purpose and connection with the community.

Investing in People and Culture

Your team is your most valuable asset. Investing in their development and nurturing a strong company culture are key to sustaining growth and adapting to future challenges.

Continuous Learning and Development: Provide ongoing training and development opportunities for your team. Encourage learning and skill enhancement that aligns with both individual career goals and business objectives.

Cultural Evolution: As your business grows, actively work to maintain a culture that reflects your core values, encourages innovation, and supports employee well-being. A strong culture is a magnet for talent and a catalyst for engagement and productivity.

Leveraging Technology and Innovation

Staying abreast of technological advancements and fostering a culture of innovation are crucial for staying competitive and relevant.

Adopting Relevant Technologies: Continuously evaluate and integrate technologies that enhance efficiency, improve customer experiences, or open new business opportunities. This might include advancements in AI, data analytics, or automation tools.

Encouraging Innovative Thinking: Create an environment where innovative ideas are welcomed and explored. Encourage your team to think creatively about solving problems and seizing new opportunities.

Conclusion

Focusing on customer and stakeholder relationships, investing in your people and culture, and leveraging technology and innovation are not just strategies for growth; they are commitments to building a business that thrives on multiple levels. It's a holistic approach that ensures your business is not just growing in size but also in depth, impact, and sustainability. By nurturing these key areas, you lay the foundation for a business that is resilient, adaptable, and primed for long-term success. Let this journey be one of continuous learning, adaptation, and unwavering commitment to the values and relationships that define your enterprise.

Conclusion: Chapter 10 - Scaling and Growth

Welcome to the conclusion of Chapter 10: Scaling and Growth, a pivotal chapter in your entrepreneurial odyssey. This journey from nurturing a nascent startup to fostering a thriving, scalable enterprise has been a masterclass in strategic expansion, resilience, and innovation. As we draw this chapter to a close, let's reflect on the key themes and insights that have illuminated the path of scaling and growth.

The Art of Scaling: A Strategic and Sustainable Approach

Scaling your business is a nuanced art, akin to cultivating a sapling into a majestic tree. It requires a blend of resource investment, strategic nurturing, and timely adaptation. This chapter has underscored the importance of sustainable growth strategies, emphasizing that scaling is more than a surge in numbers; it's a maturation in vision, approach, and execution.

Multidimensional Growth: Expanding Horizons

We've explored how growth transcends mere physical expansion to encompass customer base enrichment, product diversification, and service innovation. These multiple dimensions of growth ensure that your business doesn't just grow bigger but also becomes more robust, versatile, and responsive to market dynamics.

Building a Scalable Team: The Human Element

A significant focus of this chapter has been on the people behind the growth. Cultivating leadership within your team, hiring for scalability, and fostering a growth-conducive culture are critical to ensuring that your business's growth is supported by a strong, capable, and adaptable team.

Leveraging Technology and Innovation for Growth

In today's digital-driven world, integrating technology and nurturing a culture of innovation are imperative for scaling. We've delved into how technology acts as a catalyst for growth, streamlining processes and opening new avenues for expansion, while innovation keeps your business agile and relevant.

Measuring and Managing Growth: Keeping the Balance

The chapter has also highlighted the importance of measuring growth through key metrics and maintaining your core values as you scale. The balance between scale and maintaining the essence of what makes your business unique is crucial for long-term success.

Embracing the Journey of Scaling and Growth

As we conclude Chapter 10, remember that the journey of scaling and growth is as much about internal development as it is about external expansion. It's a path that challenges your resolve, tests your capabilities, and leads to transformation and success.

This chapter has equipped you with the strategies, insights, and perspectives necessary to navigate the complex yet rewarding path of scaling and growth. As you turn the page, do so with a renewed vision, a fortified strategy, and an enthusiastic spirit, ready to scale new heights and transform your entrepreneurial vision into a thriving reality.

Let the lessons of Chapter 10 be your guide as you continue to write your own story of entrepreneurial success, scaling your business into a legacy of lasting impact and achievement.

Chapter 11: The Entrepreneur's Journey

Welcome to Chapter 11: The Entrepreneur's Journey, a chapter that beckons you to step aboard the ship of your entrepreneurial dreams and set sail on a voyage of discovery, growth, and fulfillment. Having navigated through the ebbs and flows of challenges and setbacks in the previous chapter, you are now poised to explore the broader, panoramic view of the entrepreneur's odyssey. This chapter is a celebration of the journey itself, a tapestry of experiences that shape your path as a business creator and innovator.

The Map of the Entrepreneurial Terrain

Think of this chapter as your map, charting the terrain of the entrepreneurial world. It's a landscape filled with peaks of triumph, valleys of learning, and uncharted territories brimming with potential.

Understanding the Entrepreneurial Spirit: Delve into what drives and motivates entrepreneurs. It's about the fire that fuels the quest for innovation, the passion for creating something of value, and the relentless pursuit of your vision.
Celebrating Milestones and Achievements: Every entrepreneur's journey is dotted with milestones – moments of success, big or small, that deserve celebration. Recognize these as affirmations of your path and stepping stones to greater heights.

Navigating Through the Entrepreneurial Life Cycle

Just as every seasoned sailor understands the phases of a sea journey, this chapter helps you comprehend the stages of the entrepreneurial life cycle, from ideation to maturity and possible renewal.

The Lifecycle Stages: Explore the various stages of a business – inception, growth, maturity, and reinvention. Understand the dynamics, challenges, and opportunities at each stage.

Adapting to Each Phase: Learn strategies to adapt and thrive in each phase of your business journey. Whether you're planting the seeds of a new venture or steering a mature business towards new horizons, adaptability is key.

The Compass of Ethics and Values

In the journey of entrepreneurship, your compass is your set of ethics and values. They guide your decisions, shape your business practices, and define your legacy.

Building a Business with Integrity: Discuss the importance of ethics in business. How can you ensure that your venture not only grows in profitability but also contributes positively to society and adheres to a code of integrity?

Creating a Value-Driven Culture: Cultivate a culture in your organization that reflects your core values. This culture will be the heart and soul of your business, influencing every interaction with your team, customers, and community.

The Anchor of Work-Life Harmony

One of the most crucial aspects of the entrepreneurial journey is achieving a harmonious balance between your professional and personal life.

Striking a Healthy Balance: Learn the art of balancing the demands of your business with your personal well-being. It's about not losing sight of life's joys and responsibilities amidst the hustle of entrepreneurship.

Setting Sail into the Chapter

As we embark on Chapter 11, embrace the full spectrum of what it means to be an entrepreneur. This chapter isn't just about business strategies or management tactics; it's about understanding and celebrating the essence of being an entrepreneur.

Your journey is unique, filled with its own stories, challenges, and triumphs. It's a journey of constant learning, unending curiosity, and the courage to push boundaries. So, let's set sail on this chapter with a spirit of adventure and discovery, ready to explore the depths and breadths of the entrepreneurial journey. Here's to the paths you will tread, the seas you will cross, and the horizons you will discover in the incredible odyssey of entrepreneurship!

The Map of the Entrepreneurial Terrain

As we delve deeper into Chapter 11, let's unfold the map of the entrepreneurial terrain, a detailed chart that guides you through the varied landscapes of entrepreneurship. This map is not just a guide; it's a tool to help you understand the intricacies and dynamics of your unique entrepreneurial journey.

✧ 1. The Diverse Topography of Entrepreneurship

Welcome to the first section of Chapter 11: The Entrepreneur's Journey, where we venture into the diverse and multifaceted topography of entrepreneurship. This part of your journey invites you to explore the varied terrains of industries, markets, and niches, each presenting its unique opportunities and challenges. Just as a skilled explorer discerns the best path through different landscapes, this section empowers you to navigate the entrepreneurial world with insight and agility.

Charting the Terrain: A World of Opportunities

The entrepreneurial landscape is as vast and varied as the world itself. From the bustling metropolitan hubs of tech startups to the serene rural paths of agricultural innovations, this terrain offers a world of opportunities waiting to be explored.

Discovering Diverse Industries: Embark on an exploration of various industries. Each industry is a different terrain, with its climate, culture, and rules. Dive into understanding these industries – what makes them tick, their growth potential, and the challenges they face.

The Adventure of Market Exploration: Every market is a new adventure, teeming with its consumer behaviors, trends, and demands. It's an expedition to uncover what consumers seek, what competitors offer, and what gaps you can fill.

1. Identifying Your Niche: Your Entrepreneurial Homestead

The first step in your entrepreneurial exploration is to find your niche – your unique spot in the vast landscape where your business can flourish.

Finding the Perfect Cove: Just like finding the ideal cove for anchorage, identifying your niche involves understanding where your unique offerings meet the market's needs. It's about finding that sweet spot where your passion, skills, and customer demands intersect.

Tailoring Your Offerings: Adapt your products or services to the nuances of your niche. This customization makes your offerings more appealing and relevant to your target audience.

2. Understanding Market Ecosystems: The Dynamics of Interaction

Entrepreneurship is not just about your business; it's about how your business fits and interacts within a broader ecosystem.

Navigating the Ecosystem: Learn to navigate the complex interplay within your market. Understand how consumer trends, economic shifts, and competitive dynamics affect your business.

Adapting to Environmental Changes: Just as a navigator adjusts their course with the weather, be prepared to adapt your strategies in response to market changes. Stay informed and agile to keep your business thriving in an ever-evolving landscape.

Embarking on the Journey of Discovery

As we delve into the diverse topography of entrepreneurship, approach this journey with the spirit of a discoverer. Be ready to chart unexplored territories, to learn from each new experience, and to adapt with the changing landscapes of business.

This section of your entrepreneurial journey is about understanding the lay of the land, finding your place in it, and learning how to thrive. With curiosity as your compass and adaptability as your guide, you're set to embark on a rewarding exploration of the entrepreneurial world. Let's embrace the adventure and discover the unique path that leads to your business success!

✧   2. The Peaks of Success and Valleys of Challenge

As we continue our exploration in Chapter 11: The Entrepreneur's Journey, we venture into the second section, "The Peaks of Success and Valleys of Challenge." This section is akin to traversing a landscape of towering peaks and deep valleys, each representing the highs and lows inherent in the entrepreneurial adventure. Here, we embrace the exhilarating ascents of success and the daunting descents into challenges, recognizing them as essential facets of your business journey.

Journeying Through Varied Elevations: The Entrepreneur's Path

The path of entrepreneurship is rarely linear. It's a trek through diverse elevations, each presenting its unique vistas and obstacles.

Celebrating the Summits of Achievement: Success in entrepreneurship is akin to standing atop a majestic peak, taking in the breathtaking view that comes from hard-earned effort. It's a moment of triumph, bringing recognition, growth, and new opportunities.

Anticipating the Landscape: Success is not just a destination; it's a vantage point from which to view and plan your next move. It's about leveraging the visibility and resources gained from your successes to chart your future course.

Understanding the Valleys: Learning from Adversity

Every valley along the entrepreneurial path is a testament to resilience and learning. These are the periods that test your determination and ingenuity.
Navigating the Lowlands: Challenges, much like valleys, are inevitable and often daunting. They force you to pause, reassess, and find innovative paths forward. It's in these valleys that you learn the most about yourself and your business.

Turning Challenges into Catalysts: Each challenge is a potential catalyst for growth and change. It's an opportunity to strengthen your resolve, refine your strategies, and emerge more resilient and resourceful.
Setting Forth with Courage and Insight

As we embark on this section of your entrepreneurial journey, approach each peak with humility and each valley with courage. Celebrate your achievements, but also see them as stepping stones to further growth. Face your challenges with the knowledge that they are not insurmountable but are, in fact, integral to shaping a successful and sustainable business.

Your journey as an entrepreneur is a dynamic and evolving one, filled with moments of both triumph and trial. Embrace each with equal fervor, understanding that the peaks and valleys are what make the journey rich, rewarding, and uniquely yours.

In this section, we equip you with the tools and perspectives to navigate through these varying terrains. So, lace up your boots for the climb, prepare your gear for the descent, and let's journey through the peaks of success and valleys of challenge with an unwavering spirit of adventure and learning!

✧ 3. The Rivers of Cash Flow and Capital

As we continue our journey through Chapter 11: The Entrepreneur's Journey, we arrive at a vital section: "The Rivers of Cash Flow and Capital." This section explores the essential aspect of financial navigation within the entrepreneurial landscape. Just as rivers are crucial for the sustenance of life, managing cash flow and securing capital are the lifeblood of your business, keeping it vibrant and viable.

Sailing the Financial Currents: The Art of Cash Flow Management

Imagine your business as a vessel navigating the ever-flowing river of finance. The management of cash flow is akin to maintaining a steady course, ensuring that the waters are not too turbulent to capsize your venture or too still to stall it.

Balancing the Ebb and Flow: Learn the art of balancing income and expenses, akin to a captain balancing the sails and the rudder. Ensuring a steady cash flow is about timing, forecasting, and strategic financial planning.

Smooth Sailing through Financial Planning: Effective cash flow management involves foreseeing potential shortfalls and planning for them. It's about keeping your vessel agile and responsive to the changing currents of business.

Navigating the Streams of Capital and Investment

In the journey of entrepreneurship, capital is the stream that feeds into the river of your enterprise, essential for growth and expansion.

Exploring Diverse Funding Sources: Venture into the exploration of various funding sources. Each source, from angel investment to venture capital and loans, offers different advantages and challenges, much like the unique characteristics of streams and tributaries.

Securing the Right Kind of Capital: Choosing the right source of funding is akin to selecting the right stream that leads to a prosperous delta. It involves understanding the implications of each funding type and aligning it with your business goals and growth stage.

Embarking on the Financial Voyage

As we embark on this section of financial navigation, approach it with the mindset of a skilled navigator, understanding the nuances and rhythms of cash flow and capital. It's about more than just keeping your business afloat; it's about steering it towards prosperous shores.

Your journey through the rivers of finance will require foresight, adaptability, and strategic thinking. But fear not, for this section will equip you with the skills and knowledge to navigate these waters confidently.

So, take the helm, set your sights on the horizon of financial stability and growth, and let's navigate the rivers of cash flow and capital. These financial waters, when navigated wisely, can lead your entrepreneurial ship to the harbors of success and fulfillment. Let's chart these waters with expertise and steer your business towards a future of prosperity and achievement!

✧ 4. The Pathways of Customer Journeys

Continuing our voyage through Chapter 11: The Entrepreneur's Journey, we now set our compass towards understanding the Pathways of Customer Journeys. This section is akin to exploring the intricate network of trails that customers traverse within the market's landscape. It's about gaining a deep understanding of how customers discover, interact with, and ultimately choose to engage with your brand.

Deciphering the Routes of Customer Discovery and Engagement

Just as an explorer seeks to understand the lay of the land, this section guides you in decoding the pathways your customers take. These are the routes filled with interactions, experiences, and decisions that lead them to your business.

Mapping the Customer's Expedition: Every customer's journey is unique, yet there are common paths they tread - from initial awareness to the final decision to purchase. Grasp these paths to better align your business strategies with your customer's needs and expectations.

Identifying Key Touchpoints: Each interaction point, or touchpoint, along the customer journey is an opportunity to connect and leave a lasting impression. Whether it's your website, social media, customer service, or the checkout process, each touchpoint is a crucial stop along their journey.

Crafting a Memorable Journey for Every Traveler

Understanding your customer's journey is not just about observation; it's about actively crafting a path that is engaging, satisfying, and memorable.

Enhancing the Customer Experience: Look for ways to enhance the customer experience at every touchpoint. It's about making the journey as enjoyable and seamless as possible, ensuring that each step adds value and builds a positive relationship with your brand.

Personalizing the Path: Tailor the customer experience to meet individual preferences and needs. Personalization makes the journey feel special and unique, much like a tailor-made expedition.

Embarking on the Journey of Customer Understanding

As we explore the pathways of customer journeys, approach this exploration with a sense of curiosity and a commitment to understanding.

Your customers are the lifeblood of your business, and their journey is a critical map that guides your strategies, offerings, and interactions.

In this section, you will learn to navigate these pathways with insight and empathy, ensuring that every step of the customer journey is thoughtfully designed and executed. Remember, in the vast terrain of entrepreneurship, the paths your customers tread are as important as the destination.

So, prepare to trace these routes, understand their twists and turns, and create a journey that resonates with your customers. Your entrepreneurial map is ever-evolving, and understanding your customer's journey is key to navigating this dynamic landscape successfully. Let's embark on this insightful exploration, charting the pathways that lead to deeper customer connections and lasting business success!

The Compass of Ethics and Values

As we continue our enriching journey in Chapter 11: The Entrepreneur's Journey, we arrive at a crucial intersection: "The Compass of Ethics and Values." This section is akin to navigating the moral and ethical waters of your business venture. It emphasizes the importance of steering your entrepreneurial ship with a compass guided by core values and ethical principles. Just as a compass provides direction to sailors in the vast ocean, your business ethics and values serve as guiding principles in the complex world of entrepreneurship.

✧ Moral Mapping: Setting Your Ethical Coordinates

In the riveting narrative of Chapter 11: The Entrepreneur's Journey, we now delve into a pivotal subsection, "Moral Mapping: Setting Your Ethical Coordinates." This part of the chapter illuminates the crucial role of ethics and values in the realm of entrepreneurship. Just as a map guides a traveler through unknown terrains, a well-defined ethical framework guides entrepreneurs through the complex landscape of business decisions and interactions. Here, we focus on the art of integrating strong moral principles into the very fabric of your entrepreneurial venture.

Crafting the Ethical Compass for Your Business Odyssey

Embarking on the entrepreneurial journey requires more than just business acumen; it demands a compass of ethical integrity to navigate the myriad challenges and decisions you will face.

Sketching the Ethical Contours of Your Venture: Begin by outlining the ethical boundaries and principles that will guide your business. This process involves introspection and a deep understanding of the values you wish to espouse in your entrepreneurial journey.

Establishing Your Moral Grounds: Define what ethics mean for your business. Is it about fairness, responsibility, sustainability, or all of these? These ethical pillars will be the lighthouses guiding your business decisions and interactions.

Integrity and Transparency: The Twin Beacons of Trust

In the business world, integrity and transparency are not just ideals but essential practices that foster trust and credibility.
Navigating with Integrity: Cultivate a culture of integrity where honesty and ethical conduct are paramount. It's about making decisions that are not only profitable but also just and fair.
Illuminating Your Operations with Transparency: Emphasize transparency in all your business dealings. From clear communication with customers to openness in your internal operations, transparency builds trust and strengthens your brand reputation.

Embarking on the Ethical Expedition

As we journey through "Moral Mapping: Setting Your Ethical Coordinates," it's essential to recognize that this isn't just a subsection of a chapter; it's a fundamental aspect of your entire entrepreneurial narrative. Ethical conduct in business is a journey in itself – one that requires constant vigilance, commitment, and a willingness to do the right thing, even when it's challenging.

In this section, you'll explore how to embed ethical considerations into every aspect of your business, creating a venture that not only succeeds in the market but also contributes positively to society and sets a standard for ethical excellence.

So, let's embark on this crucial part of your entrepreneurial journey with a resolve to uphold the highest standards of ethics and integrity. Your business is not just a commercial entity; it's a vehicle for positive change, guided by the moral compass you set. Let's navigate these waters with a clear ethical vision, creating a legacy that transcends profits and stands as a testament to the power of conscientious entrepreneurship!

✧ The Role of Values in Shaping Your Business

In the ongoing exploration of Chapter 11: The Entrepreneur's Journey, we now transition to the vital subsection, "The Role of Values in Shaping Your Business." Continuing from our discussion on ethical coordinates, this section illuminates how deeply ingrained values act as guiding stars in the entrepreneurial sky, influencing and molding every aspect of your business venture. Just as navigators use stars to chart their course, your business values serve as essential beacons, guiding your company's culture, decision-making, and brand identity.

Crafting the Celestial Framework of Your Business Universe

In this dynamic and competitive business universe, your core values are the celestial bodies that provide light and direction, ensuring that your entrepreneurial journey remains true to its course.

Constellating Your Core Values: Begin by identifying and defining the core values that resonate with the heart of your business. These values are the bright stars in your enterprise's sky, shedding light on your mission, vision, and operational ethos.

Creating a Stellar Culture: Cultivate a company culture that orbits around these core values. This culture is the gravitational force that holds your team together, influencing their interactions and fostering a sense of unity and purpose.

Aligning Your Business Trajectory with Values

Your business journey should be a reflection of your values, with each decision and action aligning with these guiding principles.

Navigational Alignment: Ensure that your business strategies and actions are in harmony with your core values. It's about setting a course that consistently reflects these principles, whether in customer relations, team management, or community engagement.

Infusing Values into Business Practices: Integrate your values into all facets of your business operations. From internal policies to external communications and partnerships, let your values be the magnetic force that aligns your business practices.

Embarking on a Value-Led Expedition

As we delve into "The Role of Values in Shaping Your Business," remember that this is more than just a strategy; it's a commitment to building a business that stands out not just for its success, but for its integrity and purpose. Your values are the compass that guides you through the complex waters of entrepreneurship, ensuring that your business remains true to its founding principles.

In this section, you will discover how to weave your values into the very fabric of your business, creating an enterprise that resonates with authenticity and integrity. This journey is about aligning your business path with the values that define you, ensuring that every step you take is a step towards building a legacy that you can be proud of.

So, let's chart this course with a clear vision, guided by the stars of your core values, and navigate your business towards a future that is not only prosperous but also principled and impactful. Your values are the constellations that light up your business sky; let them guide you to new heights of success and fulfillment.

✧ Embarking on the Ethical Voyage

As we continue to navigate the rich tapestry of Chapter 11: The Entrepreneur's Journey, we embark on an integral subsection titled "Embarking on the Ethical Voyage." This journey transcends the conventional boundaries of business operations, venturing into the realm of ethics and values. It's a voyage that goes beyond mere compliance with rules and regulations, sailing towards the creation of a legacy marked by trust, respect, and integrity.

Charting a Course Rooted in Ethical Principles

This part of your entrepreneurial journey is like setting sail on uncharted waters, where the compass of your moral convictions guides you. It's about steering your business with a commitment to ethical practices that resonate deeply with your core values and the expectations of your community.

Navigating with a Moral Compass: As an entrepreneur, your moral compass is your guide. It helps you make decisions that are not only beneficial for your business but are also right and just. This section helps you define and refine this compass to ensure it points towards ethical integrity in all your dealings.

Building a Vessel of Trust and Integrity: Your business is the vessel on this ethical voyage. Construct it with the planks of trust and integrity, ensuring it stands strong against the tides of challenges and temptations.

The Captain's Responsibility: Leading with Values

Embarking on the ethical voyage requires you to lead by example. As the captain of your entrepreneurial ship, your commitment to ethics sets the course for your entire crew.

Creating a Culture of Ethical Awareness: Foster an environment where ethical awareness is part of your company's culture. Encourage open discussions about ethics and provide training and resources to help your team understand and uphold these values.

Aligning Actions with Ethical Standards: Ensure that every action, from the way you treat your employees to how you interact with clients and stakeholders, reflects your ethical standards. It's about walking the talk and embedding these values into the DNA of your business.

Embarking on a Meaningful Journey

As you set forth on this ethical voyage, approach it with the understanding that your business is a force for good. This journey is about creating a positive impact that extends beyond profit margins, influencing societal well-being and setting a standard for ethical business practices.

In this section, you'll gain insights into how to weave ethics into the fabric of your business, crafting a narrative that is not only about financial success but also about contributing positively to the world. It's a journey that demands courage, commitment, and a steadfast adherence to the principles you hold dear.

So, let's raise the sails of ethical business practices, chart a course guided by values, and embark on a voyage that will not only lead to business success but also to the creation of a legacy that is both inspiring and impactful. Navigate these waters with a sense of purpose, integrity, and responsibility, and make your entrepreneurial journey a testament to the transformative power of ethical leadership.

Personal Stories of Entrepreneurial Successes and Failures

As we further navigate the depths of Chapter 11: The Entrepreneur's Journey, we steer towards a captivating and insightful section, "Personal Stories of Entrepreneurial Successes and Failures." This segment of our odyssey takes us through the real-life tales of various entrepreneurs, echoing the undulating waves of highs and lows, successes and setbacks. Here, we draw upon the personal experiences of those who have braved the entrepreneurial seas, learning from both their triumphant voyages and their stormy encounters.

Embarking on a Voyage of Shared Experiences

In the enriching narrative of Chapter 11: The Entrepreneur's Journey, we now embark on a particularly engaging section, "Embarking on a Voyage of Shared Experiences." Picture this section as akin to gathering in an old sailor's tavern, a place brimming with stories of high seas and distant shores. Here, seasoned entrepreneurs, much like veteran sea captains, share their tales of navigating the unpredictable waters of business. Each story unfolds as a unique journey, laden with wisdom, struggles, triumphs, and invaluable lessons.

Gathering Around the Fireside of Experience

In the cozy ambiance of our metaphorical entrepreneurial tavern, let's gather close to the fireside, where stories of triumphs and tribulations in the business world are shared. This section serves as a melting pot of experiences, where the wisdom of seasoned entrepreneurs warms the spirit and guides the path of those embarking on their own ventures.

Illuminating Paths with Success Stories

First, we turn our attention to the luminaries of the entrepreneurial world, those who have navigated through treacherous waters to find success. Each tale is a beacon of inspiration, casting light on the diverse routes to achievement.

Stories of Resilience and Breakthrough: Hear tales of entrepreneurs who, against all odds, turned their visions into victorious realities. These stories often begin with humble origins, a single idea, and a relentless drive to bring it to life.

Strategies Unveiled: As they recount their journeys, pay attention to the strategies they employed. Notice how they identified opportunities, adapted to market changes, or pivoted their business models in response to unforeseen challenges.

Journeying Through the Mists of Setbacks

In equal measure, we focus on the narratives that speak of the less glorified, yet equally important, aspect of entrepreneurship - the setbacks and failures.

Tales from the Trenches: Listen to entrepreneurs who faced significant challenges - a failed product launch, a financial crisis, or a market downturn. These stories are raw and honest, often revealing the vulnerabilities and doubts faced along the way.

Lessons in Resilience: These tales are not of defeat but of resilience. They highlight the importance of learning from failure, the art of picking oneself up, and the courage to continue in the face of adversity.

Invaluable Insights: These experiences offer invaluable insights into risk management, crisis response, and the importance of maintaining a growth mindset, even in the face of failure.

Conclusion: Embracing the Spectrum of Entrepreneurial Experience

As we conclude our time around the fireside, we take with us a tapestry of experiences - the highs and lows, the victories and challenges - that define the entrepreneurial journey. This section serves as a reminder that the path to success is rarely linear and often paved with learning opportunities at every twist and turn.

So, let's carry these stories in our entrepreneurial toolkit, using them as guides and motivators. Whether you're celebrating a milestone or navigating a setback, remember the lessons shared around this fireside. Embrace every aspect of your entrepreneurial journey with the knowledge that each experience, be it a success or a setback, is a stepping stone towards your ultimate goal.

A Confluence of Diverse Journeys

In this section, we create a confluence where diverse entrepreneurial journeys intersect, offering a panoramic view of the multitude of experiences that define the business world.

Drawing Wisdom from Varied Experiences: Every entrepreneur's story adds a different hue to the canvas of business knowledge. We learn not only from their victories but also from the resilience and fortitude they displayed in the face of adversity.

Navigating the Highs and Lows: These stories encapsulate the essence of the entrepreneurial spirit – the ability to navigate both the highs of success and the lows of failure with equal grace and learning.

Commencing Our Voyage of Discovery

As we delve into "Embarking on a Voyage of Shared Experiences," let us do so with open hearts and minds, ready to absorb the wealth of knowledge and inspiration these tales offer. This is not just a section of a chapter; it's a mosaic of real-world experiences that provide a deeper understanding of the entrepreneurial journey.

Embrace these narratives as your companions and guides on your entrepreneurial quest. Learn from the wisdom of those who have journeyed before you, and use their experiences to chart your course more effectively in the vast, exhilarating ocean of entrepreneurship. Let's embark on this voyage together, gathering around the fireside of shared experiences, and set sail towards our own horizons of success and learning.

The Tapestry of Entrepreneurial Experiences

As we continue our immersive journey in Chapter 11: The Entrepreneur's Journey, we arrive at a vibrant and insightful section, "The Tapestry of Entrepreneurial Experiences." Here, we explore the rich mosaic of entrepreneurship, a tapestry interwoven with diverse experiences that span the tranquil and the turbulent in the business world. This section is a celebration of the entrepreneurial spirit in its entirety, showcasing the full spectrum of what it means to embark on this unique and often unpredictable journey.

Unraveling the Threads of Diverse Entrepreneurial Stories

In this vivid section, we weave through the rich and varied tapestry of entrepreneurship, each thread a story vibrant with color and life. Here, we unravel the diverse narratives that shape the entrepreneurial world, each one adding depth and dimension to our understanding of what it means to embark on a business venture.

Exploring the Spectrum of Journeys

The Palette of Experiences: Venture into the kaleidoscope of entrepreneurial journeys, where every color represents a different experience. From the radiant hues of triumphs and innovations to the more somber shades of challenges and setbacks, each color tells a story of resilience, creativity, and determination.

The Highs and Lows: Learn from stories that oscillate between exhilarating peaks of success – launching a breakthrough product, securing a pivotal deal, or receiving critical acclaim – and the valleys of trials, where entrepreneurs faced daunting challenges but found ways to rise again.

Drawing Inspiration from Varied Backgrounds

The Mosaic of Entrepreneurship: Each entrepreneurial story adds a unique piece to the mosaic of business endeavors. Delve into tales from diverse sectors – technology startups, social enterprises, traditional family businesses – each offering distinct perspectives and lessons.

Stories Beyond Borders: Traverse through stories that cross geographical and cultural boundaries. Learn how entrepreneurs from different parts of the world navigate their unique business landscapes, adapting to local customs, market demands, and regulatory environments.

Inspirational Journeys: Be inspired by the stories of entrepreneurs who started with little more than a dream and a steadfast resolve. Discover how their unique backgrounds – be it their upbringing, education, or previous careers – shaped their entrepreneurial vision and approach.

Conclusion: A Rich Tapestry of Entrepreneurial Wisdom
As we reach the end of this section, we step back to admire the rich tapestry of entrepreneurial stories we've explored. Each thread, each color, each pattern in this tapestry provides us with invaluable insights and lessons.

In the world of entrepreneurship, diversity is not just a buzzword – it's a reality that brings a wealth of experiences and wisdom. These stories are a testament to the boundless potential of the human spirit to innovate, overcome, and succeed.

So, let's carry these stories in our hearts, drawing inspiration and courage from them as we chart our own entrepreneurial paths. Remember, every story in this tapestry has something to teach us – about resilience, innovation, and the beauty of dreaming big. Let these narratives be your guide, your inspiration, and your reminder that in the colorful world of entrepreneurship, every experience, every challenge, and every success is a thread that adds to the beauty of the whole.

Celebrating the Essence of Entrepreneurial Resilience

In this captivating section, we raise a toast to the indomitable spirit of resilience that beats at the heart of every entrepreneurial story. Here, we delve into the depths of human endurance, adaptability, and the relentless drive that defines the essence of entrepreneurship.

Highlighting Stories of Resilience

The Odyssey of Overcoming: Unearth tales of entrepreneurs who navigated through stormy seas of business challenges. Learn how they turned formidable obstacles into stepping stones, transforming potential defeats into victories. These stories are not just narratives; they are powerful testaments to the resilience inherent in every entrepreneur.

The Art of Pivoting: Discover the art of pivoting – a skill crucial in the entrepreneurial toolkit. Read about businesses that faced dead ends and how their leaders ingeniously pivoted, finding new pathways and opportunities. These stories showcase resilience not just as enduring hardships but as the agility to change course when needed.

Honoring the Spirit of Tenacity

The Flame of Perseverance: Dive into stories that ignite the flame of perseverance. Meet entrepreneurs who, despite facing repeated setbacks, never extinguished their passion or vision. These narratives are a tribute to the relentless pursuit of dreams and goals, even in the face of adversity.

The Legacy of Grit: Embark on journeys that celebrate the legacy of grit and determination. From small businesses that fought to survive in competitive markets to startups that battled financial crises, these stories highlight the tenacity that is the lifeblood of entrepreneurial success.

Conclusion: A Symphony of Entrepreneurial Resilience

As we conclude this section, we realize that these stories form a symphony – a symphony of resilience, adaptability, and tenacity. Each entrepreneur's journey contributes a unique melody, harmonizing into a powerful composition that resonates with anyone who dares to dream.

These stories are more than just accounts of business ventures; they are narratives of human spirit and endurance. They remind us that the path of entrepreneurship, though fraught with challenges, is also paved with opportunities for growth, learning, and unparalleled satisfaction.

So, let's carry these stories forward, not just as tales of business acumen but as beacons of inspiration. Let them be a reminder that in the world of entrepreneurship, resilience is the most beautiful and powerful melody, one that plays the song of innovation, perseverance, and ultimate triumph.

Embarking on a Journey of Collective Wisdom

In "The Tapestry of Entrepreneurial Experiences," we set forth on a voyage through a rich mosaic of entrepreneurial sagas. This section transcends individual narratives, weaving together a fabric of collective wisdom that represents the diverse and vibrant journey of entrepreneurs across the globe.

The Mosaic of Shared Experiences

Gathering Wisdom: Delve into a treasure trove of experiences as we collect wisdom from myriad entrepreneurial journeys. Each story, like a unique gem, adds its brilliance to our collective understanding.

Learning from Diverse Paths: Discover the multitude of ways to navigate the entrepreneurial landscape. From the bustling city streets of tech startups to the serene paths of artisanal crafts, every journey enriches our collective knowledge.

The Power of Collective Insight

Drawing Strength from Unity: In this tapestry, every thread strengthens the other. Find encouragement in the shared challenges and triumphs, understanding that your journey, while unique, is part of a larger entrepreneurial story.

Seeing the Bigger Picture: Step back to view this tapestry in its entirety, appreciating how each entrepreneurial story contributes to a grander narrative of innovation, perseverance, and success.

Conclusion: Weaving Your Thread
As we conclude this section, we invite you to add your thread to this ever-growing tapestry. Let these stories inspire you, teach you, and embolden you on your entrepreneurial quest. Embrace this opportunity to be part of a larger, more vibrant narrative – a narrative that is continuously evolving with each new entrepreneurial venture.

Embark on this journey not just as a solitary entrepreneur but as part of a dynamic and supportive community. Together, we weave a tapestry that celebrates the spirit of entrepreneurship, a tapestry rich in diversity, color, and wisdom.

- Setting Sail into Stories of Real-World Entrepreneurs

We now hoist the sails to embark on the section "Setting Sail into Stories of Real-World Entrepreneurs" in Chapter 11: The Entrepreneur's Journey. Picture yourself navigating through a sea of authentic entrepreneurial tales, each story a vessel brimming with practical insights, hard-earned wisdom, and inspiring lessons.

Voyaging Through Authentic Narratives

Navigating Diverse Waters: Journey through a spectrum of real-world entrepreneurial experiences, from storm-tossed waves of challenges to the tranquil waters of success. These stories offer an authentic view of the highs and lows of business life.

Anchoring in Harbors of Knowledge: Each narrative serves as a harbor where we can anchor to gain insights. Learn from the strategic maneuvers of successful entrepreneurs and the course corrections made in the face of adversity.

Charting a Course of Inspiration

Guided by Lighthouses of Experience: Let these stories be your lighthouses, guiding you through the fog of uncertainty and illuminating the path to success.

Drawing Maps from Lessons Learned: Extract valuable lessons from each tale, drafting your map of entrepreneurial strategies and tactics.

Conclusion: Navigating Your Entrepreneurial Voyage
As you traverse these real-world stories, allow them to guide, inspire, and motivate you on your entrepreneurial voyage. Embrace the wisdom of those who have sailed before you, using their insights to chart your course in the vast, unpredictable ocean of business.

Set sail with a spirit of adventure and discovery, ready to navigate the exciting and challenging waters of entrepreneurship. Let these stories be your compass, leading you to uncharted territories of innovation, growth, and success. Welcome to the journey of real-world entrepreneurship, where every story is a beacon guiding you towards your entrepreneurial destiny.

Voyaging Through Authentic Entrepreneurial Seas

In the section "Voyaging Through Authentic Entrepreneurial Seas," we embark on a captivating exploration of the vast and varied ocean of entrepreneurship. Each narrative is like a distinct voyage, revealing the true essence of what it means to navigate the waters of business creation and growth.

Navigating Diverse Entrepreneurial Waters

Charting Varied Courses: Venture into the heart of entrepreneurship, where every story is a unique journey across different seas. From the serene bays of small-scale startups to the vast oceans of expansive enterprises, experience the diversity of entrepreneurial adventures.

Encountering Diverse Waters: Engage with a rich array of experiences, each characterized by its unique set of challenges and triumphs. Whether it's battling the high seas of market competition or riding the gentle currents of a niche market, these stories cover the full spectrum of entrepreneurial endeavors.

Delving into the Depths of Business Journeys

Submerging into the Realities of Entrepreneurship: Dive deep into the realities of building, managing, and growing a business. These stories take you beneath the surface, revealing the undercurrents that shape an entrepreneur's journey.

Discovering Pearls of Wisdom: In the depths of these tales lie pearls of wisdom, each offering valuable lessons learned from real-life experiences. Uncover these gems to enlighten and guide your own entrepreneurial path.

Sailing Across Uncharted Waters

Learning from the Captains of Industry: Hear from those who have captained their ships through calm and stormy weather alike. Their insights are lighthouses that illuminate your path, helping you navigate through similar waters with greater confidence.

Drawing Nautical Maps of Success and Setbacks: Use these stories as nautical maps, charting courses through successes and learning from the setbacks. Each narrative adds contours and landmarks to your understanding of the entrepreneurial landscape.

Conclusion: Embarking on Your Own Odyssey
As you conclude this section, prepare to set sail on your entrepreneurial odyssey, armed with the knowledge and inspiration gleaned from these real-world stories. Embrace the journey ahead with a spirit of exploration, ready to face the thrilling challenges and seize the boundless opportunities that lie in the unpredictable seas of entrepreneurship.

Welcome aboard this voyage through authentic entrepreneurial seas, where each story is a compass guiding you towards your own horizon of success. Let's embark on this adventure, charting a course through the diverse and dynamic waters of the entrepreneurial world.

Charting Your Course with Learned Experiences

In the realm of "Charting Your Course with Learned Experiences," we dive into the rich reservoir of knowledge amassed from the voyages of seasoned entrepreneurs. Their narratives act as guiding stars, providing invaluable insights and lessons to steer your entrepreneurial journey.

Navigating with a Compass of Wisdom

Gathering Lessons from Diverse Ventures: Embark on an exploratory mission through the tales of various business ventures. From the swift ascent of a tech startup to the steady growth of a family-owned business, each story is a chapter in the grand book of entrepreneurial wisdom.

Synthesizing Success and Resilience: Immerse yourself in accounts of triumph and endurance. Learn how entrepreneurs navigated through uncharted markets, overcame daunting obstacles, and adapted to changing tides, all while keeping their vision afloat.

Applying Seasoned Insights to Your Journey

Learning from the Captains: Draw inspiration from those who have skillfully navigated the entrepreneurial seas. Whether it's innovative problem-solving or strategic risk-taking, these tales offer a wealth of knowledge.

Mining for Actionable Nuggets: Each story is laden with actionable nuggets of wisdom. Learn how to identify potential challenges before they arise, and arm yourself with strategies that have proven effective in real-world scenarios.

Steering with Foresight and Adaptability

Adapting Lessons to Your Context: Understand how to adapt these insights to your unique entrepreneurial context. Just as a captain adjusts the sails to the changing winds, tailor these lessons to fit the needs and dynamics of your business.

Replicating Proven Strategies: Identify and replicate strategies that have led to success in other ventures. Whether it's a marketing tactic that captured a niche market or a management style that fostered team innovation, these strategies can be valuable tools in your entrepreneurial toolkit.

Conclusion: Embarking on an Informed Voyage

As you conclude this section, prepare to embark on your entrepreneurial journey with a map enriched by the experiences of those who have traversed similar paths. Embrace the wisdom gleaned from these stories, and let it guide your decision-making and strategic planning.

Chart your course with confidence, knowing that the collective wisdom of experienced entrepreneurs lights your way. Embark on your venture with a blend of enthusiasm and informed caution, ready to navigate the exciting and sometimes turbulent waters of entrepreneurship.

Embarking on a Narrative Expedition

In "Setting Sail into Stories of Real-World Entrepreneurs," we embark on a narrative expedition, a journey through the living library of entrepreneurial experiences. This section is not merely a collection of stories; it is a vibrant mosaic of dreams, challenges, innovations, and triumphs.

A Voyage Through Entrepreneurial Chronicles

Curiosity as Your Compass: Approach each narrative with the curiosity of an explorer. Each story is a new land to discover, rich with insights, strategies, and lessons learned on the front lines of business.

The Diversity of the Entrepreneurial Sea: The sea of entrepreneurship is vast and varied. From the bustling harbors of tech startups to the serene bays of artisan ventures, each story adds a unique wave to the ocean of entrepreneurial wisdom.

Learning from the Captains of Industry

Gleaning Insights from Varied Ventures: As you sail through these narratives, glean insights from a spectrum of businesses. Understand the intricacies of different industries, market dynamics, and the unique challenges they present.

Inspirational Anchors: Let these stories serve as anchors, grounding you in moments of doubt and guiding you in times of uncertainty. They are beacons of hope, resilience, and the indomitable spirit of entrepreneurship.

Charting a Course of Knowledge and Innovation

Drawing Maps from Stories: Each entrepreneur's journey offers a map of sorts. Learn to chart your course using their experiences, avoiding the storms they weathered and following the trade winds that propelled them forward.

Sparking Innovation: Let these stories ignite the fire of innovation within you. Be inspired by the creativity, the out-of-the-box thinking, and the courage to break new ground that these entrepreneurs exhibit.

Conclusion: Navigating the Entrepreneurial Waters
As you conclude this section, you stand at the helm of your own entrepreneurial journey, equipped with the collective wisdom of those who have navigated these waters before you. Embrace the vastness of this narrative expedition, and let the stories of real-world entrepreneurs guide your way.

Set sail with a heart full of ambition and a mind open to learning. Let the tales of triumph and tribulation, innovation and resilience, light your path as you navigate the thrilling and ever-evolving world of entrepreneurship.

Balancing Work and Personal Life

As we continue our exploratory voyage in Chapter 11: The Entrepreneur's Journey, we set our course towards an essential and often challenging aspect of this adventure: "Balancing Work and Personal Life."

This section sails into the delicate waters of harmonizing the demanding rhythms of your entrepreneurial endeavors with the equally important cadences of your personal life. It's about steering your ship skillfully between the dual seas of professional responsibilities and personal fulfillment.

✧ Mastering the Art of Harmonious Sailing

In the engaging journey of Chapter 11: The Entrepreneur's Journey, we now navigate to a crucial aspect of the entrepreneurial odyssey: "Mastering the Equilibrium of Work and Life." This segment of our exploration acknowledges the intricate dance between professional commitments and personal well-being. Just as a seasoned captain skillfully balances the sails and rudder in tumultuous waters, this section is dedicated to achieving a harmonious balance between the demands of your business and the needs of your personal life.

➢ Understanding the Symbiosis of Professional and Personal Realms

The intricate dance between one's professional and personal realms is a balancing act that every entrepreneur must learn to navigate. This complex interplay is not just about managing time but also about understanding how these two significant aspects of life influence and shape each other.

1. The Ripple Effect Between Work and Personal Life:

Professional Impact on Personal Life: Your work can significantly influence your personal well-being, relationships, and leisure activities. For instance, a stressful period at work might affect your mood and energy levels at home.

Personal Life Influencing Work: Similarly, events in your personal life, such as family commitments or personal hobbies, can affect your work performance and creativity. Recognizing this bidirectional impact is key to managing both spheres effectively.

2. Creating Synergy Instead of Separation:

Harmonizing Rather Than Compartmentalizing: Rather than trying to rigidly separate work and personal life, seek ways to create harmony between them. This might mean integrating personal interests into your work or finding work projects that align with your personal values.

Adapting to Life's Seasons: Acknowledge that the balance may shift at different life stages or during specific projects. Flexibility is crucial in adjusting to these changing needs.

Navigating the Tides of Responsibilities and Desires

Balancing professional obligations with personal desires requires a nuanced approach, akin to a captain navigating through shifting tides.

1. Assessing and Prioritizing Needs:

Evaluating Priorities: Regularly assess what is most important in both your personal and professional life. This evaluation will help in making decisions that reflect your current priorities.

Setting Realistic Goals: Set achievable goals in both realms. Unrealistic expectations can lead to frustration and burnout.

2. Finding Fulfillment in Both Worlds:

Professional Fulfillment: Find aspects of your work that are deeply satisfying. This could be the joy of solving complex problems, building something meaningful, or making a difference through your business.

Personal Happiness: Cultivate personal relationships, hobbies, and activities outside work that bring joy and relaxation. These elements are essential for mental and emotional well-being.

3. Creating Boundaries and Building Bridges:

    Setting Boundaries: Learn to set healthy boundaries that allow you to disengage from work to enjoy personal time, and vice versa. This might involve specific work hours or designated times for family and self-care.

    Integrating Interests: Where possible, integrate aspects of personal interest into your work. For example, a personal passion for environmental sustainability can be woven into your business practices.

➤ Charting a Sustainable Path of Balance

    Embarking further into the heart of Chapter 11: The Entrepreneur's Journey, we now approach the vital aspect of "Charting a Sustainable Path of Balance." This section is akin to navigating a ship through the narrows, requiring precision and care to maintain equilibrium. Here, we delve into the practicalities of crafting a sustainable balance between the demanding world of entrepreneurship and the equally important realm of personal life. It's about fine-tuning the art of balancing, ensuring a journey that is as rewarding personally as it is professionally.

Constructing a Blueprint for Equilibrium

    Like a skilled architect drafting a blueprint, this part of the journey involves designing and implementing strategies that foster a healthy balance between work commitments and personal fulfillment.

1. Crafting Realistic and Flexible Boundaries:

    Setting Achievable Limits: Learn how to set realistic boundaries that delineate work time from personal time, helping to prevent burnout and ensure quality time for yourself and loved ones.

    Adapting Boundaries as Needed: Understand that these boundaries may need to be flexible, adjusting to the ebb and flow of business demands and personal commitments.

2. Mastering the Art of Time Management:

   Prioritizing and Planning: Gain insights into prioritizing tasks effectively, planning your schedule in a way that maximizes productivity while leaving room for personal pursuits and relaxation.

   Embracing Efficiency: Explore techniques for working more efficiently, so you can make the most of your work hours and have more time for personal activities.

Leveraging Tools for Harmonious Living

In the quest for balance, various tools and techniques can be invaluable allies, helping to streamline work processes and enhance personal well-being.

1. Utilizing Technology for Efficiency:

   Tech Tools for Productivity: Discover how technology can aid in automating and streamlining work processes, freeing up valuable time for personal endeavors.

   Digital Detoxing: Learn when to disconnect from technology to fully engage in personal time, ensuring a complete mental and emotional break from work.

2. Incorporating Mindfulness and Stress Management:

   Mindfulness Practices: Delve into mindfulness practices that can help reduce stress and enhance focus, both at work and in personal life.
   Delegation and Outsourcing: Understand the importance of delegating tasks, both professionally and personally, to manage workload and stress levels effectively.

Embarking on the Journey of Balanced Living

As we set sail into "Charting a Sustainable Path of Balance," approach this journey with an open mind and a commitment to self-care. This section is not just about managing time; it's about cultivating a lifestyle that allows you to thrive in all aspects of life.

Engage with this section as a guide to building a life where professional aspirations and personal happiness are not in conflict but in harmony. Let's navigate these waters with the goal of creating a balanced, fulfilling life, where your entrepreneurial success is matched by personal contentment and well-being.

➤ Embarking on the Voyage of Balanced Sailing

As we navigate the deeper waters of Chapter 11: The Entrepreneur's Journey, we set our sights on a crucial and transformative section: "Embarking on the Voyage of Balanced Sailing." This part of our journey is dedicated to mastering the delicate art of balancing the demands of a thriving business with the needs of a fulfilling personal life. It's a voyage that calls for not only skillful navigation but also deep wisdom and self-awareness.

Steering Towards a Fulfilling Work-Life Harmony

In the realm of entrepreneurship, balancing work and life is like steering a ship through ever-changing seas – it requires vigilance, adaptability, and a keen understanding of when to push forward and when to pull back.

1. Juggling the Dual Roles with Skill and Insight:

    Mastering the Juggle: Learn the intricate art of juggling your roles as a business leader and as an individual with personal aspirations and relationships. This section offers insights into maintaining equilibrium, ensuring neither role overshadows the other.

    Crafting a Fulfilling Professional Journey: Discover how to make your work journey fulfilling and rewarding, turning professional challenges into opportunities for growth and satisfaction.

2. Rejuvenating through Personal Time:

    Valuing Personal Rejuvenation: Understand the importance of valuing and investing in your personal time. It's about recognizing that periods of rest and relaxation are not just breaks from work but essential elements that recharge and inspire.

    Creating Joyous Personal Experiences: Explore ways to enrich your personal life with activities, relationships, and hobbies that bring joy, relaxation, and a sense of fulfillment outside the confines of your professional responsibilities.

Setting Sail on the Voyage of Balance

As we embark on this journey of "Mastering the Equilibrium of Work and Life," approach it with a mindset geared towards holistic success – success that encompasses both professional achievements and personal contentment.

In this section, you'll be equipped with strategies and insights that enable you to strike a balance between the demands of your entrepreneurial pursuits and the pleasures of your personal life. It's about charting a course that leads to a life where your business thrives, and your personal well-being flourishes.

So, let's set sail with an open heart and a commitment to achieve balance in all aspects of life. Embrace this voyage as an opportunity to create a life that is as rewarding and enriching personally as it is professionally. Here's to a journey that is productive, satisfying, and joyous in equal measure!

✧ Creating a Culture of Balance in Entrepreneurship

As we continue our insightful voyage through Chapter 11: The Entrepreneur's Journey, we arrive at a pivotal segment, "Creating a Culture of Balance in Entrepreneurship." This section underscores the profound influence an entrepreneur's approach to balance has on the entire organizational ecosystem. Here, we delve into how you, as a business leader, can set a powerful precedent and foster a work culture where balance is not just encouraged but ingrained. It's about leading a voyage where every crew member feels valued, both professionally and personally.

➢ Charting the Path for a Balanced Organizational Culture

As we continue our navigational journey through Chapter 11: The Entrepreneur's Journey, we turn our compass towards a critical destination, "Charting the Path for a Balanced Organizational Culture." In the ever-evolving and dynamic landscape of entrepreneurship, fostering a balanced work environment is akin to a captain charting a careful course—one that ensures all members of the crew can effectively manage their professional tasks while also pursuing personal growth and fulfillment. This section delves into the art of cultivating a workplace where balance is not an afterthought but a fundamental principle that guides every action and decision.

Navigating the Waters of Work-Life Integration in Organizations

Creating a balanced organizational culture is like navigating a vessel through both calm and stormy seas, ensuring that every crew member remains safe, motivated, and on course.

1. Building a Culture that Values Balance:

    Cultivating an Environment of Mutual Respect and Support: Explore strategies to create a workplace culture where respect for individual needs and support for work-life balance is ingrained in the company ethos.

    Innovative Approaches to Work-Life Integration: Learn about innovative organizational practices that encourage a healthy blend of work and personal life, acknowledging that a well-rounded employee experience leads to enhanced creativity and productivity.

2. Implementing Policies that Foster Equilibrium:

    Developing Supportive Policies and Benefits: Investigate the various policies and benefits that can be implemented to promote work-life balance, such as flexible working hours, remote work options, and mental health initiatives.

    Adapting to the Changing Needs of Employees: Understand the importance of continuously adapting organizational policies to meet the evolving needs of your team, especially in response to life changes and external factors.

Embarking on the Voyage of Creating Balanced Workspaces

As we set sail into "Charting the Path for a Balanced Organizational Culture," approach this journey with the vision of creating not just a successful business, but a thriving community of individuals who feel valued and supported. This section is about taking proactive steps to ensure that your organizational culture actively promotes and supports the well-being of each team member.

In this part of the chapter, you will discover the key elements and practices that contribute to building a balanced and healthy workplace. It's a voyage towards establishing an environment where professional aspirations and personal well-being coexist in harmony, leading to a more engaged, content, and productive team.

So, let's navigate this path with commitment and foresight, crafting an organizational culture that sets a benchmark for balance in the entrepreneurial world. Here's to charting a course that leads to a workplace where every member feels empowered to excel in their professional roles while also enjoying a fulfilling personal life!

➢ Leading by Example in Work-Life Harmony:

In the unfolding narrative of Chapter 11: The Entrepreneur's Journey, we now navigate towards a critical aspect of organizational leadership, "Leading by Example in Work-Life Harmony." In this section, we explore the influential role of the entrepreneur as a captain, not just in steering the business towards success but also in exemplifying the significance of a balanced life. This journey is about embodying the principles of work-life harmony, demonstrating to your team that integrating professional diligence with personal well-being is not only possible but also beneficial for overall productivity and satisfaction.

Charting a Personal Example of Equilibrium

As an entrepreneurial leader, your approach to balancing work and life serves as a guiding light for your team, illuminating the path to harmonious living.

1. Embodying the Role of a Balanced Leader:

The Captain's Balance: Embrace the responsibility of being a role model in work-life harmony. Illustrate through your behavior and choices how a balanced approach leads to a more fulfilled and productive life, both personally and professionally.

Inspiring Through Action: Inspire your team by actively practicing balance. Show that you value your time outside of work as much as your time within it, thereby encouraging your team to do the same.

2. Integrating Balance into Everyday Leadership:

Practicing What You Preach: Ensure that your daily actions reflect your commitment to a balanced life. This could be through maintaining regular work hours, prioritizing mental health, engaging in hobbies, or spending quality time with family and friends.

Communicating the Value of Balance: Openly discuss the importance of work-life harmony with your team. Share your practices and encourage dialogue on how the organization can support each member in achieving this balance.

➤ Embarking on the Leadership Voyage of Balance

As we venture deeper into the enriching realms of Chapter 11: The Entrepreneur's Journey, we steer our focus towards a critical and transformative leadership role in "Leading by Example in Work-Life Harmony: Embarking on the Leadership Voyage of Balance." This section delves into the profound influence that entrepreneurial leadership has on shaping a culture of balance within an organization. It emphasizes the pivotal role of leaders in demonstrating, through their actions and attitudes, how to successfully navigate the often challenging waters of maintaining equilibrium between professional diligence and personal well-being.

Setting the Sail for a Balanced Leadership Approach

The journey of a leader in the entrepreneurial world is twofold: steering the business ship towards success while also ensuring the holistic well-being of the team. This section explores how to master this dual responsibility with grace and effectiveness.

1. The Captain's Dual Role:

Charting a Balanced Course: Embrace the role of a leader who exemplifies balance. Understand that your approach to managing work and life significantly shapes the work culture and sets a standard for your team.

Influencing Through Personal Practice: Demonstrate the importance of work-life harmony by integrating it into your own life. Show your team that achieving professional success does not require sacrificing personal happiness and health.

2. Cultivating a Culture of Holistic Success:

Beyond Policies to Practice: Move beyond mere policy implementation to cultivating a culture where work-life balance is a lived experience. This involves creating an environment where the team feels encouraged and supported to find their own equilibrium.

Empathetic Leadership for Sustainable Growth: Adopt an empathetic leadership style that acknowledges and addresses the diverse needs of your team members, recognizing that each individual's path to balance may look different.

Embarking on the Balanced Leadership Journey

As we embark on "Leading by Example in Work-Life Harmony," approach this journey with an understanding of the transformative power of empathetic and balanced leadership. Recognize that as a leader, your actions, choices, and the work environment you foster have a ripple effect, influencing not just the business outcomes but also the personal lives of your team members.

In this section, you will uncover the strategies and insights needed to lead a team that is not only successful in achieving business goals but also in maintaining personal well-being. It's about championing a leadership style where professional accomplishments and personal contentment are not mutually exclusive but are interwoven into the fabric of your organizational culture.

So, let's commence this leadership voyage with a commitment to balance, empathy, and holistic well-being. Here's to setting an example that inspires and motivates, creating an entrepreneurial journey that is as rewarding personally as it is professionally, for you and your entire crew.

> ➢ Cultivating a Workplace Environment Conducive to Balance:

In the continuing exploration of Chapter 11: The Entrepreneur's Journey, we now navigate to a critical aspect of leadership, "Cultivating a Workplace Environment Conducive to Balance." This section builds on the concept of leading by example in work-life harmony, focusing on the active development of a workplace culture that deeply values and facilitates the balance between professional responsibilities and personal well-being. It's about crafting an environment where the principles of flexibility, understanding, and holistic wellness are not just encouraged but are integral to the organizational ethos.

Laying the Foundations for a Balanced Workplace

As the captain of your entrepreneurial ship, this segment guides you in laying down the foundations of a workplace culture where balance is not just a concept but a practiced reality.

1. Building a Culture of Understanding and Flexibility:

    Creating an Empathetic Work Environment: Delve into the importance of fostering an empathetic workplace where each team member's need for balance is recognized and respected. This involves creating policies and an atmosphere that support flexible work arrangements and encourage employees to voice their work-life balance needs.

    Adapting to Individual Needs: Understand that work-life balance looks different for each person. Embrace a flexible approach that adapts to the diverse needs and life circumstances of your team, enabling them to thrive both at work and in their personal lives.

2. Promoting a Holistic Approach to Employee Well-being:

    Beyond Traditional Benefits to Total Well-being: Explore ways to extend your support for your team beyond the conventional work benefits. Implement initiatives like wellness programs, mental health days, and activities that promote a healthy integration of work and life.

    Cultivating a Well-being Oriented Culture: Learn how to embed a culture that prioritizes the overall well-being of your employees. This involves not just providing resources but also creating an environment where mental health, physical well-being, and personal growth are valued and supported.

Embarking on a Journey of Creating Balanced Workspaces

As we set sail into "Cultivating a Workplace Environment Conducive to Balance," approach this task with a commitment to nurturing a workplace where every member feels supported in achieving their ideal work-life harmony. This section is about translating the concept of balance into actionable practices and policies that actively contribute to the well-being of your team.

In this part of the chapter, you will be equipped with strategies to build a work culture that genuinely embraces flexibility, understanding, and a holistic approach to well-being. It's about leading a journey where your team is empowered to find their unique balance, fostering a workplace that is not only productive but also supportive and nurturing.

Let's embark on this endeavor with the vision of creating a balanced, healthy, and thriving workplace. Here's to cultivating an environment where the well-being of your team is as much a priority as the success of your business!

➢ Embarking on the Journey of Creating Balanced Workspaces

In the enlightening passage of Chapter 11: The Entrepreneur's Journey, we now embark on an integral and transformative segment, "Leading by Example in Work-Life Harmony: Embarking on the Journey of Creating Balanced Workspaces." This section extends beyond the realm of personal balance to the broader scope of cultivating a work environment where harmony between professional demands and personal fulfillment is not just an aspiration but a lived reality. It's about charting new horizons where the concept of work-life balance transcends individual practice and becomes an organizational ethos.

Navigating the Course of Balanced Work Culture

In this part of the journey, we focus on how entrepreneurial leadership plays a pivotal role in shaping a workspace that inherently supports and promotes balance.

1. Setting the Tone for Organizational Balance:

Influencing Organizational Perception of Balance: As a leader, your approach to balancing work and life significantly influences how balance is perceived and integrated within your organization. This section guides you in setting the tone for a culture where balance is valued and actively pursued.

Leading the Way in Practice and Policy: Discover how to implement policies and demonstrate practices that reflect a commitment to work-life harmony. It's about leading by example and creating systems that enable your team to achieve balance.

2. Cultivating Spaces of Equilibrium and Growth:

Building Environments That Foster Balance: Learn how to create physical and emotional spaces within your organization that encourage a healthy blend of work and personal life. This involves considering workspace design, flexible schedules, and an atmosphere of respect and understanding.

Promoting Well-being as a Pillar of Success: Emphasize the importance of well-being as a fundamental component of business success. Understand that a team that is well-balanced is more engaged, creative, and productive.

Setting Sail on a Transformative Voyage

As we set sail on "Leading by Example in Work-Life Harmony," approach this voyage with a vision of transformative leadership. This journey is about more than just achieving business objectives; it's about creating a workplace where each member of the team feels empowered and supported to pursue both professional success and personal well-being.

In this section, you will gain the tools and insights necessary to build a workplace that not only thrives in its business endeavors but also champions the well-being of its people. It's about pioneering a path where the workplace becomes a haven of balanced living, reflecting the values and practices of a holistic approach to work and life.

So, let's embark on this mission with dedication and a forward-thinking mindset. Here's to leading the way in creating workspaces that are not just centers of productivity but also sanctuaries of balance and well-being. Let's chart a course towards a future where businesses excel and people thrive in unison.

> ✧ Embarking on the Journey of Balance

As we set our course into the insightful section "Balancing Work and Personal Life" in Chapter 11: The Entrepreneur's Journey, we embrace the critical and enriching challenge of finding equilibrium in our professional and personal lives. This journey, often as demanding as it is rewarding, calls for a thoughtful exploration into the delicate art of balancing the intense demands of entrepreneurship with the equally important aspects of personal fulfillment and happiness.

Charting a Course Toward Holistic Fulfillment

In this segment, we delve into the intertwined nature of work and personal life, recognizing that the journey of entrepreneurship is not solely defined by business achievements but also by the quality of life experienced along the way.

1. Mastering the Dynamics of Work-Life Integration:

Understanding the Interplay: Gain insights into how professional commitments and personal life can complement and enhance each other, rather than exist in constant conflict. It's about finding synergy in the overlap of these two worlds.

Developing Strategies for Equilibrium: Learn to develop and implement strategies that allow for a fulfilling professional life without compromising personal well-being and relationships.

2. Embracing a Philosophy of Balanced Living:

Adopting a Holistic Approach: Embrace a philosophy that views success not just in terms of business metrics but also in the richness of personal experiences and relationships.

Navigating the Practicalities and Philosophies: Explore both the practicalities of managing time and responsibilities, and the philosophies that underpin a truly balanced life, providing a compass for decision-making and priority-setting.

Setting Sail on a Voyage of Work-Life Harmony

"Leading by Example in Work-Life Harmony" is not just a chapter in a book; it's the beginning of an enlightening voyage. A voyage where the dual horizons of professional success and personal fulfillment converge, creating a panorama of balanced living.

Navigating the Seas of Balance

Embarking with a Vision: Set sail on this journey with a clear vision – one where your entrepreneurial ambitions and personal aspirations sail in harmony. Visualize a life where professional achievements and personal contentment are not at odds but in a beautiful symphony.

Charting the Course: Charting the course in this journey involves more than just plotting points on a map; it's about introspection and understanding your priorities. Balance is personal and subjective; it's about finding what equilibrium looks like for you.

The Tools for a Harmonious Journey

Equipping Your Ship: Equip yourself with the tools of mindfulness, time management, and self-awareness. These are your compass, sextant, and map, guiding you through the choppy waters of entrepreneurial challenges and the calm seas of personal life.

Learning from Navigators: Learn from the seasoned navigators who have mastered this art. Draw inspiration from entrepreneurs who have successfully balanced intense professional demands with rich personal lives.

Embracing the Winds of Challenge and Opportunity

The Winds of Challenge: Just as a skilled sailor uses the wind, no matter its direction, use the challenges you face to propel you forward. See each challenge as an opportunity to refine your balancing skills.

The Currents of Opportunity: Similarly, when favorable currents of opportunity flow, navigate them with foresight. Seize opportunities that align with your vision of balance.

A Journey of Self-Discovery and Growth

Discovering Uncharted Waters: This voyage is as much about self-discovery as it is about achievement. It's about exploring the uncharted waters of your potential, both as an entrepreneur and as an individual.

Growth on All Fronts: Embrace growth in every aspect of your life. Grow your business, but also grow in your relationships, in your passions, and in your understanding of yourself.

Conclusion: Arriving at a Destination of Balance
As you conclude "Leading by Example in Work-Life Harmony," understand that this voyage never truly ends. It's an ongoing journey of balancing, adjusting, and growing. It's about creating a life where your business's success fuels your personal happiness, and your personal well-being underpins your professional achievements.

Set forth on this journey with enthusiasm and determination, ready to navigate the ever-changing tides of life. Here's to a voyage that brings you not just to the shores of success but also to the harbors of happiness and well-being. Let's raise our sails and embark on this transformative journey of harmonious living.

The Future of Entrepreneurship

As we progress further into Chapter 11: The Entrepreneur's Journey, we turn our gaze towards a visionary segment, "Leading by Example in Work-Life Harmony: The Future of Entrepreneurship." This section invites us to contemplate the evolving landscape of entrepreneurship, where the integration of work-life balance is not just a trend but a fundamental shift in the entrepreneurial ethos. Here, we explore how the principles of work-life harmony are becoming integral to the future success and sustainability of entrepreneurial ventures.

- ❖ Envisioning a New Era of Entrepreneurial Leadership

In this era of entrepreneurship, there is a paradigm shift towards a more comprehensive and humane approach to business leadership. This shift is redefining what it means to be successful, emphasizing a balanced approach that values personal well-being just as much as business achievements.

- ➤ Redefining Success in Entrepreneurial Ventures:

Holistic Success Metrics: The concept of success is evolving beyond traditional financial metrics to include factors like mental health, employee well-being, social impact, and personal fulfillment. Entrepreneurs are now seen as successful not just by their company's profit margins but also by their ability to create a positive and balanced work environment.

Impact on Entrepreneurial Mindset: This change is influencing the entrepreneurial mindset, encouraging leaders to prioritize their health and happiness and to foster a culture where such priorities are respected and valued.

Embracing Work-Life Integration as a Norm:

Integration Over Separation: The traditional view of work-life balance as a strict separation between professional and personal life is giving way to a more integrated approach. This involves creating work environments that accommodate personal life responsibilities and encourage a healthy blend of work and life activities.

Innovation and Employee Satisfaction: Integrating work-life balance into business operations is proving to drive innovation and employee satisfaction. Companies that adopt flexible work policies, for instance, often see increased creativity, loyalty, and productivity among their teams.

> Leading the Charge Towards a Harmonious Future

The role of the entrepreneur in the future of business is expanding to include being a vanguard of work-life harmony, setting an example for current and future generations.

The Entrepreneur as a Beacon of Balance:

Setting Precedents for Future Leadership: Entrepreneurs who prioritize work-life balance set a powerful precedent, demonstrating that it's possible to achieve business success without sacrificing personal well-being. They become role models, inspiring a new generation of leaders to adopt a more balanced approach.

Advocating for a Balanced Lifestyle: Entrepreneurs have the unique opportunity to advocate for and implement policies that support work-life balance, not only within their organizations but also in the broader business community.

Conclusion: Shaping the Future of Entrepreneurial Leadership

As we explore this new era of entrepreneurial leadership, it becomes evident that the future of business will be shaped by leaders who understand the importance of balancing professional achievements with personal well-being. This forward-looking approach is about more than just individual success; it's about creating a sustainable, healthy, and innovative business culture that benefits everyone involved.

The journey toward this future is both challenging and exciting, offering entrepreneurs the chance to redefine what it means to be successful. By embracing work-life integration and setting a positive example, entrepreneurial leaders can spearhead a movement towards a more balanced, fulfilling, and humane approach to business. This is the future of entrepreneurship – a future where success is measured not just in financial terms, but in the overall well-being and satisfaction of every individual it touches.

Innovating for a Balanced Business World: Contemplate the innovations and changes necessary to support this shift towards a more balanced entrepreneurial world, including technological advancements, policy reforms, and cultural shifts within the business community.

✧ Embarking on a Journey Towards Balanced Entrepreneurial Futures

The section "Leading by Example in Work-Life Harmony: The Future of Entrepreneurship" serves as a call to action for current and aspiring entrepreneurs to embrace a transformative approach to their professional and personal lives. This future-oriented perspective envisions a world where entrepreneurial success is inextricably linked to the well-being and balance in every aspect of life.

1. Envisioning a Holistic Model of Success:

Broadening the Definition of Entrepreneurial Achievement: This future envisages a paradigm where success is redefined to include mental and emotional health, personal growth, and community engagement alongside traditional business milestones.

Integrating Personal Values and Business Goals: The new entrepreneurial model encourages the integration of personal values, such as sustainability, mindfulness, and social responsibility, into business practices and goals.

2. Shaping a Supportive Entrepreneurial Ecosystem:

Cultivating Support Networks: A key aspect of this future is the development of robust support systems within the entrepreneurial community, including mentorship programs, wellness initiatives, and collaborative networks that emphasize balance and holistic growth.

Advocating for Policy and Cultural Change: Entrepreneurs are positioned as advocates for change, influencing policies and cultural norms that promote work-life harmony, both within their organizations and in the wider business landscape.

Leading the Voyage Towards a Balanced Future

As we embark on this journey, we recognize the role of entrepreneurs as trailblazers in this new era of business, setting the course for a future where balance and well-being are central to entrepreneurial success.

1. Embracing the Role of Change-Makers:

Pioneering New Practices: Entrepreneurs are encouraged to experiment with innovative business practices that foster balance, such as flexible working models, employee wellness programs, and a focus on mental health.

Leading with Empathy and Understanding: The entrepreneurial leader of the future is empathetic, understanding, and attuned to the needs of their team, promoting a culture where work-life harmony is actively pursued and celebrated.

2. Creating a Legacy of Balanced Entrepreneurship:

   Building Businesses with a Human Touch: The focus is on building businesses that are not only economically successful but also enhance the lives of those they touch – employees, customers, and the broader community.

   Leaving a Legacy of Well-being: Entrepreneurs are invited to consider the legacy they wish to leave, envisioning businesses that contribute positively to societal well-being and set a standard for future generations.
   Conclusion: Embarking on a Transformative Entrepreneurial Era

   As we set sail towards this new horizon, the journey invites us to be both dreamers and doers, envisioning a future where the entrepreneurial spirit is synonymous with balance, innovation, and holistic well-being. This is more than just a shift in business practices; it's a cultural and personal revolution, reimagining the essence of entrepreneurship.

   So, let's embrace this exciting and meaningful voyage, forging ahead as pioneers of a new entrepreneurial era. An era where the pursuit of business success is harmoniously aligned with personal fulfillment and societal well-being, creating a legacy that transcends traditional measures of success and paves the way for a prosperous, sustainable, and fulfilling future.

Chapter Conclusion: Chapter 11 - The Entrepreneur's Journey

As we close the final pages of Chapter 11: The Entrepreneur's Journey, we reflect on the vast and varied landscapes we have traversed. This chapter has been a comprehensive exploration of the entrepreneurial spirit, a deep dive into the heart and soul of what it means to embark on this unique and exhilarating journey. From understanding the intricate dynamics of the entrepreneurial terrain to navigating the delicate balance between professional and personal life, this chapter has illuminated the path for aspiring and seasoned entrepreneurs alike.

A Voyage of Discovery and Growth

The Entrepreneur's Journey is not just a business venture; it's a personal odyssey of discovery, growth, and fulfillment. We have charted the diverse topography of entrepreneurship, unveiling the myriad opportunities and challenges that lie in the varied industries and markets. We have climbed the peaks of success, understanding their exhilarating heights, and descended into the valleys of challenges, learning invaluable lessons from their depths.

Navigating the Entrepreneurial Lifecycle

Understanding the entrepreneurial lifecycle has been akin to recognizing the changing seasons of a sea voyage. We have learned to adapt and thrive at each stage, from the nascent beginnings of a startup to the maturity and possible reinvention of a well-established enterprise. The lifecycle of a business, much like the journey of a ship, requires constant vigilance, adaptability, and strategic foresight.

Steering with Ethics and Values

Our compass throughout this journey has been our ethics and values. These have guided our decisions, shaped our interactions, and will ultimately define our legacy. We have embarked on the ethical voyage with a commitment to upholding the highest standards of integrity, understanding that the true measure of success extends beyond profit margins to the positive impact we have on society and the world.

The Anchor of Work-Life Harmony

One of the most crucial insights from this journey has been the importance of work-life harmony. We have delved into the art of balancing the demands of entrepreneurship with personal well-being, recognizing that this balance is essential for long-term success and happiness. As leaders, we have learned to set the sails for our teams, creating cultures where balance is not just an aspiration but a practiced reality.

Conclusion: Sailing into the Future

As we conclude Chapter 11, we do so with a renewed sense of purpose and a deeper understanding of the entrepreneurial path. This journey has equipped us with the knowledge, tools, and insights to navigate the entrepreneurial seas with confidence and clarity. We have learned that the journey of entrepreneurship is as much about the destination as it is about the journey itself - a journey of constant learning, unending curiosity, and the courage to push boundaries.

We set forth from here with our maps charted, our compasses set, and our sails hoisted high, ready to embrace the challenges and opportunities that lie ahead. Let this chapter be a beacon that guides you through your entrepreneurial voyage, illuminating your path with the wisdom, strategies, and inspiration needed to navigate the dynamic and exhilarating world of entrepreneurship.

Here's to the paths you will tread, the seas you will cross, and the horizons you will discover in your incredible odyssey of entrepreneurship. Let's sail forth with the spirit of adventure, discovery, and determination. The entrepreneurial journey awaits!

Chapter 12: Social Responsibility and Ethical Entrepreneurship

Welcome aboard Chapter 12: Social Responsibility and Ethical Entrepreneurship, an essential chapter that charts a course through the vital waters of ethics and social impact in the entrepreneurial journey. As we embark on this chapter, we delve deep into the heart of what it means to be not just a successful entrepreneur but a responsible and ethical one. This chapter is a call to navigate the business world with a compass calibrated not only to profitability but also to principles and purpose.

Navigating the Waters of Business Ethics

Our journey begins with exploring the fundamental role of ethics in business. In this realm, ethics are like the beacon lights guiding ships through dark nights, ensuring safe and responsible passage. We delve into the complexities and challenges of maintaining ethical integrity in today's competitive and rapidly evolving business landscape. This section provides the tools and insights necessary for entrepreneurs to make decisions that are not only smart but also right and just.

Charting the Course of Social Entrepreneurship

As we sail further, we encounter the rising tide of social entrepreneurship - a powerful movement where business meets societal impact. This part of the chapter is an odyssey into businesses that are driven not just by the desire to profit but by the mission to solve social problems and contribute positively to the world. We explore how social entrepreneurship is redefining the purpose of business, transforming entrepreneurs into agents of change and innovation for social good.

Building a Legacy Beyond Profits

In the quest to build a lasting and meaningful business, we understand that success is measured not only in financial terms but also in the legacy we leave behind. This section of the chapter focuses on how entrepreneurs can create businesses that do more than generate revenue; they generate positive change. We examine how embedding social responsibility into the core of your business can lead to a legacy that transcends profits, one that impacts communities, environments, and future generations.

Conclusion: Sailing into a Future of Ethical Business

As we set sail on Chapter 12, we do so with the understanding that our journey in the world of entrepreneurship is intertwined with the larger journey of our society. This chapter is not just about understanding the importance of ethics and social responsibility in business; it's about embodying these values in every aspect of your entrepreneurial endeavor.

So, let us embark on this journey with a sense of purpose and a commitment to ethical excellence. Here's to navigating the entrepreneurial seas with a vision that goes beyond the horizon of profits, towards creating a better world through responsible and ethical business practices. Welcome to the chapter where you not only chart the course of your business but also contribute to charting a course for a more ethical and socially responsible business world.

The Role of Ethics in Business

Setting the Compass: The Vitality of Ethics in Entrepreneurship

In the heart of Chapter 12, we delve into the crucial role that ethics plays in the realm of business. As entrepreneurs, we are not just building enterprises; we are shaping the fabric of society. This section explores the indispensable function of ethics as the guiding compass in this endeavor, ensuring that our business practices not only lead to success but are also aligned with moral and ethical principles.

Understanding the Landscape of Business Ethics

1. The Foundation of Trust and Credibility:

The Strategic Value of Trust:

Direct Impact on Customer Loyalty: Exploring how ethical business practices directly influence customer loyalty. Ethical companies often see a higher rate of customer retention due to the trust they build. This trust stems from consistent ethical behavior, transparency, and integrity in all business dealings.

Enhanced Employee Engagement and Retention: Discussing how a strong ethical foundation contributes to a positive workplace culture, leading to higher employee satisfaction and retention. When employees trust their employer, they are more engaged, productive, and committed to the organization's success.

Investing in Ethical Practices as a Business Strategy:

Long-Term vs Short-Term Gains: Addressing the misconception that ethical practices are costly or reduce profitability. On the contrary, in the long run, ethical practices can lead to sustainable business growth and profitability through customer loyalty and brand reputation.

Risk Mitigation: Ethical practices help in mitigating risks related to legal issues, reputational damage, and potential financial losses due to unethical behavior.

Illustrating Ethics in Action:

Case Study of Fair Labor Practices:

Company Profile: A detailed profile of a company renowned for its fair labor practices, such as providing fair wages, ensuring safe working conditions, and respecting workers' rights.

Impact on Business: Analyzing the tangible benefits seen by the company, such as increased market share, improved customer loyalty, and a stronger brand image.

Research Findings on Ethics and Customer Loyalty:

Survey Data: Presenting survey data that links ethical practices with customer loyalty. For example, data showing that a significant percentage of consumers prefer buying from companies known for their ethical practices.

Consumer Behavior Analysis: An analysis of consumer behavior trends demonstrating a growing preference for ethically responsible companies.

Ethical Practices Leading to Employee Satisfaction:

Employee Testimonials and Feedback: Incorporating employee testimonials from companies with strong ethical standards to illustrate how these practices contribute to job satisfaction and employee morale.

HR Metrics: Presenting HR metrics from such companies, showcasing lower turnover rates, higher employee engagement scores, and other indicators of a healthy workplace environment.

Long-Term Financial Success Tied to Ethical Practices:

Financial Analysis: A financial analysis of companies that prioritize ethical practices, showing how these practices correlate with long-term financial success and resilience in the market.

Comparative Study: A comparative study of companies with strong ethical practices versus those with poor ethical records, highlighting the differences in their financial performance over time.

Conclusion:

In this expanded exploration of the role of ethics in trust-building, the aim is to provide a comprehensive understanding of how ethical practices are not just moral obligations but strategic business assets. Through case studies, research data, and real-world examples, this section underscores the tangible benefits of ethics in building customer loyalty, employee satisfaction, and long-term financial success. It aims to inspire businesses to view ethics as a foundational pillar for building a sustainable and successful business model, where trust is both a key driver and an outcome of ethical practices.

Credibility in the Market:

Ethics as a Brand Differentiator: In a marketplace where consumers are increasingly values-driven, a company's ethical stance can set it apart from competitors. Ethical practices can be a significant differentiator, akin to a badge of honor that marks a business as trustworthy and reliable.

Building a Reputation of Integrity: Detailed examples of how companies have enhanced their market reputation through ethical conduct, such as transparent communication during crises or consistent commitment to environmental sustainability.

2. Navigating the Challenges of Ethical Dilemmas:

Introduction to Decision Frameworks: Detailing decision-making frameworks like the Ethical Decision-Making Matrix, which helps evaluate the ethical dimensions of business decisions, or the Triple Bottom Line approach, which focuses on balancing social, environmental, and financial outcomes.

Practical Application: Demonstrating how these frameworks can be applied in real-world business scenarios, providing a structured approach to navigating complex ethical dilemmas.

Real-World Scenarios and Resolutions:

Case Studies: Presenting case studies of businesses that have encountered ethical grey areas, such as conflicts of interest, and how they navigated these challenges using ethical decision-making frameworks.

Lessons Learned: Extracting key lessons from these case studies, highlighting the importance of a structured approach to ethical decision-making in business.

Balancing Profit with Principles

The Intersection of Profit and Ethics:

Synergistic Relationship: Exploring the synergy between ethical practices and profitability. Case studies of businesses that have successfully integrated ethical considerations into their profit-making strategies, showing that ethics and profits can coexist and enhance each other.

Long-Term Benefits: Discussing how ethical business practices can lead to sustainable long-term growth, enhanced brand loyalty, and reduced risks.

Strategies for Ethical Profitability:

Ethical Investment and Sourcing: Exploring strategies such as ethical sourcing of materials, investing in sustainable practices, and engaging in fair trade, which can contribute to profitability while upholding ethical standards.

Corporate Social Responsibility (CSR): Discussing how CSR initiatives can enhance a company's reputation, strengthen customer loyalty, and ultimately contribute to profitability.

Conclusion

This expanded exploration into the challenges of ethical dilemmas in business underscores the importance of integrating ethical decision-making into the core business strategy. It highlights that ethical considerations are not merely about adhering to regulations or avoiding negative outcomes but are fundamental to building trust, credibility, and sustainable success. By navigating the intricate balance between ethics and profitability, businesses can thrive in the market while contributing positively to society and setting a precedent for responsible business conduct. This section aims to empower business leaders with the knowledge, tools, and inspiration to embed ethical practices into their business models, ensuring a journey that is not only commercially successful but also ethically sound and socially responsible.

Implementing Ethical Practices in Business Operations

1. Creating an Ethical Framework

Developing Ethical Policies:

Crafting Ethical Guidelines: Detailing the process of developing a comprehensive set of ethical policies tailored to the business's specific needs and industry standards. These policies should serve as a clear guide for acceptable behaviors and decision-making processes.

Customization and Relevance: Emphasizing the importance of customizing these guidelines to be relevant and applicable to various aspects of the business, ensuring they address specific ethical challenges pertinent to the industry and operational context.

Institutionalizing Ethics:

Embedding Ethics into Organizational Culture: Strategies for integrating ethical principles into the very fabric of the organization. This involves leadership commitment, policy integration, and creating a culture where ethical considerations are a part of everyday business operations.

Leadership Role: Highlighting the critical role of leadership in setting the tone for ethical behavior and decision-making. Leaders should not only endorse these policies but also demonstrate them through their actions.

2. Training and Awareness

Educating Your Team:

Comprehensive Training Programs: Developing and implementing comprehensive training programs that educate employees about the company's ethical policies and their practical application. This training should be an ongoing process, incorporating regular updates and refreshers.

Interactive Learning: Utilizing interactive and engaging methods for ethical training, such as workshops, role-playing scenarios, and discussion forums, to ensure better understanding and retention of ethical principles.

Fostering an Ethical Work Culture:

Recognition and Reward Systems: Establishing recognition and reward systems for ethical behavior to reinforce and encourage adherence to ethical standards. This can include acknowledging ethical decision-making in performance reviews and team meetings.

Addressing Unethical Behavior: Setting up clear procedures for addressing and rectifying unethical behavior. This includes creating a safe and confidential environment for employees to report unethical practices without fear of retribution.

Conclusion

Implementing ethical practices in business operations is a dynamic and ongoing process that requires commitment from all levels of the organization. By creating a robust ethical framework and instilling a culture of ethical awareness and behavior, businesses can ensure that their operations are not only compliant with legal standards but also aligned with moral and ethical principles. This commitment to ethical business practices fosters trust, credibility, and sustainability, ultimately contributing to the long-term success and reputation of the business. The aim is to transform ethical guidelines from mere documents into lived values and practices that define the organization's identity and operations.

Ethics as a Driver of Innovation and Growth

1. Innovating with Integrity

Ethics-Driven Innovation:

Integrating Ethics in R&D: Exploring how ethical considerations can be integrated into research and development processes. This includes assessing the societal impact of new products or services and ensuring they contribute positively to social welfare.

Case Studies: Presenting case studies of companies that have successfully integrated ethical considerations into their innovation processes, resulting in products or services that not only meet market needs but also address social or environmental issues.

Sustainable Practices:

Eco-friendly Innovations: Discussing how adopting sustainable practices can lead to innovative solutions in product design, packaging, and production processes. This includes using renewable resources, reducing carbon footprint, and promoting circular economy principles.

Impact on Brand Image: Highlighting how sustainable practices enhance the brand image, attracting customers who prioritize environmental consciousness, and setting the business apart in the market.

2. The Competitive Advantage of Ethics

Standing Out in the Market:

Ethics as a Brand Differentiator: Delving into how ethical practices can distinguish a company in a competitive marketplace. This includes exploring how ethics in marketing, supply chain management, and customer service can elevate a brand's reputation.

Consumer Trends: Analyzing current consumer trends that show a growing preference for ethically responsible companies. Demonstrating how businesses that prioritize ethics are better positioned to capture market share in increasingly socially conscious consumer bases.

Building Long-term Relationships:

Ethical Supply Chains: Discussing the importance of ethical supply chains in building long-term supplier relationships. This includes fair trade practices, ensuring fair labor conditions, and fostering transparency.

Customer Loyalty: Detailing how ethical practices contribute to building customer loyalty. Customers are more likely to remain loyal to brands that align with their values and demonstrate ethical behavior in their operations.

Partner Alliances: Exploring how a commitment to ethics can lead to stronger and more meaningful partnerships with other businesses, non-profits, and government entities. These alliances can open up new opportunities for collaboration and market expansion.

Conclusion:

Innovating with integrity and leveraging the competitive advantage of ethics are not just about doing what is right; they are strategic imperatives in today's business landscape. Companies that embrace these principles find themselves at the forefront of innovation and market leadership. They are able to forge deeper connections with their stakeholders, from employees to customers and partners, based on shared values and trust. By prioritizing ethical practices, businesses not only contribute to a more sustainable and equitable society but also position themselves for enduring success and relevance in a rapidly evolving global market.

Social Entrepreneurship and Its Impact

Definition and Concept: Social entrepreneurship refers to the practice of establishing businesses with the primary goal of addressing social or environmental issues. Unlike traditional businesses, where profit is the main driver, social entrepreneurs prioritize social impact while maintaining financial sustainability.

Evolution of the Concept: Tracing the evolution of social entrepreneurship from philanthropic efforts to a robust business model that combines innovation, resourcefulness, and a deep commitment to societal betterment.

The Impact of Social Entrepreneurship

Addressing Societal Needs

Filling Critical Gaps: Social entrepreneurs are often the bridge between the needs of a community and the available resources. They step in where governments and traditional businesses may not, offering solutions to pressing social issues. This section will explore various examples where social entrepreneurs have effectively addressed issues like homelessness, food insecurity, and lack of access to education and healthcare.

Targeting Underserved Communities: Many social enterprises focus on underserved or marginalized communities, bringing essential services and products to those who might otherwise be overlooked. We'll delve into case studies of enterprises that have made significant impacts in such communities, showcasing the transformational changes they've achieved.

Innovative Solutions

Creative Problem-Solving: Social entrepreneurs often think outside the box, using innovation to tackle complex social challenges. This part of the section will showcase examples of unique business models and innovative products or services that have successfully addressed social issues.

Leveraging Technology for Social Good: Technology plays a crucial role in scaling and enhancing the impact of social enterprises. Here, we'll explore how social entrepreneurs are using technology to increase efficiency, reach more people, and create more significant impact.

Economic Benefits

Job Creation in Local Communities: Social enterprises are vital in creating employment opportunities, especially in regions with high unemployment. This subsection will focus on how these jobs not only provide income but also skills training and personal development, leading to the overall upliftment of individuals and communities.

Boosting Local Economies: By keeping profits within local communities and focusing on local development, social enterprises stimulate economic growth. We'll examine the ripple effect of these enterprises on local economies, including increased spending power and improved quality of life.

Environmental Sustainability

Champions of Sustainability: This part will highlight case studies of social entrepreneurs who have integrated environmental sustainability into their business models. From renewable energy projects to sustainable agriculture practices, these stories will illustrate how businesses can operate while respecting and preserving the environment.

Educating and Raising Awareness: Social entrepreneurs often play a crucial role in raising public awareness about environmental issues. This subsection will focus on initiatives aimed at educating communities about sustainable practices and the importance of environmental conservation.

Conclusion

In conclusion, this section will reinforce the idea that social entrepreneurship is a powerful tool for driving social change. By addressing societal needs, offering innovative solutions, creating economic benefits, and promoting environmental sustainability, social entrepreneurs demonstrate that it's possible to build successful businesses that also make the world a better place. This exploration aims to not only celebrate their achievements but also inspire future entrepreneurs to consider the social impact of their business ventures.

Challenges and Opportunities in Social Entrepreneurship

Financial Challenges

Securing Sustainable Funding: One of the primary challenges for social entrepreneurs is securing funding that aligns with their social mission. This section will delve into innovative funding strategies, including grants, impact investments, and crowdfunding, which have proven effective for various social enterprises.

Balancing Mission and Money: A critical discussion on how social entrepreneurs can maintain their social objectives while ensuring financial viability. Case studies will illustrate successful models where businesses have managed to achieve this delicate balance.

Scaling Impact

Strategies for Expanding Reach: Scaling impact is a significant milestone for social entrepreneurs. This part will explore various approaches such as forming strategic partnerships, leveraging technology for wider reach, and adopting scalable business models that can amplify their social impact.

Challenges in Scaling: Addressing the unique challenges that come with scaling a social enterprise, from maintaining the quality of service to ensuring that the core social mission remains intact during expansion.

The Future of Social Entrepreneurship

Emerging Trends and Innovations: This section will examine the latest trends in social entrepreneurship, such as the integration of AI and blockchain for social good, the growing popularity of social impact bonds, and the shift towards more inclusive business models.

The Influence of Digital Transformation: Discussing how digital technologies are enabling social entrepreneurs to reach new audiences, improve operational efficiency, and measure the impact more effectively.

Policy and Institutional Support

The Role of Government and Policy: Highlighting the importance of government support in creating a conducive environment for social enterprises. This includes tax incentives, legal frameworks, and funding opportunities.

Collaboration with Traditional Business and Academia: Exploring the growing trend of collaborations between social enterprises, traditional businesses, and academic institutions. These collaborations can lead to shared resources, research advancements, and a broader impact.

Conclusion

Social entrepreneurship is not just a business model; it's a movement towards a more inclusive and sustainable future. By overcoming financial and scaling challenges, and leveraging emerging trends and institutional support, social entrepreneurs can continue to drive profound and lasting change. As the sector evolves, it presents an opportunity for traditional businesses, governments, and communities to play a pivotal role in supporting these changemakers. The future of social entrepreneurship holds exciting potential for innovation, impact, and the reshaping of the business landscape towards greater good.

Building a Legacy Beyond Profits

In the realm of entrepreneurship, there's a horizon that extends far beyond the conventional metrics of success. "Building a Legacy Beyond Profits" navigates this expansive vista, where the true measure of a business's worth transcends financial gains and delves into the impactful and enduring contributions it makes to society and the environment. This section is an odyssey into the heart of purpose-driven business practices that create a legacy of positive change.

Crafting a Purpose-Driven Business Model

In the landscape of modern entrepreneurship, crafting a business model that transcends the pursuit of profit to embrace a greater purpose is not just commendable; it's transformative. This section of the chapter delves deep into the art of infusing your business with a purpose that resonates beyond the confines of traditional business goals, exploring the realms of social change, environmental stewardship, and community upliftment.

Defining a Greater Purpose

Vision Beyond Profit: Here, we explore the initial steps of defining a purpose that aligns with your core values and the needs of the world around you. It's about asking the profound questions: What change do you wish to see? How can your business be a vehicle for this change?

Integrating Purpose with Business Goals: This part discusses strategies for intertwining your newfound purpose with your business objectives. It's about ensuring that every business decision and strategy is a step towards fulfilling this greater purpose.

Building a Brand Around Purpose: Learn how to communicate your purpose effectively to your audience. It's about building a brand narrative that authentically reflects your mission and resonates with your customers, employees, and stakeholders.

Stories of Purpose-Driven Leaders

Inspirational Narratives: Here, we present a collection of stories from visionary entrepreneurs who have successfully merged profitability with purpose. These tales span various industries and scales, from small local businesses to large corporations, each illustrating the power of a purpose-driven approach.

Lessons from the Field: Each story is dissected to uncover the lessons, strategies, and insights that these leaders used to build their purpose-driven enterprises. It's a treasure trove of real-world wisdom and practical tips for aspiring purpose-driven entrepreneurs.

Challenges and Triumphs: These narratives also delve into the challenges faced by these leaders and how they overcame them. It's an honest look at the hurdles inherent in aligning business with a social mission and how these can be transformed into opportunities for growth and impact.

Conclusion: A Call to Purposeful Entrepreneurship

The section concludes with a compelling call to action for current and aspiring entrepreneurs. It emphasizes that embedding a deeper purpose into your business model is not just a path to differentiation and success; it's a journey towards creating meaningful and lasting impact in the world.

This call to action is a reminder that businesses have the power to be catalysts for positive change. Entrepreneurs are invited to embrace this power, to envision and build enterprises that not only achieve financial success but also contribute to a better, more sustainable, and equitable world.

In crafting a purpose-driven business model, you are not just setting the foundation for a successful enterprise; you are joining a movement of forward-thinking leaders who are redefining the very essence of success in the business world. This is an invitation to embark on a journey that transcends traditional business goals and enters the realm of impactful, purposeful entrepreneurship.

The Ripple Effect of Social Impact

In the realm of modern entrepreneurship, the concept of creating a business that serves a greater good has moved from a niche idea to a central tenet for many. The 'Ripple Effect of Social Impact' section of this chapter highlights how businesses can serve as catalysts for broad, positive change, touching lives and ecosystems far beyond their immediate scope. It's a deep dive into the transformative power of businesses that prioritize social and environmental well-being alongside profitability.

Creating Waves of Change

In an era where businesses are increasingly scrutinized not just for their financial performance but also for their impact on society and the environment, the concept of 'Creating Waves of Change' has never been more pertinent. This section delves into the realms beyond the traditional boundaries of business, examining how ethical practices, community engagement, and environmental stewardship can amplify the positive impact of a business well beyond its immediate operational sphere.

Ethical Business Practices

Building on Integrity: Ethical business practices form the bedrock of trust and reliability, both within and outside the company. We explore how integrity in operations, transparency in dealings, and fairness in practices not only build a strong internal culture but also resonate with external stakeholders, creating a positive ripple effect in the broader business landscape.

Ethical Decision-Making: At the heart of ethical business practices lies the process of decision-making. This part discusses how choices made at various levels within the business can have far-reaching consequences. We provide insights into creating decision-making frameworks that prioritize ethical considerations, ensuring that every choice aligns with the core values of the business.

Community Engagement

Fostering Connections: Community engagement goes beyond philanthropy; it's about establishing meaningful connections with the community. Here, we discuss strategies for businesses to actively participate in community development, from local initiatives to global collaborations, and how these efforts can lead to sustainable societal growth.

Case Studies of Community Impact:

In a world where business dynamics are intricately tied to societal and environmental well-being, the stories of businesses that have made a positive impact are both inspiring and instructive. This section presents detailed case studies of diverse businesses that have successfully harnessed their resources, creativity, and influence to create significant social and environmental impacts. These real-life examples serve as vivid illustrations of how businesses, regardless of size or industry, can contribute to meaningful and sustainable change.

1. Renewable Energy Innovator: GreenTech Solutions

Background: GreenTech Solutions, a small startup founded in a garage, has now become a leader in renewable energy technologies. Initially focusing on solar panel installations, they expanded their portfolio to include wind and hydro energy solutions.

Impact: GreenTech Solutions has played a pivotal role in transforming energy consumption patterns in several underserved communities, providing affordable and sustainable energy alternatives. Their initiatives have not only reduced carbon footprints but also fostered local job creation and skill development.

Key Takeaways: This case study highlights the importance of innovation in addressing environmental challenges and underscores the potential of small startups to drive big changes.

2. Community-Centric Retailer: FairMart

Background: FairMart, a retail chain, differentiated itself by committing to fair trade practices and prioritizing locally sourced products. They partnered with local artisans and farmers, ensuring fair prices and ethical procurement.

Impact: FairMart's approach revolutionized the local retail sector, significantly boosting the local economy. Their commitment to fair trade practices enhanced the living standards of their suppliers and set a new standard in the retail industry for ethical sourcing.

Key Takeaways: This case study showcases the power of ethical supply chain practices in creating economic opportunities and enhancing community well-being.

3. Tech for Good: EduTech Innovations

Background: EduTech Innovations, a technology company, developed educational software aimed at making learning accessible in remote and underprivileged areas. They collaborated with NGOs and governments to deploy their solutions.

Impact: Their technology has bridged educational gaps, providing thousands of children with access to quality education. The company's initiative has been instrumental in enhancing literacy rates and opening new opportunities for underserved communities.

Key Takeaways: This case study demonstrates the role of technology in addressing social challenges and the impact of collaborative efforts in amplifying reach and effectiveness.

4. Sustainable Fashion Pioneer: EcoWear

Background: EcoWear, a clothing brand, emerged as a pioneer in sustainable fashion by using eco-friendly materials and championing ethical labor practices. They focused on minimizing environmental impact throughout their production process.

Impact: EcoWear's approach has not only reduced environmental harm but also raised awareness about sustainable fashion. Their success has influenced other brands to adopt more environmentally friendly practices.

Key Takeaways: This case study illustrates how a commitment to sustainability can lead to industry-wide changes and foster a culture of environmental consciousness.

Conclusion

The stories of these impactful businesses underscore the diverse ways in which companies can be agents of positive change. From addressing environmental issues to driving social development, these case studies serve as compelling evidence that business success and societal progress can go hand in hand. They provide practical insights and inspiration for businesses aspiring to make a difference, illustrating that impactful change is achievable and beneficial for both the company and the wider community.

Environmental Stewardship

In an era marked by environmental challenges, environmental stewardship in the business world has evolved from a mere ethical choice to a strategic necessity. This section probes into how adopting sustainable practices is not just about fulfilling a moral obligation but also about securing a competitive edge, fostering innovation, and building a resilient brand.

Key Areas of Focus:

Resource Efficiency and Management:

Exploration of techniques for efficient resource utilization, such as water conservation, energy efficiency, and waste reduction.

Case studies of businesses that have significantly lowered operational costs and reduced environmental impact through resource management strategies.

Innovation through Sustainability:

Analyzing how environmental challenges have spurred innovation in product design, service delivery, and operational processes.

Examples of cutting-edge sustainable technologies and business models that have emerged as a response to environmental concerns.

Enhanced Brand Reputation and Customer Loyalty:

Discussion on how green business practices contribute to building a strong, positive brand image.

Insights into consumer trends showing increased loyalty towards environmentally responsible brands.

Innovative Green Initiatives: A Global Perspective

Renewable Energy Adoption: Leading the Charge to a Greener Future

Transitioning to Renewable Energy Sources:

Case Studies of Success: Presenting a variety of companies, from small businesses to large corporations, that have successfully shifted to renewable energy sources like solar and wind power.

The Journey and Challenges: Detailing the process of transitioning, including the initial investment, infrastructural adjustments, and overcoming logistical challenges.

Outcomes and Benefits: Highlighting the environmental impact, cost savings, and long-term sustainability achieved through this switch. Real-world data to showcase the return on investment and environmental benefits.

Circular Economy in Action: Redefining Waste and Value

Embracing Circular Economy Models:

Businesses Leading in Circular Economy: Featuring companies that have adopted circular economy models, emphasizing product life-cycle extension, reuse, and recycling.

Innovative Practices: Showcasing creative approaches to converting waste into resources, such as using recycled materials in production or creating new products from waste.

Impact Assessment: Evaluating the environmental and economic impact of these practices, including reduced waste footprint and creation of new revenue streams.

Sustainable Supply Chains: Balancing Efficiency and Responsibility

Revamping Supply Chain Operations:

Sustainable Sourcing: Exploring how companies are sourcing materials in an ethically and environmentally responsible manner, including the use of fair trade and organic products.

Green Logistics: Delving into the adoption of green logistics practices, such as optimizing transportation routes for lower emissions and using eco-friendly packaging materials.

Case Profiles: Highlighting companies that have successfully optimized their supply chains for sustainability, detailing the strategies employed, challenges faced, and benefits reaped.

Global Perspectives and Diverse Approaches

Cross-Continental Initiatives:

Diversity in Green Efforts: Bringing forward examples from different continents and industries, showcasing how diverse businesses are implementing green initiatives unique to their contexts and markets.

Collaborative Efforts: Highlighting instances of cross-industry and international collaborations in green initiatives, showing how partnerships can amplify environmental impact.

Conclusion: A Call to Green Action

The section concludes by affirming that the shift to green business practices is not just a trend but a necessity for the future of our planet. It serves as an inspiration and a guide for businesses worldwide to understand the feasibility, benefits, and transformative impact of adopting green initiatives. This global perspective aims to motivate businesses to innovate and adapt, playing a pivotal role in driving the shift towards a more sustainable and environmentally responsible world.

Conclusion: The Transformative Power of Business in Environmental Stewardship

The 'Environmental Stewardship' section concludes by emphasizing the powerful role businesses can play in addressing environmental challenges. It underscores that when companies go beyond compliance and proactively engage in environmental stewardship, they don't just contribute to the health of the planet but also position themselves for long-term success and resilience.

By showcasing the tangible benefits and real-world examples of environmental stewardship in business, this section aims to inspire and guide companies to embrace sustainability not as an optional extra but as an integral part of their business strategy. It calls for a transformative approach where environmental consciousness becomes a core tenet of business operations, driving innovation, efficiency, and a positive brand image, thereby creating a more sustainable and prosperous future for all.

Case Studies of Impactful Environmental Practices

This section presents an in-depth analysis of various businesses, ranging from startups to established corporations, that have successfully incorporated environmental stewardship into their core operations. These case studies serve as a testament to the potential of businesses to drive significant positive change in environmental conservation and sustainability.

1. Renewable Energy Pioneers

Case Study A: A small startup that transitioned its entire operation to renewable energy sources, significantly reducing its carbon footprint. The study details the challenges faced during this transition, the innovative solutions adopted, and the long-term benefits realized, both environmentally and economically.

Case Study B: A global corporation that invested in large-scale renewable energy projects, contributing to a reduction in greenhouse gas emissions and setting a new standard in its industry for environmental responsibility.

2. Circular Economy and Waste Reduction

Case Study C: An innovative company that adopted circular economy principles, focusing on waste reduction and resource efficiency. This case study highlights their approach to recycling materials, designing products for longer life, and reducing overall environmental impact.

Case Study D: A retail giant implementing a comprehensive waste management strategy, including recycling programs and partnerships with suppliers to minimize packaging waste. The study examines the impacts of these initiatives on the environment and customer perception.

3. Sustainable Supply Chain Management

Case Study E: A case study of a fashion brand that revolutionized its supply chain to ensure ethical sourcing and environmental sustainability. It details the brand's journey towards using sustainable materials, fair labor practices, and transparent supply chain operations.

Case Study F: An electronics manufacturer that implemented a green supply chain strategy, focusing on reducing the environmental impact of its components and manufacturing processes. The study explores the challenges, strategies, and outcomes of this approach.

4. Community and Environmental Engagement

Case Study G: A local business that actively engages in community-based environmental projects, such as tree planting and local conservation efforts. The case study discusses the impact of these activities on the community and the company's brand.

Case Study H: A multinational company with a global environmental program that supports various sustainability projects around the world. The study analyzes the program's structure, implementation, and the measurable impact on global environmental conservation.

Conclusion: Lessons and Inspirations

Each case study concludes with key takeaways and lessons learned, providing valuable insights and inspiration for other businesses seeking to integrate environmental sustainability into their operations. These real-life examples demonstrate that environmental stewardship can be successfully implemented across different industries and company sizes, leading to a positive impact on the planet while also enhancing business performance

Sustainable Business Practices

We explore a variety of sustainable business models and practices that go beyond minimizing harm to actively benefiting society and the environment. This includes eco-friendly manufacturing processes, fair labor practices, and initiatives that foster community development.

Measuring and Reporting Impact

Tools and Methodologies for Impact Assessment

This section introduces tools and methodologies for measuring social and environmental impacts, transforming qualitative aspects of social good into quantifiable metrics.

Balancing Metrics with Mission

We discuss how businesses can balance impact metrics with financial performance, illustrating that measuring social and environmental impact can align with and enhance business objectives.

Reporting and Transparency

Learn about the importance of transparently reporting impacts to stakeholders, building trust and credibility, and inspiring other businesses and individuals to make positive changes.

The Long-Term View: Building a Sustainable Legacy

Creating a Lasting Positive Impact

This part delves into how prioritizing social and environmental impacts can shape the enduring legacy of a business, creating a lasting impression that extends beyond mere products or services.

Sustainability as Core Business Strategy

We position sustainability as a fundamental aspect of long-term business success, offering strategies for integrating sustainability into the heart of business operations.

Influencing Industry Practices

Understand how your business can set new benchmarks and influence broader industry standards, driving change across your sector.

Conclusion: A Call to Transformative Action

The section concludes with a call to action for businesses to embrace their power in shaping societal and environmental landscapes. Entrepreneurs are encouraged to envision enterprises that not only prosper economically but also significantly contribute to societal well-being and environmental preservation.

This vision challenges businesses to redefine success, emphasizing a holistic approach that recognizes the interconnectedness of business, society, and the natural world. It invites businesses to join a transformative movement, pioneering a future where success is measured by the positive impact left on the world.

Legacy Building through Community Engagement

Fostering Community Partnerships: Explore strategies for engaging with communities, understanding their needs, and building partnerships that are mutually beneficial. It's about weaving your business into the fabric of the community it serves.

Empowering Through Involvement: Discuss ways to involve employees, customers, and local communities in your social mission. This inclusive approach not only amplifies impact but also strengthens bonds and loyalty with your business.

Sustainability: The Cornerstone of Legacy

Adopting Sustainable Practices: Examine how integrating sustainability into every aspect of your business operations can ensure the longevity of both the business and the planet. It's a commitment to future generations, ensuring that the business thrives in harmony with the environment.

Innovations in Sustainability: Highlight innovative sustainable practices and technologies that are shaping the future of environmentally conscious business operations.

Conclusion: Envisioning the Future

In concluding this section, reflect on the powerful notion that the legacy of a business is not etched in its financial achievements but in the positive impact it leaves on the world. As entrepreneurs, the opportunity to build a legacy beyond profits is not just an aspiration but a responsibility. This journey into creating a purpose-driven business model, fostering community partnerships, and embracing sustainability paves the way for a new era of business where success is measured in the richness of its contributions to society and the environment.

Embrace this path with passion, creativity, and determination. The future of business is not just about thriving in the marketplace but thriving in a way that uplifts, sustains, and honors the world we live in. Let's embark on this journey to build a legacy that transcends profits and stands as a testament to the transformative power of ethical, sustainable, and socially responsible entrepreneurship.

Conclusion: Embracing the Essence of the Entrepreneurial Mindset

As we conclude our exploration of "The Entrepreneurial Mindset," we reflect on a journey that has taken us through the multifaceted landscape of entrepreneurship. From laying the foundations to embracing social responsibility and ethical entrepreneurship, this book has been a guide, a mentor, and a source of inspiration, charting a course through the complexities of the entrepreneurial world.

Integrating the Chapters: A Harmonious Symphony

Harmonizing Knowledge and Action:

Each chapter, from understanding the basic tenets of entrepreneurship in Chapter 1 to the profound insights of social responsibility in Chapter 12, is akin to a unique note in a grand symphony. Together, they create a harmonious melody that resonates with the spirit of entrepreneurship.

The Interconnectedness of Concepts:

The chapters, though distinct, are interconnected, each building upon the other. The creativity explored in Chapter 4 is as vital as the financial acumen discussed in Chapter 6 or the team-building strategies in Chapter 7. Each chapter is a piece of the puzzle, essential to completing the picture of entrepreneurial success.

The Continuous Journey of Learning and Growth

A Lifelong Process:

The entrepreneurial mindset is not a static state but a continuous journey of learning, adapting, and growing. This book is not just a one-time read but a lifelong companion, offering insights and guidance as you navigate the ever-evolving challenges and opportunities of entrepreneurship.

Adapting to Change:

As the world of business continuously transforms, so must the entrepreneur. This book equips you with the mindset to embrace change, to see challenges as opportunities, and to constantly evolve in your entrepreneurial pursuits.

Beyond Business: A Broader Impact

Influencing Society and the Environment:

The final chapters, particularly Chapter 12, underscore the broader role of entrepreneurs in shaping societal and environmental landscapes. Entrepreneurship is not just about individual success but about contributing to a better world.

Building Legacies:

The book concludes with a call to envision entrepreneurship as a pathway to building legacies that transcend profits – legacies of innovation, ethical conduct, social responsibility, and sustainable growth.

Conclusion: The Call to Action

As we close this book, consider it not as an end but as a beginning – the start of a journey filled with discoveries, challenges, and triumphs. Embrace the entrepreneurial mindset in its entirety: be visionary, innovative, resilient, responsible, and ethical. Let this book be your guide as you carve your path in the dynamic world of entrepreneurship.

"The Entrepreneurial Mindset" is more than a collection of concepts; it's a manifesto for action, a blueprint for success, and a catalyst for change. So, step forth with confidence, armed with the insights and knowledge from these pages, and embark on your entrepreneurial adventure. The world awaits the unique mark that only you, as an entrepreneur, can make.

Key Takeaways and Final Thoughts

As we close the pages of "The Entrepreneurial Mindset," let us reflect on the key takeaways from each chapter and the overarching messages that bind this journey together.

Chapter 1: The Foundations of Entrepreneurship

Key Takeaway: Understanding the fundamental principles of entrepreneurship is crucial. It involves recognizing opportunities, assessing risks, and being prepared for the entrepreneurial journey.

Chapter 2: Cultivating an Entrepreneurial Mindset

Key Takeaway: An entrepreneurial mindset is characterized by resilience, adaptability, and a relentless pursuit of goals. Cultivating this mindset is essential for overcoming challenges and seizing opportunities.

Chapter 3: Vision and Goal Setting

Key Takeaway: Clarity of vision and setting achievable goals are the cornerstones of entrepreneurial success. They provide direction and a roadmap for the journey ahead.

Chapter 4: Innovation and Creativity

Key Takeaway: Innovation and creativity are the lifeblood of entrepreneurship. They drive progress and differentiation in a competitive market.

Chapter 5: Decision-Making and Problem-Solving

Key Takeaway: Effective decision-making and problem-solving skills are vital. They enable entrepreneurs to navigate complex situations and turn challenges into opportunities.

Chapter 6: Financial Acumen

Key Takeaway: Financial literacy is not optional; it's fundamental. Understanding financial metrics and managing resources effectively are key to sustainability and growth.

Chapter 7: Building and Leading Teams
Key Takeaway: Successful entrepreneurship involves building and leading effective teams. Collaboration, communication, and leadership skills are essential for fostering a productive and motivated team.

Chapter 8: Marketing and Branding

Key Takeaway: Mastering marketing and branding is critical for making a mark in the market. It's about connecting with your audience and building a strong, recognizable brand.

Chapter 9: Navigating Challenges and Setbacks

Key Takeaway: Challenges and setbacks are inevitable. Resilience, grit, and a positive outlook are key to navigating through them and emerging stronger.

Chapter 10: Scaling and Growth

Key Takeaway: Scaling a business requires careful planning and execution. It involves understanding market dynamics, managing resources, and maintaining quality during growth.

Chapter 11: The Entrepreneur's Journey

Key Takeaway: The entrepreneurial journey is unique and multifaceted. Embrace the entire spectrum of experiences - successes, failures, learning, and growth.

Chapter 12: Social Responsibility and Ethical Entrepreneurship

Key Takeaway: Entrepreneurs have a responsibility beyond profits. Ethical practices, social responsibility, and environmental stewardship are integral to modern entrepreneurship.

Final Thoughts

"The Entrepreneurial Mindset" is more than a guide; it's a mirror reflecting the multifaceted nature of entrepreneurship. As you embark on or continue your entrepreneurial journey, remember that this journey is one of continuous learning and adaptation. Embrace each aspect of entrepreneurship - from the foundational skills to the ethical responsibilities - as part of a holistic approach to business.

Entrepreneurship is not just about creating businesses; it's about creating value that transcends profits. It's about impacting lives, shaping societies, and leaving a legacy. Let the principles and insights from this book light your path, and may your entrepreneurial journey be as rewarding as it is challenging.

Remember, the journey of entrepreneurship is not a solo venture. It's a collaborative effort, a dance with the market, a relationship with society, and a stewardship of the environment. As you turn each page and apply these learnings, may you find success, fulfillment, and the joy of making a difference in the world.

Encouragement for Aspiring Entrepreneurs

Embarking on the journey of entrepreneurship is akin to setting sail on an uncharted ocean. It is a voyage filled with both exhilarating discoveries and challenging storms. Aspiring entrepreneurs, standing on the shoreline of this vast and unpredictable sea, may feel a mixture of excitement and apprehension. This section is dedicated to you, the courageous souls ready to embark on this remarkable journey.

Embrace the Adventure

Embrace Uncertainty: Entrepreneurship is about embracing the unknown. Each step is an opportunity to learn and grow. Accept that uncertainty is not a barrier but a doorway to possibilities.

Celebrate Small Victories: Every milestone, no matter how small, is a step towards your dream. Celebrate these moments. They are the building blocks of your future success.

Journey of Self-Discovery: Entrepreneurship is as much a journey of self-discovery as it is of business creation. You will discover strengths you never knew you had and overcome fears you thought were insurmountable.

Cultivate Resilience

Overcome Fear of Failure: Failure is not the end; it's a vital part of the learning process. Each failure brings invaluable lessons that pave the way for success.

Build Resilience: Resilience is the armor of the entrepreneur. Cultivate it by facing challenges head-on and learning from setbacks.

Seek Support: You are not alone. Seek mentors, join entrepreneur networks, and surround yourself with people who encourage and challenge you.

Harness Your Passion

Follow Your Passion: Let your passion be the guiding light of your entrepreneurial journey. It will fuel your persistence and creativity.

Stay True to Your Vision: Your vision is your north star. Keep it in sight, even when the seas get rough. It will guide you back on course.

Innovate and Adapt: The world of business is constantly evolving. Stay open to new ideas, adapt to changes, and always be on the lookout for ways to innovate.

Embrace Learning

Lifelong Learning: Entrepreneurship is a continuous learning experience. Embrace every opportunity to acquire new knowledge and skills.

Learn from Others: Listen to the stories of those who have walked this path before you. Their experiences are a treasure trove of wisdom.

Stay Curious: Curiosity is a powerful tool. It drives innovation, opens new doors, and keeps you engaged in your entrepreneurial journey.

Building a Network

Cultivate Relationships: Build strong relationships with customers, suppliers, and other entrepreneurs. These connections are invaluable assets.

Networking is Key: Attend industry events, join professional groups, and engage on social media. Networking can lead to opportunities, partnerships, and friendships.

Balance and Well-being

Work-Life Harmony: While entrepreneurship demands much, remember to balance work with personal well-being. Your health and relationships are as important as your business.

Practice Self-care: Take time for yourself. Exercise, meditate, pursue hobbies, and spend time with loved ones. A well-balanced life fuels a healthy business.

Conclusion: A Call to Courageous Action

To the aspiring entrepreneurs standing at the threshold of this grand adventure: you are about to embark on a journey that few dare to take. It is a path filled with challenges, but also with immense rewards. Your journey will be unique, marked by your own experiences, triumphs, and lessons.

Remember, entrepreneurship is not just about building a business; it's about building a life that is rich in meaning and purpose. It's about creating something that matters, not just to you, but to the world.

So, take that first step with courage and confidence. Embrace the journey with all its ups and downs. Believe in yourself, in your vision, and in the difference you can make. The world of entrepreneurship awaits you, full of opportunities and possibilities. Let your entrepreneurial journey be a reflection of who you are and what you aspire to be.

Here's to your success, your growth, and the remarkable journey ahead. Welcome to the world of entrepreneurship!

Resources for Entrepreneurs

The journey of entrepreneurship is filled with challenges and opportunities. To support this voyage, a wealth of resources is available, offering guidance, insight, and inspiration. Below is a curated list of essential resources for entrepreneurs at various stages of their journey:

1. Educational Materials

Coursera: Offers a wide range of courses in entrepreneurship, business management, digital marketing, and more, taught by professors from leading universities. Website: coursera.org

Udemy: Features an extensive collection of courses on various aspects of entrepreneurship, from startup fundamentals to advanced business strategies. Website: udemy.com

LinkedIn Learning: Provides professional courses focused on business skills, leadership, and personal development. Website: linkedin.com/learning

Khan Academy: Offers free courses on economics, finance, and entrepreneurship basics. Website: khanacademy.org

Harvard Online Learning: Explore a variety of courses offered by Harvard University, including those on entrepreneurship and business. Website: online-learning.harvard.edu

Recommended Books for Entrepreneurs:
"The Lean Startup" by Eric Ries: A revolutionary approach to business startup and management.

"Good to Great" by Jim Collins: Insights on what makes businesses excel and how good companies can transition into great ones.

"Zero to One" by Peter Thiel: A unique perspective on innovation, competition, and starting a business.

"The $100 Startup" by Chris Guillebeau: A guide to starting small businesses with minimal investment.

"The E-Myth Revisited" by Michael E. Gerber: Explains why most small businesses don't work and what to do about it.

Podcasts for Entrepreneurs:
How I Built This with Guy Raz: Fascinating stories behind some of the world's best-known companies.

The Tim Ferriss Show: Tim Ferriss, the author of "The 4-Hour Workweek," interviews world-class performers to extract tactics and routines listeners can use.

Masters of Scale with Reid Hoffman: LinkedIn co-founder explores how companies grow from zero to a gazillion.

The GaryVee Audio Experience: Hosted by entrepreneur Gary Vaynerchuk, featuring a mix of interviews and chats about marketing and business.

Entrepreneurs on Fire with John Lee Dumas: An award-winning podcast where successful Entrepreneurs share their journey.

2. Business Planning Tools

Business Plan Templates: Access to customizable business plan templates that can help in structuring and presenting business ideas effectively.

Market Research Tools: Resources for conducting market research, including access to market analysis reports, consumer behavior studies, and competitive analysis tools.

Financial Planning Software: Recommendations for software tools that assist in financial planning, budgeting, and forecasting. Examples include QuickBooks, FreshBooks, and Xero.

3. Networking and Community

LinkedIn: The world's largest professional network, ideal for connecting with other business professionals, joining industry groups, and sharing insights. Website: linkedin.com

Meetup: Great for finding and attending local events and networking groups tailored to entrepreneurs and specific business interests. Website: meetup.com

Eventbrite: Find and register for business and networking events, workshops, and seminars in your area. Website: eventbrite.com

Bizzabo: A platform to discover new business events and conferences, offering opportunities for networking. Website: bizzabo.com

AngelList: A platform for startups, investors, and job seekers looking to work in startups. Great for networking in the startup ecosystem. Website: angel.co

Entrepreneurial Communities and Forums:
StartupNation: Offers a rich online forum where entrepreneurs can share advice, feedback, and support. Website: startupnation.com

Entrepreneurs' Organization (EO): A global network exclusively for entrepreneurs, offering peer-to-peer networking, mentorship, and professional growth. Website: eonetwork.org

Founder Institute: An early-stage startup accelerator and global launch network for entrepreneurs. Website: fi.co

Y Combinator Startup School: An online forum where startup founders can learn from each other and YC partners. Website: startupschool.org

Reddit Entrepreneur: A subreddit dedicated to discussing all aspects of starting and running businesses. Website: reddit.com/r/Entrepreneur

Indie Hackers: A community where independent entrepreneurs and startups can share experiences and advice. Website: indiehackers.com

4. Funding and Investment

Venture Capital and Angel Investors:
AngelList: A platform for startups to meet investors, and for investors to find promising startups. It's a great resource for discovering angel investors and venture capitalists. Website: angel.co

Crunchbase: Offers data on companies, startups, and investors. You can research potential investors and track industry trends. Website: crunchbase.com

Gust: Connects startups with a large pool of investors across the world to raise early-stage funding. Website: gust.com

VC Firms Directory: Many directories list venture capital firms, such as the National Venture Capital Association (NVCA) in the U.S. Website: nvca.org

SeedInvest: A leading equity crowdfunding platform that connects startups with investors. Website: seedinvest.com

Crowdfunding Platforms:
Kickstarter: Well-known for creative projects, it's a great platform for consumer-focused products and ideas. Website: kickstarter.com

Indiegogo: Offers more flexibility than Kickstarter in terms of funding models and is open to a wide variety of projects. Website: indiegogo.com

GoFundMe: Popular for personal fundraising but also used for business projects and startups. Website: gofundme.com

Crowdcube: UK-based crowdfunding platform that allows individuals to invest in small companies in exchange for equity. Website: crowdcube.com

Fundable: Focuses exclusively on helping startups raise capital from investors, customers, and friends. Website: fundable.com

Government Grants and Support:
Grants.gov (U.S.): A comprehensive database of grants offered by various U.S. federal government agencies. Website: grants.gov

SBIR/STTR (U.S.): Programs that provide funding for research and development for technology innovation. Website: sbir.gov

Canada Business Network (Canada): Offers resources for Canadian entrepreneurs, including information on grants and financing. Website: canadabusiness.ca

European Union Grants (EU): Provides information on grants and funding from the European Union. Website: europa.eu

Business.gov.au (Australia): Offers information on grants and assistance for Australian businesses. Website: business.gov.au

5. Legal and Regulatory Guidance

Legal Resources:
LegalZoom: Provides a range of legal services for small businesses, including company formation, intellectual property, and legal document review. Website: legalzoom.com

Nolo: Offers a vast library of legal articles, do-it-yourself legal books, and software on a variety of business topics. Website: nolo.com

Rocket Lawyer: An online legal technology company that provides legal documents and advice for businesses and individuals. Website: rocketlawyer.com

FindLaw for Small Business: Contains information on starting a business, operations management, and legal issue resolution. Website: smallbusiness.findlaw.com

U.S. Patent and Trademark Office (USPTO): Essential for intellectual property guidance, especially for patents and trademarks in the United States. Website: uspto.gov

Regulatory Guidelines:
U.S. Small Business Administration (SBA): Offers guidance on federal regulations for small businesses and provides resources for compliance. Website: sba.gov

GOV.UK (United Kingdom): Provides information on business and self-employed regulations in the UK, including tax, licensing, and legal requirements. Website: gov.uk

Business.gov.au (Australia): Offers guidance on Australian business laws and regulations, including licenses, registrations, and legal obligations. Website: business.gov.au

Canada Business Network (Canada): Provides resources on Canadian business regulations, including permits, licenses, and legal requirements. Website: canadabusiness.ca

European Commission - Business: Offers information on EU business regulations, including market rules, contracts, and competition laws. Website: ec.europa.eu

6. Marketing and Branding

Digital Marketing Tools:
Hootsuite: An excellent tool for managing and scheduling posts across multiple social media platforms. Great for increasing online engagement. Website: hootsuite.com

Google Analytics: Essential for tracking website traffic and user engagement, helping you understand your audience better. Website: analytics.google.com

Mailchimp: A user-friendly platform for email marketing campaigns, newsletters, and automated messages. Website: mailchimp.com

SEMrush: Offers SEO tools and resources to improve your website's visibility and ranking on search engines. Website: semrush.com

Canva: A graphic design tool that's ideal for creating visual content for social media, advertisements, and marketing materials. Website: canva.com

Branding Guides:
Brandwatch: Provides insights on brand perception and consumer trends. Useful for developing informed branding strategies. Website: brandwatch.com

HubSpot Brand Kit: Offers branding templates and resources, useful for creating a consistent brand image across various platforms. Website: hubspot.com

99designs: A platform to connect with professional designers for branding materials like logos, business cards, and website design. Website: 99designs.com

Adobe Spark: Useful for creating branded graphics, web pages, and video stories. It offers a variety of templates and design options. Website: spark.adobe.com

Advertising for Trient Press Magazine:
Google Ads: To reach a wider audience through targeted online advertising campaigns. Website: ads.google.com

Facebook Ads Manager: For targeting specific demographics and interests on Facebook and Instagram. Website: facebook.com/business/tools/ads-manager

LinkedIn Marketing Solutions: Ideal for B2B advertising and reaching a professional audience. Website: linkedin.com/marketing-solutions

Twitter Ads: Useful for engaging with audiences in real-time and boosting the reach of tweets. Website: ads.twitter.com

Pinterest Ads: For visually-driven advertising, particularly effective if your content is design, lifestyle, or inspiration-focused. Website: ads.pinterest.com

7. Productivity and Efficiency Tools

Project Management Software:
Trello: A visual tool using boards, lists, and cards to organize and prioritize projects in a fun, flexible way. Ideal for workflow visualization. Website: trello.com

Asana: A project management tool that helps teams orchestrate their work, from daily tasks to strategic initiatives. Great for team collaboration. Website: asana.com

Monday.com: A Work Operating System (Work OS) that powers teams to run projects and workflows with confidence. It's highly customizable. Website: monday.com

Jira: Best suited for software development projects, it offers agile project management tools, including scrum and kanban boards. Website: atlassian.com/software/jira

Basecamp: Known for its simple interface, it combines all the tools teams need to get work done in a single, streamlined package. Website: basecamp.com

Time Management Apps:
Todoist: A task manager and to-do list app that helps you organize and prioritize your tasks and projects. Website: todoist.com

Evernote: A note-taking app that organizes your notes, lists, and tasks, making them easily accessible and searchable. Website: evernote.com

RescueTime: Automatically tracks the time you spend on applications and websites and gives you detailed reports and data. Website: rescuetime.com

Focus@Will: A unique productivity tool that uses music to boost concentration and focus. Website: focusatwill.com

Forest: An app that helps you stay focused by planting a virtual tree which grows while you work and dies if you leave the app. Website: forestapp.cc

Each of these tools offers unique features that can help streamline your project management and enhance time management. By incorporating these tools into your daily routine, you can significantly improve your productivity and efficiency in managing your business tasks and projects.

8. Personal Development

Work-Life Balance Tips:

Mindful.org: Offers resources on mindfulness and meditation techniques that can help manage stress and improve work-life balance. Website: mindful.org

Lifehack: Provides a wide range of articles and tips on improving productivity and achieving a better work-life balance. Website: lifehack.org

Tiny Buddha: Focuses on simple wisdom and stress reduction, offering insights into mindfulness and contentment in daily life. Website: tinybuddha.com

Zen Habits: A blog by Leo Babauta focusing on finding simplicity and mindfulness in the daily chaos of our lives. Website: zenhabits.net

The Muse: Offers career advice and tips on work-life balance, including strategies for time management and stress reduction. Website: themuse.com

Leadership Development:
Harvard Business Review (HBR): Features articles, podcasts, and webinars on leadership and management from world-renowned experts. Website: hbr.org

Leadership Now: Provides a wealth of resources, articles, and tools on leadership development. Website: leadershipnow.com

TED Talks Leadership: A collection of TED Talks on various aspects of leadership, featuring speakers from various fields. Website: ted.com/topics/leadership

Coursera Leadership Courses: Offers online courses in leadership and management from top universities and institutions. Website: coursera.org

Center for Creative Leadership: Provides research, tools, and training for leaders at all levels. Website: ccl.org

Recommended Reading

The following list comprises a selection of books that are highly recommended for entrepreneurs. These books cover a range of topics critical to entrepreneurial success, from leadership and innovation to strategy and personal development:

1. Business Strategy and Entrepreneurship

"The Lean Startup" by Eric Ries: A revolutionary approach to business development, which introduces the concept of 'Lean' thinking in startups.

"Zero to One" by Peter Thiel with Blake Masters: Offers unique insights into startup innovation and building a future-focused business.

"The E-Myth Revisited" by Michael E. Gerber: Explores the myths surrounding starting your own business and walks you through all stages of a business life.

2. Leadership and Management

"Good to Great" by Jim Collins: This book explores what elevates a company from mediocrity to excellence, drawing on research from various companies.

"Dare to Lead" by Brené Brown: Focuses on developing brave leaders and creating courageous cultures, a crucial read for managing teams effectively.

"Start with Why" by Simon Sinek: Encourages leaders to find their 'why' – the purpose that drives them and their business.

3. Marketing and Brand Building

"Contagious: How to Build Word of Mouth in the Digital Age" by Jonah Berger: Offers key insights into why certain things go viral and how to harness the power of word of mouth.

"Building a StoryBrand" by Donald Miller: Guides businesses in clarifying their message and creating a brand story that resonates with customers.

4. Personal Development and Productivity

"Deep Work" by Cal Newport: Focuses on the ability to focus without distraction and how it can be cultivated for massive productivity and success.

"The 7 Habits of Highly Effective People" by Stephen R. Covey: A holistic approach to personal and professional effectiveness and leadership.

5. Innovation and Creativity

"The Innovator's Dilemma" by Clayton M. Christensen: Discusses how successful companies can do everything "right" and still lose market leadership.

"Creativity, Inc." by Ed Catmull: Offers insights into fostering a creative culture, as experienced by the co-founder of Pixar Animation Studios.

6. Financial Acumen

"Profit First" by Mike Michalowicz: Introduces a simple yet effective formula to ensure profitability from your business's next deposit forward.

"Rich Dad Poor Dad" by Robert T. Kiyosaki: Offers perspectives on investing and personal finance that challenge conventional wisdom.

7. Social Responsibility and Ethics

"Conscious Capitalism" by John Mackey and Raj Sisodia: Promotes a business philosophy that values ethical considerations alongside financial success.

"The Triple Bottom Line" by Andrew Savitz: Explores how companies can succeed in the market by focusing on social, economic, and environmental sustainability.

These books offer invaluable lessons and insights that can aid entrepreneurs in navigating the complex business landscape, fostering personal growth, and driving sustainable success.

Glossary of Key Terms

This glossary provides definitions for key terms and concepts that are essential in the entrepreneurial world. Understanding these terms can greatly enhance an entrepreneur's ability to navigate the business landscape effectively.

A

Angel Investor: An affluent individual who provides capital for a business start-up, usually in exchange for convertible debt or ownership equity.

Agile Methodology: A project management approach, primarily in software development, that emphasizes flexibility, customer satisfaction, and iterative progress.

B

Bootstrapping: Starting and growing a business using limited resources or personal finances, without external help.

Burn Rate: The rate at which a new company spends its venture capital to finance overhead before generating positive cash flow from operations.

C

Cash Flow: The total amount of money being transferred into and out of a business, especially as affecting liquidity.

Crowdfunding: The practice of funding a project or venture by raising small amounts of money from a large number of people, typically via the Internet.

D

Disruptive Innovation: An innovation that significantly alters the way that businesses operate, often displacing established market-leading firms and products.

E

Entrepreneurship: The process of designing, launching, and running a new business, often initially a small business.

Equity: Ownership interest in a business, usually in the form of shares.

F

Fiscal Year: A business's operating year, used for financial reporting purposes, which may or may not coincide with the calendar year.

Franchising: The practice of licensing a business model and brand for a prescribed period within an agreed territory.

G

Growth Hacking: Strategies focused solely on growth, often used by startups, involving marketing, development, and design.

H

Human Capital: The skills, knowledge, and experience possessed by an individual or population, viewed in terms of their value or cost to an organization or country.

I

Innovation: The process of translating an idea or invention into a good or service that creates value or for which customers will pay.

Incubator: A company that helps new and startup companies to develop by providing services such as management training or office space.

J

Joint Venture: A business arrangement in which two or more parties agree to pool their resources for the purpose of accomplishing a specific task.

K

Key Performance Indicator (KPI): A measurable value that demonstrates how effectively a company is achieving key business objectives.

L

Lean Startup: A methodology for developing businesses and products, which aims to shorten product development cycles and rapidly discover if a proposed business model is viable.

M

Market Penetration: The extent to which a product is recognized and purchased by customers in a particular market.

Minimum Viable Product (MVP): A product with enough features to attract early-adopter customers and validate a product idea early in the product development cycle.

N

Networking: Interacting with others to exchange information and develop professional or social contacts.

O

Outsourcing: The business practice of hiring a party outside a company to perform services and create goods that traditionally were performed in-house by the company's own employees.

P

Pitch: A presentation in which a startup founder explains their business idea to potential investors.

Profit Margin: A measure of a company's profitability, calculated as the net income divided by the revenue.

Q

Quality Assurance (QA): A way of preventing mistakes and defects in manufactured products and avoiding problems when delivering solutions or services to customers.

R

Return on Investment (ROI): A performance measure used to evaluate the efficiency or profitability of an investment.

Risk Capital: The funds allocated for speculative, high-risk, high-return investments.

S

Scale-Up: The process of increasing the size or scope of a business, typically after validating the business model and achieving product-market fit.

Seed Capital: The initial capital used to start a business, often coming from the company founders.

T

Target Market: A particular group of consumers at which a product or service is aimed.

Traction: The progress of a startup company and the momentum it gains as it grows.

U

Unique Selling Proposition (USP): The factor or consideration presented by a seller as the reason that one product or service is different from and better than that of the competition.

V

Venture Capital: Financing that investors provide to startup companies and small businesses that are believed to have long-term growth potential.

Value Proposition: An innovation, service, or feature intended to make a company or product attractive to customers.

W

Working Capital: The capital used in day-to-day trading operations, calculated as current assets minus current liabilities.

X

X-Efficiency: The degree of efficiency maintained by firms under conditions of imperfect competition.

Y

Yield: The income return on an investment, such as the interest or dividends received from holding a particular security.

Z

Zero-Sum Game: A situation in which one person's gain is equivalent to another's loss, so the net change in wealth or benefit is zero.

www.ingramcontent.com/pod-product-compliance
Lightning Source LLC
LaVergne TN
LVHW030311070526
838199LV00008B/375